From Situated Selves to the Self

From Situated Selves to the Self

*Conversion and Personhood among
Roman Catholics in Tokyo*

Hisako Omori

Published by State University of New York Press, Albany

© 2020 State University of New York

All rights reserved

No part of this book may be used or reproduced in any manner whatsoever without written permission. No part of this book may be stored in a retrieval system or transmitted in any form or by any means including electronic, electrostatic, magnetic tape, mechanical, photocopying, recording, or otherwise without the prior permission in writing of the publisher.

For information, contact State University of New York Press, Albany, NY
www.sunypress.edu

Library of Congress Cataloging-in-Publication Data

Names: Omori, Hisako, author.
Title: From situated selves to the self : conversion and personhood among Roman Catholics in Tokyo / Hisako Omori.
Description: Albany : State University of New York Press, 2020. | Includes bibliographical references and index.
Identifiers: LCCN 2019028199 | ISBN 9781438478159 (hardcover : alk. paper) | ISBN 9781438478142 (pbk. : alk. paper) | ISBN 9781438478166 (ebook)
Subjects: LCSH: Catholics—Japan—Tokyo. | Catholic Church—Japan.
Classification: LCC BX1670.T65 O46 2020 | DDC 282/.5209051—dc23
LC record available at https://lccn.loc.gov/2019028199

10 9 8 7 6 5 4 3 2 1

To My Mother

Contents

List of Illustrations	ix
A Note on Transliteration and Translation	xi
Acknowledgments	xiii
Introduction	1
Chapter 1 Setting the Stage	17
Chapter 2 Propriety, Virtues, and Social Obligations	53
Chapter 3 Breaking the Barrel and Becoming Catholic	81
Chapter 4 Housewives, *Nippon Danji*, and the Church	129
Chapter 5 Private Faith and the Legacy of Persecution	159
Conclusion and Implications	179
Notes	193
Works Cited	205
Index	217

Illustrations

Figure 1.1 Map of Sixteen Dioceses in Japan.   35

Figure 1.2 Items for Sale at the Angel's Forest Shop.   44

Figure 3.1 Business Card Reception Box at Cemetery.   89

Figure 3.2 Business Card Reception Box at Cemetery.   89

Figure 3.3 "Paper Oracles."   95

Figure 3.4 "Paper Oracles."   95

A Note on Transliteration and Translation

When I refer to Japanese terms, I use the conventional transliteration form called the Hepburn romanization system. Transliterated words are italicized.

In transliterating Japanese words, I use a diacritic mark to indicate a long vowel. I omit a macron when the word is already used commonly without a mark. For example, Tokyo and Osaka are spelled as such, instead of Tōkyō and Ōsaka.

All the English translations found in the text are my own unless otherwise indicated. Reference to Japanese names follows the Japanese convention of placing the family name first, unless the author's published name follows a different format.

For Japanese individuals who appear in this ethnography, I use their family names followed by an honorific -san at the end. I use the first name followed by -san for only one person. This choice was based on which name was used by others in the specific ethnographic context.

Acknowledgments

This book had a long gestation period, and I must first and foremost thank Ellen Badone, who shepherded it through all the stages of its production: the conception of the first research question, ethnographic fieldwork, writing, and publishing of this ethnography. Ellen accompanied me on my intellectual journey, initially as my advisor at McMaster University and later as a mentor and friend, always giving freely of her time to discuss ideas and showing her unwavering support. Without her guidance and encouragement, this book would never have come into existence.

Over the course of its production, many people have read various drafts of this manuscript in its entirety or parts of it and offered advice, criticism, and suggestions to improve the text. I thank James A. Benn, Mark Rowe, John W. Traphagan, and Laurel Kendall for sharing their insights. I also thank Aubrey Cannon for introducing me to historical thinking and Eileen Schuller for awakening me to the perspectives of the Roman Catholic Church. I should state, however, that responsibilities for any errors or omissions remain strictly mine. Some passages of this book appeared in altered form in "Private Faith: Social Memory, Gender and the Roman Catholic Church in Contemporary Tokyo," *Culture and Religion* (https://www.tandfonline.com/toc/rcar20/current). These passages are reproduced by permission of Taylor and Francis Group.

During my ethnographic research in Tokyo, I was affiliated with the Sophia University Institute of Comparative Culture. I thank Mark R. Mullins and David H. Slater for welcoming me into vibrant intellectual communities at Sophia University. Back in Canada, Joseph H. Kary helped me to sharpen my writing at various points in the preparation of the manuscript. At Akita International University, Patrick N. Shorb constantly showed his support and reminded me that I should take the necessary time to complete this book, and Ken Ogasawara provided me with technical support to prepare figures. I am also indebted to my anonymous reviewers. They challenged me to reframe my argument in a significant way, and I am genuinely grateful for their insight into my work. Exchanges with reviewers enriched my thinking, and I hope the book reflects the results of this process. My thanks are also due to my editor, Christopher Ahn, of SUNY Press, who was always calm and lighthearted in providing support and guidance during the production of this book.

Several organizations financially supported various aspects of this research. The fieldwork on which the book is based was generously funded by the Japan Foundation. My studies at McMaster University and trips to various conferences were supported by Ontario Graduate Scholarships, the Department of Religious Studies, the Mary Margaret Scammell Scholarship, and the Toshiba International Foundation. I thank all of these organizations, which enabled me to complete this project.

Without the hospitality and friendship of Roman Catholics in Japan, this work could have never come into fruition. I am deeply indebted to the Roman Catholic communities in Tokyo, Nagasaki, Yokohama, and beyond. Not only did people from these communities generously share their stories of faith, but they were also willing to discuss what makes Roman Catholicism so valuable in the context of Japanese society. I can only hope that I have done justice to their stories.

I am also grateful to my friends and family. I especially thank Joyce Y. Mitamura, Lev Jaeger, Lily Vuong, Yukihisa and Sumiko Nogami, Ewan Whyte, and Maria Eusebia da Silva for providing me with a home away from home and always keeping my spirits up during writing. More recently, I am indebted to my husband, Omori Toshinori, who has constantly supported me both through cooking and humor so that I may finish the final stretch of this long marathon. I also thank the members of my family, Tanaka Hiroko, Furuya Mikiko, Matsuura Yumi, and Tanaka Shigeki, who allowed me to remain in Canada during the course of my studies. In Canada, I was able to put my relational self in secondary place in order to pursue my individual intellectual questions. Finally, I would like to thank my parents—especially my mother. Born in a different era, my mother was unable to continue her studies. As a member of her natal household, her sense of self was deeply rooted in her family role, which did not allow her to pursue education beyond junior college. Instead of pursuing her own dreams, my mother devoted her life to the family business and the education of her children. It is my mother to whom I dedicate this work.

Introduction

It was my first day in the "Introduction to Catholicism" class on Thursdays at Our Lady of the Assumption Church[1] in central Tokyo. I carefully approached a vacant seat that was located near the back of the room so that I could see the entire room. The class was to begin at 10:30 a.m., and there were about forty or so women and a few men present. Surprisingly, the room was full of older people. I was hoping that I was dressed nicely enough to blend in with the people here, who I anticipated were from the affluent strata of Japanese society. Before taking up an empty seat, I asked a woman next to me whether it was okay to sit there. She appeared to be in her sixties or early seventies, wearing her permed hair short. Like so many people in Japan, her hair was dyed, making it darker than it would be naturally. She pleasantly told me that the seat was empty, and when I sat down next to her, she asked whether this was my first day of class. Upon hearing that I was there to conduct ethnographic research on the Japanese Catholic community, she was intrigued and whispered to her neighbor: "Did you hear? She came all the way from Canada to study Catholicism in Japan!" Without being prompted, my neighbor went on to share her story with me.

> "Once I started praying, you know, so many wondrous things [*fushigi na koto*] happened around me! They are such trifling things that nobody would care, but I know those things are happening not randomly but as a response to my prayer. This is something I cannot explain with words. You cannot see it, but there exists something that we cannot see with our eyes. They are like, you know, magic! One thing after another, things would happen! I can't explain how fun it is!"

As if she were a sixteen-year-old, she could hardly contain her excitement. After saying all this, with an expression of slight embarrassment on her face, she stole a peek at me as if to check my reaction toward her candid confession to a complete stranger. This encounter was not within the range of my expected scenarios for fieldwork. My research proposal, prepared in Canada, outlined how I had planned to study, using the contemporary Roman Catholic community in Tokyo as a window, the influence of recent globalization in Japan, as well as the many historical layers of Westernization discourses that have impacted the Japanese people. Gradually, however, it became apparent to me that at the heart of the experience of becoming Roman Catholic in Tokyo lies the matter of submitting one's will to a new authority, the Christian God. Although this might not sound particularly novel to readers who are familiar with the Christian worldview, accepting a new authority has unique and significant implications for the idea of personhood, one's sense of self, and agency in the Japanese context.

As George E. Marcus and Michael M. J. Fischer (1986) have pointed out, the study of personhood[2] can potentially be the most fertile area of investigation in revealing how cultures differ from one another. The study of personhood counters the "subtly ethnocentric assumptions about human agency embedded in the frameworks with which anthropologists have represented their subjects" (1986, 45). Since Marcus and Fischer's evocative question, scholars have made various attempts to question and complicate the analytical categories of individual, agency, and the self (Mahmood 2005; Ortner 2006; Robbins 2004). The current study of Japanese Roman Catholic people in Tokyo is my attempt to enrich ongoing investigation of these categories.

In contemporary Tokyo, members of the Roman Catholic Church are exhorted to surrender to divine will. When these Japanese members of the Church become successful in trusting in the divine, they often simultaneously leave behind the popular Japanese virtue of striving hard to fulfill one's social roles. For these Japanese Catholics, this decision to submit to divine will rather than to live up to society's expectations is often validated by extraordinary mystical experiences or signs, such as communication with the unseen through prayers or being surrounded by the sudden, unexplained scent of roses. I argue that through this process of surrendering to divine will, converts[3] experience a new power structure in which human authority is significantly diminished. This restructuring of authority results in a sense of liberation and elation for these Japanese Catholics, whose sense of self has previously been shaped by social obligations and by the Japanese[4] emphasis on the social order and the authority of human beings. Furthermore, I suggest that Neo-Confucian values and idioms that have repeatedly been mobilized within Japan's discursive processes underpin a relational sense of self so salient in Japan. As the laity deepen their understanding of the Catholic worldview, the culturally sanctioned, relational sense of self that is constructed based on one's social context is often realigned to accommodate the non-human divine. With this reconfiguration of authority figures, the relationship with the divine is awarded the most prominent position. As a result, this Catholic sense of self finds an inner compass from which one can act, giving rise to a more integral sense of self.

While on the surface, this sense of self among Japanese Catholics resembles an oft-discussed sense of individuality associated with the conversion to Christianity found in many non–Euro-American cultural contexts (Robbins 2004; Keane 2007), I suggest that perhaps it is more fruitful to look at this Japanese Catholic sense of self as a "realigned self" that is relational. This realigned self is a subjectivity positioned in relation to the non-human divine. As the Christian deity is invisible, however, the person who espouses this sense of self appears independent, as his or her relationship with the divine is invisible to others.

As the reader will find in subsequent chapters in this ethnography, Roman Catholics in Tokyo welcome this change in one's self and enjoy their relationships with the divine. It is perhaps right to situate these joyous converts in the context of the post–Vatican II era of the Roman Catholic Church. Although I also depict many Roman Catholics in Tokyo hiding their Christian identities from their peers at work and some even from their own family members (Omori 2014), many Catholics stay for hours in the church after Sunday masses, organizing talks by guest priests, transcribing sermons for distribution over the Internet, and actively involving themselves in various church activities. A significant number of Catholics cherish the notion of God as love and talk about their relationships with the unseen with fondness. It can be said that, in the twenty-first century, Catholics in Tokyo are enjoying the fruits of the various debates and changes devised and implemented through the Second Vatican Council of the 1960s. I should also caution the reader that I do not extend this claim to describe Roman Catholics in other parts of Japan, such as in Nagasaki, as I did not have many opportunities to spend time with the parishioners of other areas.

Before I turn to the discussion of the ways in which laypeople in Tokyo undergo changes in their sense of self, I first turn to further theoretical orientations to set up the framework for my discussion of Roman Catholics in Tokyo.

Theoretical Orientations

This work is largely inspired by a Foucauldian insistence on examining historical processes to understand the "mode by which [. . .] human beings are made subjects" (Foucault 1984, 7). In his search for the mode in which distinct subjectivities are produced, Foucault emphasizes notions of truth and power. In his introduction to Michel Foucault's work, Paul Rabinow points out that Foucault is "highly suspicious of claims to universal truth" (4). He approaches a claim to a universal truth by historicizing the category in question. By doing so, he eventually unmasks its claim to authenticity and as a result dismantles its power. Foucault insists that "truth isn't the reward of free spirits, the child of protracted solitude, nor the privilege of those who have succeeded in liberating themselves" (72), but that truth is "produced" through various processes of sanctioning. He claims that "[e]ach society has its regime of truth" (73), and the current work is my attempt to discern it in the context of Japanese society.

Following a Foucauldian model, the present study explores the historical processes through which contemporary Japanese and, in particular, Roman Catholics are shaped through various discursive processes. In historicizing my own subjects, I adapt the approaches taken by the French *Annales* school of history. In particular, my work uses the *Annales* ideas of the *longue durée* and the conjuncture[5] (Braudel 1980) in discussing various historical periods that differently, and sometimes simultaneously, have shaped the lives of contemporary Japanese Roman Catholics. According to this scheme, I discuss the era starting with the Edo Period (1603–1868) and ending at the Pacific War in 1945 as a *longue durée* in which certain values were propagated and inculcated among Japanese people using Neo-Confucian idioms. I also consider another era from the Meiji Period (1868–1912) to the end of the Pacific War as a conjuncture, or a shorter period of social development, in which the state pursued an intense application of similar ethics using Confucian ideas, with the Japanese emperor as the pinnacle of the Confucian hierarchy. Furthermore, I look at several historical periods in which governmental policies had a significant impact on the lives of the laity in order to analyze aspects of lay religious practice and the self-consciousness of lay Catholics. Most notably, I look at anti-Christian discursive process at another conjuncture, when, in the early seventeenth century, the Tokugawa government banned Christianity altogether[6] and, at the same time, ordered all residents of the Japanese islands to maintain a Buddhist altar in the home (Hur 2007). Along with other anti-Christian decrees of the Tokugawa government, these policies had a long-lasting impact on the populace, both making the domestic sphere a cultic domain (Takeda 1976) and transforming Christianity into a symbolic, anti-national villain.[7]

My analysis often focuses on the geopolitically bounded notion of Japan as a nation-state so that I can direct my attention to policies to govern its internal subjects. Like Foucault, I am interested in the question of how certain subjects are made; not the outcome but the process of producing them. In this line of inquiry, I realize the state and other influential leaders within the state have often played major roles in shaping certain discourses. To trace state-led discourses that contributed in noteworthy ways to forming subjects in this study, I need to use the adjective "Japanese" frequently. I am aware that this emphasis on the unit of "Japan" may create the impression that my work belongs to the line of scholarly and popular discourses labeled as *nihonjinron* or the study of Japanese uniqueness. I would like to clarify that I do not assume that the Japanese are a single "race" that has a peculiar ability and unique qualities, as many writers whose works belong to the genre of *nihonjinron* tend to assume. My necessary usage of the term "Japanese society" and the adjective "Japanese" should be understood, instead, as referring to those people who are affected unevenly by various regulations and constraints imposed by the state through taxation, law, freedom of speech, and freedom to practice religion, among other constraints. Historically, the state also controlled the languages used within the Japanese archipelago. Although minor languages such as Okinawan and Ainu existed in the periphery of Japanese society, these languages have never become a dominant language of the media. As a result, the Japanese language played a vital role in shaping the discourse of the populace. Now, having laid down the framework for this study, I turn to my central topic: the sense of self among Japanese members of the Roman Catholic Church in Tokyo.

The "Relational" Sense of Self and Neo-Confucian Values

Describing the sense of freedom that she gained through baptism, Hashimoto-san, an older female convert to Catholicism, compared the experience of baptism to being liberated "as if the barrel hoop had come off" (*taga ga hazureru mitai*). This phrase, "the barrel hoop had come off," is an idiomatic expression used in the modern Japanese language to describe an ungoverned state of being that should be regulated by a proper set of rules. In other words, this idiom normally describes a negative condition. Hashimoto-san, however, deliberately used this idiomatic expression in a contradictory and playful way. In Tokyo, many members of the laity find that the experience of espousing the Catholic worldview is a liberating experience precisely because of its difference from social ideals that dictate appropriate behaviors. As the normal usage of the term "barrel hoop" indicates, there are socially sanctioned rules and ideals that one ought to adhere to in becoming a "mature" member of Japanese society. As I show in chapter 2, the constant effort to keep up with societal ideals is often a taxing experience for many people and is frequently a source of emotional and psychological difficulties. These socially conceived sets of rules and ideals, however, can be relegated to secondary importance once one completely immerses oneself in the Catholic worldview.

There are two dissimilar worldviews at play in many of my interlocutors' narratives. Before converting to Catholicism, they often strived hard to be dutiful daughters-in-law, ideal wives, and caring mothers. Later on, through their conversions to Catholicism, they leave behind this emphasis on their social roles and conceive of who they are in terms of the Catholic worldview. In this latter worldview, the Christian God plays a central role in interpretations of one's position vis-à-vis other human beings. For example, the experience of sitting right next to somebody could be the work of God[8] according to the Catholic understanding of the world. This same person, however, might rather quickly change seats if he or she were concerned with seating order according to the Confucian-based understandings of the social hierarchy. Whereas it is a norm to defer to the social order and human society as the voice of moral authority, by converting to Catholicism, it becomes possible instead to defer to the Christian God as one's absolute moral authority.

The emphasis in Japanese society on one's social role as the center of one's subjectivity has received much scholarly attention among anthropologists of Japan in the recent past (Borovoy 2005; Kondo 1990; Lebra 1984; Rosenberger 1992; Smith 1983). Going back even further, the Japanese sense of self has enjoyed significant scholarly attention since the inception of Japanese Studies (e.g., Benedict 1974 [1947]; Doi 1971).[9] After Japan's rapid economic growth in the 1960s and 1970s, there were numerous scholarly inquiries into the economic sphere of Japanese society. Kondo argues that the Japanese sense of self centers on the self's "relational" character as compared to that of the typically American, and more individualistic, sense of self (Kondo 1990). Kondo maintains that "contextually constructed, relationally defined selves are particularly resonant in Japan." In her seminal work *Crafting Selves* (1990), Kondo eloquently depicts the ways in which one is "defined by obligations and linked to others" and is thus "'always already' caught in webs of relationships" (Kondo 1990, 26).

She further discusses the structure of the Japanese language and says that "awareness of complex social positioning is an inescapable element of any utterance in Japanese, for it is utterly impossible to form a sentence without also commenting on the relationship between oneself and one's interlocutor" (1990, 31). For example, there are a variety of male pronouns for "I," including *watakushi*, *watashi*, *washi*, *boku*, and *ore*, that can be used in conversation. However, one needs to choose which pronoun to use depending on the context (Kondo 1990, 27). This choice demands an instant judgment on the part of the speaker who initiates the conversation as to which individual should be located in a higher position in a given social hierarchy and who is to be located lower. For example, no employee should use *ore* in describing himself when talking to the president of his company. It is proper to use *watakushi* or *watashi* in this context. *Ore* is an informal expression that allows the speaker to talk to his peers and possibly to his girlfriend and wife. In addition to the pronouns, one needs to decide which mode of speech to use in conversing with an interlocutor, as the verbs also change depending on social relationships. Many other scholars have pointed out that one's sense of self in Japan is often constructed through interactions with others (Kuwayama 1992; Ohnuki-Tierney 1990, 2001). Jane Bachnik has called this constantly shifting idea of the self the "sliding scale" of the self and other (quoted in Kondo 1990, 26). In Japanese society, the mastery of language reflecting proper social relationships is considered to be a sign of maturity. It is common practice in the hospitality industry to train the newly employed in the proper usage of the language so that they will not offend their customers. It should be noted that Kondo emphasizes selves *in the plural* and their relationship to power. Using her ethnographic data, she depicts the ways in which selves are constructed and reconstructed according to context. She emphasizes the relations of power in complicating this process of self-construction in various Japanese contexts.

Scholars have agreed that there is a pronounced gender divide in Japanese society (Brinton 1993; Kelsky 2001; Lebra 1984; Rosenberger

1992, 2001). Many have argued that this gender divide further reinforces the prescribed role-playing aspects of the Japanese sense of self (Allison 1991, 1994; Borovoy 2005; Ogasawara 1998; Rosenberger 2001). Although I did not exclude men from my investigation of Japanese Roman Catholic communities in Tokyo, this research is, to a large extent, concerned with women, women's lives, and their religious expressions in contemporary Japan.

This focus on women was not intentional, but rather an artifact of my empirical research. In addition to the fact that my position as a woman facilitated my rapport with research participants of the same gender, approximately 90 percent of those who attend church activities during the daytime in Tokyo are women. As a result, my data reflect more on the experience of women than those of men.[10] While this study is not motivated by a feminist agenda such as a discourse on gender equality in religious traditions (cf. Kawahashi 2006; Yamaguchi 2003), I hope that by depicting the concerns and practices of women and describing their lives, I have produced a culturally sensitive account of notions of selfhood in contemporary Japan.[11]

Although the scholars referenced here have emphasized the importance of contexts in which people define themselves, the dynamic roles that Neo-Confucian idioms played in shaping and reshaping the Japanese sense of self have not been explored to a large extent. Confucian-derived values have often been used as symbols or, the model of, and model for, reality. In this book, I link Neo-Confucian values to the "relational" trait of the sense of self in Japan and point to two discursive periods in which Neo-Confucian idioms became deeply embedded in Japanese society. As previously mentioned, I identify the era starting with the Edo Period and ending at the Pacific War in 1945 as a *longue durée* in which Neo-Confucian ethics became one of the important intellectual currents of the state. Second, I identify another era from the Meiji Period to the end of the Pacific War as a conjuncture, or a shorter period of social movement, in which the state pursued an intense application of Neo-Confucian ethics, with the Japanese emperor as the pinnacle of the Confucian hierarchy. Using both ethnographic examples and historical documents, I illustrate various efforts to instill Neo-Confucian values, such as the importance of social hierarchy, fulfilling of one's social roles, the subordinate position of woman, and filial piety. By juxtaposing Japanese renditions of Neo-Confucian idioms in historical contexts with the present-day experience of Roman Catholic laypeople, I demonstrate the dynamics of the discursive processes whereby the Japanese elites shaped and reshaped their subjects.

The Christian God as an Anchor

When I trace the conversion of Japanese individuals to Roman Catholicism, or the deepening of Catholic faith among people who received infant baptism, a similar pattern emerges. As I stated earlier, Catholics in Tokyo shift their allegiance from human authority to that of the Christian God when espousing the Catholic faith. By placing the Christian God at the pinnacle of the hierarchy of the moral authority, these Catholics are able to create a central position within themselves, an anchor or center of gravity, which roots their otherwise constantly shifting contextual sense of self defined by social hierarchies based on Neo-Confucian values. As Kondo puts it eloquently in her work, Japanese contexts constantly demand one to locate oneself in a social hierarchy. As we will see in this ethnography, Christianity, in particular Roman Catholicism, enables individuals to break away from the constant demands of positioning in Japanese society. When embraced by a Japanese person, a Roman Catholic identity functions as an anchor for one's positioning in a world otherwise dictated by human hierarchies. As one is able to develop a center of gravity, a stable position from which one can see the world, this enables the person to embrace a solid standpoint.

This allegiance to a new authority generates tremendous relief for many converts and devout Catholics in Tokyo. It also creates a sense of liberation and elation. As noted above, many Catholics whom I encountered in Tokyo were jubilantly exultant and cheerful about being Catholic, in stark contrast to numerous lay Catholics whom I encountered in North America. Many lay Catholics in Canada have been embarrassed by the scandal associated with pedophile priests and express ambivalence toward the Church. On the contrary, Tokyo Catholics have maintained their sense of reverence towards priests[12] and see Jesus and the Christian God as their personal center of gravity.

Perhaps because of its strong presence in the West, anthropology has had a complex relationship with Christianity as the subject of investigation (Bialecki et al. 2008; Canell 2006). It did not attract much scholarly attention, especially during the discipline's infancy. This situation has changed over time, for example, when scholars turned their attention to the study of popular Catholicism and peasant society (Badone 1989, 1990; Christian 1996; Taylor 1995). In recent years, the study of personhood has been invigorating theoretical discussions in the field of anthropology of Christianity (Bialecki and Daswani 2015; Mosko 2010; Robbins 2010).

As Bialecki and others have put it, "in cultures that have recently adopted Christianity, conversion often triggers a partial abandonment of social and cultural forms oriented toward the collective in favor of individualist models of social organization" (Bialecki et al. 2008, 1141). Several scholars have associated conversion to Christianity with the development of a more bounded, individualistic sense of self (Barker 2007; Keane 2007; Robbins 2004) as opposed to the pre-conversion "relational" or "dividual" sense of self. These discussions are partially built on the works of Dumont (1985, 1986), who argues that Christianity has been a cultural force contributing to the rise of a Western notion of individualism (see also Mauss 1985). In Melanesian contexts in particular, this pre-conversion personhood is characterized as "dividual" (see Mosko 2010 for a summary). My work on conversion to Roman Catholicism in Tokyo adds to the discussions generated by several anthropologists who have observed the development of a more bounded, individualistic sense of self as a result of conversion to Christianity. While some anthropologists question the wisdom of seeing too much of a clear division between the two models (Chua 2012; Elisha 2011; Ikeuchi 2017; Mosko 2010), for my part, I attempt to complicate this binary model of personhood by depicting the "realigned sense of self" among Roman Catholics in Tokyo, which is still relational, but the relationship formed is that with the divine.

Are These Changes Only Seen among Roman Catholics?

Some readers may wonder if the transformative processes in one's sense of self that I describe in this book are specifically Roman Catholic. More specifically, would people change their sense of self through other means? This is an important and interesting question. Specialists on Japanese religion may notice that there are some similarities between the descriptions of religious expressions of Roman Catholics and those of personal experiences recorded in the study of so-called new religious movements in Japan (Davis 1980; Shimazono 2004; Young 1993). Mullins has noted in the case of what he calls "indigenous Christian movements" that these groups resemble new religious movements (1998). It is also possible to see similarities between Roman Catholicism in Tokyo and other new religious movements.

Furthermore, other readers may wonder if transformative processes one undergoes through deepening of a Catholic faith may be similar to what some Japanese people may feel through other practices outside religious spheres. For example, would practicing a tea ceremony bring a similar effect? How about those who are in the world of the arts? By deepening one's involvement in a creative world of artistic expressions—such as painting, playing musical instruments, and dancing—can one be able to transcend the mundane and bring about changes in one's relational selves?

It has been a long time since the expression *jibun sagashi*, or "the search of one's self," became a buzzword in Japan (Cave 2007, Rosenberger 2001). Scholars have studied various ways in which people attempt to maintain socially ascribed roles while continuing their exploration that may go beyond such roles. Postponing marriage (Rosenberger 2013), looking toward opportunities relating to the "West" through emotional and physical intimacy (Kelsky 2001), and taking dance lessons such as ballet (Ono 2015) are some of the avenues through which they try to go beyond the socially ascribed narrow sense of self imposed on them. The kind of changes that I describe in this book may resemble some of the cases discussed by these researchers. However, a clear realignment of values Japanese Roman Catholics undergo as well as the discovery of ultimate authority outside the human sphere, in my mind, departs from these examples.

Take a tea ceremony, for example—somewhat of a favored topic among cultural anthropologists of Japan. Through practicing the tea ceremony, many middle-aged and older women were reportedly gaining cultural and symbolic capital with which they feel they can stand on an equal footing with their male family members (or even daughters) who have other social and symbolic capital such as higher education (Chiba 2011; Kato 2004). According to these researchers, these women feel empowered through their involvement in the world of the tea ceremony. It seems to me, however, that this empowerment occurs because they all subscribe to the values popular among members of Japanese society at large. In other words, these women take a yardstick created by the society at large and measure themselves against that yardstick.

On the contrary, metaphorically speaking, Japanese Catholics decidedly exchange their yardstick with that created by the Roman Catholic Church, whose values in many ways are contrary to popular values found in Japanese society. In this way, Japanese Roman Catholics' transformation seen in the sense of self is at a different level from at least those who practice the tea ceremony. Whereas the tea ceremony practitioners continue to remain within the spheres dictated by the authority of humans, Roman Catholics can find their source of legitimacy outside human spheres. Admittedly, it is difficult to compare the cases of Roman Catholics with those who practice other art forms, such as painting and music. It is interesting, however, that I met many musicians and artists who became Roman Catholics at Our Lady of the Assumption Church. This is something that can be pursued by later research.

A Vantage Point

In her article "Dissolution and Reconstitution of Self," Kondo (1986) writes about a few key moments in which she, as a third-generation Japanese American, realized that her sense of self was fragmented, pushed around by the expectations of others, and eventually collapsed. She discusses being torn between her American sense of self and the Japanese sense of self. Through these difficult experiences, Kondo explains, the main focus of her research on the sense of self in Japanese society emerged. She further discusses the epistemological implications of her position(s) in her research. In my own case as a Japanese woman born and culturally trained in Japan but who has also spent more than ten years in North America, my background came with its own set of privileges, disadvantages, and questions.

As a Japanese native using English as a second language for many years, I have frequently wondered about the precise meaning of the word "integrity." When I look up the word in the *Kenkyusha's New College English-Japanese Dictionary*, there are two different entries. The first entry lists the following Japanese words: *kōketsu, seijitsu, seiren*. Here are the English translations of each word in the *New College Japanese-English Dictionary*:

> *kōketsu*—high minded, principled, noble (minded), a person of noble character
>
> *seijitsu*—good faith, reliability, fidelity, reliable, faithful, trustworthy
>
> *seiren keppaku*—absolute honesty, upright

The second entry gives me the following concepts: a perfect state, no damage. In a square bracket, the dictionary says integrity means "perfect" and "healthy" in Latin.

Whenever I look up this word in a dictionary, I halfheartedly say "okay" to myself. I have pretended for many years that I know the word "integrity," making a mental note of these ostensibly equivalent ideas, such as "high-minded" (*kōketsu*) and "faithful" (*seijitsu*). According to the aforementioned two dictionaries, "a person of integrity" would be somebody who is high-minded. I was, however, unsure of whether the dictionaries produced by Japanese academics provided an adequate understanding of this word. After all, my translation of "integrity" has often failed to explain specific situations in Canada or the United States. It was only when somebody pointed out the word's association with the idea of an "integer"—a number that cannot be divided further—that I finally put my finger on the meaning of this word. "Aha!" I nodded. A person of integrity is reliable because she would be grounded in certain moral values or/and committed to her position, and therefore would not waver. Similar to an integer as a numeric value, you cannot divide this person's allegiance in two or three. This concept was rather new for me as a Japanese person and seemed as foreign and novel as Tibet's polyandry or Sudan's female circumcision. I added a mental footnote to the English word "integrity" in my head: in English-speaking cultures, singular allegiance and a determined, committed attitude are positively sanctioned. When I started feeling confident about my understanding of the concept of integrity, several questions emerged. How could people always view integrity in a positive light? Wouldn't integrity hurt people's feelings, as it would in Japanese contexts? Was maintaining integrity always good in English-speaking cultures? Why is this concept not so popular in Japanese contexts?

In situating myself as an investigator into the sense of self in Japanese society, I follow the position advocated by Neni Panourgiá (1994), who studied her own grandfather's death in Greece. Although I am not as intensely "native" as Panourgiá—she studied her own family—I share her experience of the complexity and difficulties of being both the studied and the student simultaneously. I agree with Panourgiá when she states: "humanity deserves the right and the privilege to be communicated, perhaps translated (sometimes even interpreted), from every possible angle, that of the native included, so that we will finally attain the ever-elusive heteroglossic and polyphonic texts we desire" (Panourgiá 1994, 48).

Notes on Fieldwork and Chapter Outline

This is a qualitative ethnographic study. Specifically, I conducted participant-observation fieldwork over a twelve-month period in Tokyo from September 2006 to August 2007 by attending regular masses, other Catholic gatherings, and small weekly study groups led by priests and members of religious orders. I also attended weekly Catholic charismatic meetings.[13] The majority of my field data come from three major sites, all located in central Tokyo: two popular, yet different parishes and one Catholic Charismatic Renewal group. In each of these three research sites, I had approximately twelve to eighteen people—hence altogether roughly fifty—with whom I could regularly talk and ask questions. They also helped me to reach out to other segments of the Roman Catholic Church in Tokyo and surrounding areas.

The two parishes differ in institutional setup; one parish is entrusted to a religious order that has its headquarters in Rome, and the other parish is overseen by local priests who belong to the Archdiocese of Tokyo. The third site, a Catholic Charismatic Renewal group, is what I call a supra-parish organization that attracts people from many different parishes. Interestingly, this group does not enlist any individual as a leader. The details of these three sites are discussed in the next chapter. Through my fieldwork among parishioners in Tokyo, I was able to participate in two pilgrimages to Nagasaki and the Gotō Islands in the Kyushu region.

In addition to participant observation, data for my project come from in-depth interviews, the collection of life histories, and the study of material culture. I conducted thirty structured interviews that each lasted between one and four hours. The age of interviewees varied. They ranged from those in their twenties to eighties, but the majority of them are women in their forties and seventies. Outside the official contexts of the churches and meetings, I spent many hours with my respondents talking about their faith experience and personal situations over cups of tea, and occasionally over glasses of beer or wine. My close relationships with respondents often involved text messages, and it was not unusual to receive text messages on my cell phone until midnight.

Although the Roman Catholic Church and its clergy constitute a part of my study, my primary research focus is on the laity. I am particularly interested in the ways in which laypeople form their sense of self. For this reason, the Church and clergy provide the context rather than the content of my study. Furthermore, I seek to examine the construction of Japanese historical consciousness through the lens of Japanese Catholicism, and thus my study is not primarily concerned with lay Catholics who immigrated to Japan from foreign countries. Because there has been a recent influx of Roman Catholics from overseas that has doubled the Catholic population in Japan (Mullins 2011; Terada 2010), it may seem unreasonable to ignore this segment of the Roman Catholic Church in Tokyo. My fieldwork among Japanese members of the Church, however, did not lead me to the domain of these migrant Catholics in any significant way. In my attempt to integrate with the majority of Japanese Catholics in the metropolitan Tokyo area, I unintentionally kept a distance from "foreigners." These members of the laity are approached indirectly from the perspective of Japanese Catholics, my primary subjects, whose historical consciousness is situated within the geopolitical boundaries of Japan.

The data collected through these methods are analyzed, and the construction of identity and personhood among Roman Catholics is discussed in six chapters. In depicting the transformation in the sense of self that the laity experience, it is necessary to describe two almost opposing social ideals upheld by these individuals at different stages in their lives: a Japanese social ideal on the one hand and a Roman Catholic ideal on the other hand. Before discussing this transformation, however, I first set the stage for my research in chapter 1, discussing the environment and population of Tokyo and providing a brief history of Japanese Catholicism, as well as a bird's-eye view of Japanese religious life after World War II. By discussing the distinctly urban lifestyle of metropolitan Tokyo, where consumers almost always have a wide variety of products to choose from, chapter 1 argues for a notion of the parish that is urban, individually oriented, and in a sense uniquely post–Vatican II with an abundance of resources for individuals to explore their spirituality.

In chapter 2, I depict the conventional values emphasized in contemporary Japanese society. These values include the importance of social hierarchy, fulfilling one's social roles (such as wife, daughter-in-law, and caregiver), and the virtue of striving hard or *ganbaru*. I discuss these values using Confucian teachings expressed in historical contexts. I also provide ethnographic examples in which we learn how these values are understood and manifested as governing ideas in the daily lives of contemporary Japanese. In addition, I analyze the notion of *seken*, according to which human beings and society are invested with ultimate moral authority.

In chapter 3, using the previous chapter as a foil, I depict the ways in which Roman Catholics consider themselves liberated when they find ultimate moral authority in the figure of the Christian God. This chapter illustrates how the laity understands the Catholic faith vis-à-vis Japanese social ideals. Whereas the Neo-Confucian–based worldview is dictated by person-to-person relationships, the Catholic worldview introduces a new "third person": God. By examining popular Catholic notions such as entrusting, "rejoice always," and God as love, I characterize Tokyo Catholics as embracing a new identity marked by a joyous attitude.

Chapter 4 is concerned with the issue of gender within the Church. In exploring the female-dominated nature of parish life, I contextualize Tokyo Catholics in the background of the political economy of Japanese society. Having been designated by postwar governments as the backstage supporters of full-time male workers and as the caretakers of children and the sick (Allison 1991; Lebra 1984; Rosenberger 2001), women can afford to use their leisure hours during the daytime for spiritual pursuits. Men, on the other hand, often convert on their deathbed or in their retirement.

Chapter 5 deals with the issue of concealed identity among Roman Catholics in Tokyo. Many converts decide not to reveal their Christian identity, even to their family members. This chapter situates contemporary Catholics within the context of Japan's genealogy of religion, in which Christianity was represented both officially and unofficially as a villain for centuries. The chapter explores the ongoing implications of the anti-Christian decrees issued in the seventeenth century, whose legacy is still felt through the strong ties maintained between local Buddhist temples, especially with their graveyards, and Japanese households. In the conclusion, I summarize the arguments made throughout the book and extend my discussions to implications on the historical relationship between religion and the self (or the individual).

Chapter 1

Setting the Stage

I was standing at the end of the platform of the Yamanote Line in Gotanda Station. The Yamanote Line circles around central Tokyo, of which the royal palace dominates the very core. I needed to go to the Komagome Station, which is located roughly at the opposite end of the Yamanote circle. Just like any Tokyoite, I have researched the best option to reach my destination. I use one of the common websites that many Tokyoites use for navigating the city. Before I reached the Gotanda Station to transfer to the Yamanote Line, I checked the schedule using my cell phone. It was past 4:30 p.m. in the afternoon. If I took the Yamanote Outer Circle Line, the train that would arrive at 4:34 p.m. at Gotanda Station would take me to Komagome Station at 5:05 p.m., taking thirty-one minutes. If I missed this train, on the opposite platform, I could take the next train of the Yamanote Inner Circle Line, which would arrive at 4:35 p.m. and go around the other way to reach Komagome Station at 5:10 p.m. But this would take slightly longer—thirty-five minutes to reach my destination. If I preferred a shorter trip, according to the website, I could take the next Yamanote Outer Circle Line, which would arrive at 4:38 p.m. at Gotanda Station and would take me to Komagome Station by 5:08 p.m., two minutes earlier than if I took the Inner Circle option.

  As I rehearsed these available options, I missed the first option of departing Gotanda at 4:34 p.m. Now I was pressed to decide whether to wait until 4:38 p.m. to take the same route or to jump on the one, that had just slid into the other side of the platform. I had only one minute to decide to catch this train, which was due to depart at 4:35 p.m. Meanwhile, the 4:35 p.m. train slid into the other side of the platform. In reality, I needed to focus on the train schedule at hand, but instead, I was impressed by how punctually the trains run in Tokyo. I was also impressed by the way in which the train schedule listed on the website that I was checking on my cell phone corresponded to the actual operation of the train.

As this ethnographic vignette indicates, punctuality and efficiency are highly valued qualities in central Tokyo. With the availabilties of cell phones that provide information regarding train connections in a precise manner, one is expected to be punctual. In this city, whose population during the daytime swells to almost 15 million (Tokyo Metropolitan Government 2008), accommodating commuters from neighboring prefectures, transportation systems need to run smoothly and punctually to ensure the security and safety of passengers. If a train is delayed, platforms can become overcrowded with people waiting for the next available trains. For many reasons, orderliness is highly valued, and to a large extent it is in place.

In this chapter, I discuss several themes to contextualize my research. As this opening story illustrates, the urban life of Tokyo, which is characterized by mobility, orderliness, and punctuality, provides the context to this study. I also depict this scene in the train station as foreshadowing my further discussion of the importance of order in Japanese society in this book.

City Life in Tokyo

One of the elements that distinguishes my study from other works on Catholicism is its context, Tokyo. Life in Tokyo, the biggest urban center of Japan, is impersonal, highly mobile, and fast paced. Japan holds roughly 127 million people in a landmass roughly the size of California. Japan's landscape is dominated by mountains. More than 70 percent of the land is mountainous, leaving the remaining small portion of the area for agriculture and urban settlement. The Kanto Plain, in which Tokyo is situated, is the largest lowland in Japan (16,172 square kilometers). The Kanto Plain technically contains seven prefectural-level political entities that include metropolitan Tokyo. In my research, I was concerned only with the Greater Tokyo area, which consists of metropolitan Tokyo and the three surrounding prefectures of Chiba, Saitama, and Kanagawa. This extended area is crisscrossed by well-developed webs of subways and trains, and it accommodates millions of people who commute to the center of the city. According to United Nations (UN) statistics, the Greater Tokyo Area ranks as the number-one global megacity, with its approximately 38 million inhabitants, followed by Delhi, with roughly 26 million inhabitants, and Shanghai, with 24 million people (UN DESA 2016). In this section, I discuss some characteristics of Tokyo that shape the experience of my research participants.

This area was thoroughly destroyed as a result of intensive air bombing at the end of World War II (WWII), and the damage, ironically, facilitated development of the area. Although my research was conducted within the Archdiocese of Tokyo, parishioners and parishioners-to-be commute to sites within the Archdiocese from anywhere in the Greater Tokyo Area. Because subway and train routes are highly developed, it is not difficult to move about in the area.

One of the characteristics of urban life in Tokyo is its anonymity. For example, it is highly unlikely to see people you know when you are walking on a crowded sidewalk in central Tokyo in the vicinity of the Shinjuku and Shibuya stations. This anonymity is intimately connected to the Japan's high population density, which, according to a 2007 UN statistic, is 338 people per square kilometer. This statistic is similar to 348 for Belgium and 345 for India, but slightly less than 439 for the Netherlands (United Nations 2009). When one considers Tokyo, however, a different picture emerges. In the twenty-three wards of Tokyo, which constitute the core part of metropolitan Tokyo, the population density goes up to a remarkable 8,490 people per square kilometer. This level is more than double the 3,580 for Yokohama city in neighboring Kanagawa prefecture (Statistics Bureau Japan 2007). In central Tokyo, there is such an exceedingly large number of people living, working, and conducting their daily lives that even if somebody you know is walking nearby, you might miss this person because of the sheer numbers of people there. Although this may sound overwhelming to those who are used to a tightly knit rural community, the anonymity associated with living among such a dense population has an upside for some Japanese. Many of those who live in Tokyo say that they feel freer in this anonymous context, in which people do not care about what other people are doing. As I discuss later in chapter 2, because people have to deal with the importance of "human relationships" in Japanese society, many people appreciate the anonymity that one can maintain in Tokyo.

This densely populated urban space discourages people from communicating with strangers. People generally believe that those who approach you to talk on the street are "out there to make money" through the bogus services that they are offering. This perception is based somewhat on reality. For example, in the Harajuku area, one may be "discovered" as a prospective fashion model only to find out that he or she has to pay a large sum of money to have photographs taken. In the Ginza area, one may be given "spiritual advice" by a "medium" who insists on selling a special vase that has a magical quality to placate the angry spirits of one's ancestors.[1] Presumably, these angry spirits are the main source of one's current problems (cf. Davis 1980). People are also suspicious of one's neighbors in this densely populated area where occupants of apartments constantly change. For example, in my apartment building in central Tokyo, I attempted to introduce myself to my neighbors in two units that were located on the same floor. I tried knocking on the door or ringing the doorbell several times throughout the year that I stayed there. Even if my neighbors were inside their apartments, none of them took the chance to come out to see me. In the end, I was not successful in meeting any of my neighbors in the building. People seemed to take extra care not to bump into each other by listening to the noise of the neighbors' doors.

Another characteristic of urban life in Tokyo is its "convenience" and efficiency. *Benri* (convenience) is a word that has been worshipped in the postwar era. People pay money for convenience, sacrifice their work hours for convenience, and admire the cleverness of a new service for its convenience. "Convenience stores" (*konbini*, a short form of "convenience store") can be found throughout commercial and residential areas. Most of the stores are open twenty-four hours a day and seven days a week. After working until midnight in one's office in central Tokyo, one can take the subway home, drop by a convenience store, and buy a bentō box with organic vegetables, seaweed salad, and one's favorite sweet snack. Another impressively convenient service is the home delivery courier. Over the past few decades, several home delivery courier companies have become extremely popular. The delivery people for these companies work from early morning to late at night, delivering goods right to the recipients' doorsteps. If the recipient is not home, the delivery person leaves a slip with his or her cell phone number in the mailbox so that, when the recipient returns home, he or she can call the delivery person. If one calls early enough, the delivery can be arranged for the same day.

The cost for the cult of convenience, however, is significantly high. Long work hours and irregular shift work add stress to the lives of many people. A 2004 report from the International Labour Organization says that 28.1 percent of Japanese employees worked more than fifty hours per week in 2001 (Iwasaki et al. 2006). According to Iwasaki et al., this figure is substantially higher than in many European nations such as the Netherlands (1.4 percent), Sweden (1.9 percent), Finland (4.5 percent), and Germany (5.3 percent). This 28.1 percent translates into approximately 15 million workers, most of whom are male employees. Additionally, more than 6 million employees worked more than sixty hours per week between 2002 and 2005 (Iwasaki et al. 2006, 537). *Karōshi* (death by overwork) has long been a household term in Japan.[2] A friend of mine made the analogy that working overtime is like riding a car on a highway. You cannot reduce your speed, as doing so may cause problems for other cars. When the other cars (i.e., employees) are running at a certain speed (i.e., working at a certain rate), you are not able to reduce your own speed (i.e., by leaving work early). Furthermore, as the data in the Iwasaki et al. article show, the majority of this extensive overtime work is done by male employees.

Men are not the only people who work long hours in Japan. It is not uncommon to see school-aged children taking the subway alone to commute to cram schools late at night. Many children are expected to go to cram schools in preparation for fierce entrance examinations for high school or university. Tokyo is known as a place where even toddlers go to cram schools to prepare for entrance exams for prestigious kindergartens. The wives of employees who work overtime assume many household responsibilities to fill the gap created by the absence of their male partners. Taking care of children is one of the top priorities for these women (Allison 1991, 1996; Borovoy 2005). However, women tend to have more flexible hours during the day when their husbands are at work and their children are at school. It is during these daytime hours that I saw women at one of the parishes where I did fieldwork.

Although Japan entered a long period of economic stagnation after its bubble economy had gradually collapsed in the early 1990s, those people I met during the fieldwork for this research seemed to have maintained the clearly delineated gender roles that characterized most of the postwar period. This is partly because the women who frequent Catholic churches are older, many in their retirement. As Nancy Rosenberger has argued, the successive postwar governments had envisaged different roles for these women, and the women more or less have lived up to the governments' agendas. They are expected to be avid consumers of international goods, learn to express their "individual taste," and devote themselves to childcare and the care of the elderly (Rosenberger 2001). The city is filled with numerous shops where one can explore fancy merchandise collected from all over the world. Women frequent these shops to maintain their sense of material fulfillment (Goldstein-Gidoni 2012) or to purchase gifts to smooth out human relationships (Rupp 2003).[3] Husbands delegate these shopping tasks to their wives, who fulfill these duties during daytime.

As briefly described above, despite its fancy exterior, life in Tokyo can be stressful. Men are expected to work long hours, and women are to manage their households without their male partners. It is assumed that wives are nurturers who are in charge of taking care of children, the elderly, and husbands all at the same time. Although women can have free time during the day, they are still part of the larger economic system in which convenience takes priority over people's welfare. Tokyo continues to be an overcrowded city with an immensely high population density. Although there are a number of benefits to living in the ultra-urban center of the nation—for example, one can enjoy world-class art exhibitions that tour major world cities such as Paris, New York, and London—life in Tokyo is not without many restrictions. Now, having provided this necessary context, I turn to the primary focus of this study: Roman Catholicism in Japan.

A Brief History of Roman Catholicism in Japan

Since its introduction by Jesuit missionaries in 1549, Roman Catholicism has never disappeared from Japanese society. The history of Roman Catholicism in Japan can be divided in three major periods: the initial successful "Christian century" (1549–1639); the subsequent proscription period when the laity went underground (1640–1873); and the Meiji Period to the present, in which the practice of faith is officially permitted (1873–present). In this section, I highlight some major events that have shaped the contours of each period.

It is fair to state that the initial phase of evangelization was a success (Boxer 1951; Drummond 1971; cf. Gonoi 1990; Ohta 2004). Christianity was officially brought to Japan by a Jesuit missionary, Francis Xavier, in 1549. At this time, Japan was in the Warring States Period (1460–1573), during which powerful warlords were competing with each other to ascend to the pinnacle of power in the country's political unification process. With the aid of a Japanese interpreter, Xavier had some success in evangelizing. The work started by Xavier was taken over by his successors in a few years, and gradually Japanese followers of Catholicism increased in number, and their population spread over the southwest part of Japan.

Historical evidence suggests that missionaries were successful in collaborating with provincial feudal lords in this initial phase (Elisonas 1991). Most notably, the first political unifier of Japan, Oda Nobunaga (1534–1582), collaborated with mission work largely inspired by his hostility toward powerful Buddhist groups. Under Nobunaga's influence, the Jesuits were able to build a famous three-story church called Nanbandera (literally, "Western Temple") in Kyoto and a Christian school near his castle in Azuchi (present-day Shiga Prefecture). On the southern island of Kyushu, the significant gain in followers was most conspicuous in the area surrounding the southern port city of Nagasaki. This success was partly because missionary work was intertwined with the commercial trade between the Portuguese and the Japanese. The area quickly flourished after this port was opened up for the Portuguese. In 1562, the feudal lord Ōmura Sumitada (1533–1587) was baptized and became the first *kirishitan daimyō* (Christian feudal lord). Most interestingly, he later donated part of Nagasaki to the Jesuit Order in 1580, and another kirishitan *daimyō*, Arima Harunobu (1567–1612), followed suit by donating another part of the city to the Jesuits in 1584. Other *daimyōs*, such as Takayama Ukon (1553–1615) and Ōtomo Sōrin (1530–1587), also converted to the Christian faith. These feudal lords subsequently converted a large number of their retainers (Miyazaki 2003, 7).

After a few decades of missionary work, the Jesuits constructed two institutions for primary education, *seminario*; an institution for higher learning, *collegio*; and the novitiate, *novitiado*, for religious candidates (Miyazaki 2003, 9). In 1582, to show the fruit of their successful evangelization in Japan, the Jesuits sent four young Japanese Christians to Rome in hope of securing funding for further evangelization; this mission is known as the Tenshō Mission to Europe. By the time these boys returned to Japan eight years later, however, the ruling shogun, Toyotomi Hideyoshi (1537–1598), issued a decree to expel all foreign missionaries (Ohta 2004, 59).[4] According to the Jesuits' historical records, prior to the expulsion of foreign priests, there were more than two hundred thousand Roman Catholic converts, two hundred churches, and twenty religious institutions in Japan (Gonoi 1990, 9). The Japanese historian Gonoi Takashi estimates that there were approximately 370,000 converts when the proscription decree of 1614 was issued by Tokugawa Ieyasu (1542–1616), the successor to Hideyoshi (Gonoi 1990, 206).

After enjoying the honeymoon phase of initial evangelization, Christianity entered a period of proscription and persecution.[5] In the eyes of the successive ruling shoguns, Toyotomi Hideyoshi and Tokugawa Ieyasu,

Christianity came to be regarded as a threat to their political ambitions to unify the archipelago. Hideyoshi departed from his early favorable treatment of Christianity and initiated persecution by ordering the expulsion of the missionaries in 1587. While Hideyoshi did not strictly enforce anti-Christian policies during his reign, his successors took various measures to ensure the systematic uprooting of Christianity from Japan. In 1614, Ieyasu's government issued a total ban of Christianity nationwide. This ban included the expulsion of missionaries as well as influential leaders, and the demolition of Christian edifices (Miyazaki 2003, 12). Later in 1623, the ruling shogun Tokugawa Iemitsu (1604–1651) further expanded the system of eradication. The official policy to proscribe Christianity was disseminated nationwide through notice boards (*takafuda/kōsatsu*) on which different reward sums were promised to those who reported finding lay Christians (*kirishitan*), brothers (*iruman*), and priests (*bateren*). The authorities also instituted the temple certification system (*terauke seido*), in which all family members had to receive certification from a local Buddhist temple that there were no Christians in the household (Gonoi 1990, 231–35). Furthermore, the authorities forced residents to step on sacred Christian icons (*fumie*) to prove that they were not Christians (Gonoi 1990, 235–36).[6] Most of these anti-Christian policies continued until the end of the Edo Era.[7]

During the persecution period, many Christians were captured, tortured, and, when they did not abandon their faith, killed. In the face of severe torture and impending death, many decided to conceal their religious affiliation with Christianity and disguised it through their affiliation with Buddhist and Shinto institutions. Those who disguised their Christian identity are called hidden Christians (*kakure kirishitan*, shortened to *kakure*). While practicing their Christian faith underground, the laity developed a system to keep track of the liturgical calendar, transmit important information regarding their faith community, and conduct important rituals such as baptism and funeral rites. In this way, the hidden Christians managed to practice their faith for many generations without clergy. Although numerous losses and alterations were inevitable in the course of transmission over centuries without clergy, the extent to which earlier traditions were kept is remarkable.[8] The explicit ban on Christianity continued for roughly two and a half centuries until 1873, when the government reluctantly rescinded the decree of proscription in response to Western condemnation of the ban (Gonoi 1990, 266).

The rescinding of the decree at the beginning of the Meiji Period came as a byproduct of Japan's growing recognition of the need to establish stable diplomatic and commercial relationships with the powerful European nations and the United States. Particularly interesting is that prior to the rescinding of the decree, hidden Christian communities resurfaced, and their plight came to be known in the West. Toward the end of the Edo Period, Japan was forced to end its national seclusion policy in 1854 by signing the Treaty of Amity and Commerce with the United States, providing opportunities to other European nations such as France and England to procure the same treaty conditions.[9] Among the conditions that these Western nations procured was their right to practice their religion in Japan. With the arrival of various Europeans and Americans, the building of churches for resident aliens started. On March 17, 1865, a group of *kakure kirishitan* in the Urakami region of Nagasaki managed to sneak in to the "French Temple," which was a Roman Catholic church officially built for French residents of Japan. Here, to the astonishment of the French priest, they told him that they too believed in the same religion. As if to clear any doubts that the French priest may have had, one of the women asked the priest: "Where is the statue of Santa Maria?" (Gonoi 1990, 249; Ohta 2004, 196) Immediately after this incident, the two resident priests started their pastoral work in secret so that these hidden Christians could be reincorporated into the Roman Catholic Church. Not surprisingly, however, these activities soon caught the attention of local authorities. As a result, many of these resurfaced hidden Christians from the Urakami region were again captured, tortured until they renounced their faith, and sent into exile, where many died from severe living conditions and torture (Gonoi 1990, 260).

Subsequently, the plight of these hidden Christians caught media attention overseas, and this story became a cause célèbre among Western nations (Ohta 2004, 200; Hardacre 2006). Coincidentally, the new Meiji government had just dispatched its foreign mission, led by Iwakura Tomomi (1825–1883), to several major Western countries to study overseas conditions and also to negotiate more equal terms for the treaties that Japan had signed earlier. This series of diplomatic visits is known as the Iwakura Mission (1871–1873). In the meetings with foreign dignitaries, Iwakura and his companions were strongly urged to lift the ban on Christianity. Despite the Japanese ministers' insistence that the treatment of Christians should be considered an internal matter (and therefore was unrelated to the diplomatic issues at hand), for the Europeans and Americans, the oppression of Christians was a sign that Japan was an uncivilized country (and therefore should not be considered an equal diplomatic partner). Judging that the proscription of Christianity was not worth continuing in light of the pressing international agenda for Japan, in 1873 the government quietly removed the decree of proscription from street corners.[10]

Scholars point out that removing the decree from street corners did not necessarily mean acceptance of Christianity in practice. From 1873 to 1889, the government took an ambivalent position in dealing with matters relating to Christianity. This ambivalence came to an end in 1889, when the Meiji Constitution, which included the limited "freedom of religion" clause, was enacted (Hardacre 1989, 114). Freedom of religions was guaranteed "within limits not prejudicial to peace and order, and not antagonistic to their duties as subjects" (Hardacre 1989, 119–20). In reality, however, the missionaries started their work when the notice boards were taken down in 1873. From the Meiji Era onward, unlike the previous era of evangelization before proscription, the Christian market was no longer a monopoly for the Roman Catholic Church. The Japanese "market" was open for other Christian denominations, including various American, English, Canadian, and Dutch Protestant and Russian Orthodox churches operating in the hope of gaining some Japanese converts (Ballhatchet 2003).

There was one significant issue that all the Christian denominations had to deal with from the early Meiji Period to the end of World War II: their relationship with Japan's newly devised emperor-centered "theocracy" and the associated ideology of the emperor's divinity. In other words, the churches were pressed to deal with Japan's State Shinto, the state-sponsored religion that upheld the reigning emperor as a "living deity" (*arahitogami*). In discussing possible sources for the idea of *arahitogami* in Japan, Sueki Fumihiko (2006) points to influences that political elites in Japan may have received from the Christian characterization of God as the powerful ruler. He points to the deification of Toyotomi Hideyoshi and Tokugawa Ieyasu in the earlier periods may have been influenced by this Christian characterization of the deity. Sueki suggests that the budding ideas of the veneration of political leaders as divine began earlier, and then the same current contributed to a later creation of *arahitogami* during the Meiji Period (2006, 140), thus giving rise to a Japanese case of the diffusion of the temporal and spiritual realms. For scholars of religion, this era is a fascinating one to study, as it is the time when Japan was struggling to understand the category of "religion," which appeared so significant to the Western mind (Josephson 2012). The government devised its own "religion" that it saw as being analogous to Christianity.[11] For conscientious

Christians in Japan at the time, however, State Shinto created an enormous problem. The essential question asked by the government was whether one could be Japanese and Christian at the same time. Many intellectuals who converted to the Christian faith wrote treatises in defense of their faith. Uchimura Kanzō, founder of an independent Japanese Christian movement called Mukyōkai-shugi or Non-Church Principle, for example, wrote an essay titled "Two J's," Jesus and Japan (Ballhatchet 2003, 51). The degree to which the state ideology interfered with the life of Christians varied from period to period. Generally, however, in the cultural milieu of new beginnings in the country, patriotism was overtly visible among new Protestant converts in the early period. This gradually waned as the marginalization of Christianity intensified with the nationalistic turn in the later years of the early Shōwa Era (1926–1989) up to the defeat of the war. When Japan entered WWII, anything Western was suspect, and Christianity was often detested as part of Western civilization.[12]

To focus more specifically on the Roman Catholic Church, before the ban on Christianity was lifted, the Sacred Congregation for Propagation of the Faith in the Vatican entrusted the evangelization of Japan to the hands of the Société des Missions Etrangères (hereafter the Paris Foreign Missions Society, or Paris Mission for short).[13] In 1844, its member Fr. Forcade managed to land on Okinawa Island, and in 1846 the Vatican made Japan an apostolic vicariate[14] prior to the lifting of the ban on Christianity. Re-evangelization of Japan largely fell under the responsibility of the Paris Mission. Until the arrival of the Spanish Dominicans in 1904, all of the Catholic groups that evangelized in Japan were French in origin, leaving unmistakable influences of nineteenth-century France on churches in Japan (Ohta 2004, 178). As previously discussed, the church edifices were built initially for resident aliens. After the first Catholic church was built in Yokohama, churches were constructed in other port cities, including Nagasaki (which led to the "discovery" of the hidden Japanese Catholics), and these places became hubs of various evangelistic activities.

In the re-evangelization period (1873–present), the Roman Catholic Church expanded its work in the areas of social welfare and education. In the southern region of Kyushu, missionaries' efforts were divided between the care of returnees from exile and the reincorporation of hidden Christian community members back into the Church. In other parts of Japan, missionary work was initially focused on the disadvantaged in rural areas, such as the poor and abandoned children (Ballhatchet 2003, 40). In the project led by de Rotz of the Paris Mission, for example, we see these two themes coming together. When dysentery spread in Nagasaki, de Rotz organized several Christians returned from exile to identify, isolate, and give medical treatment to the afflicted. He used lay volunteers as nurses and produced remarkable results, saving many people from death caused by dysentery.[15] Later, some of these laywomen started raising abandoned children, and this project eventually developed into an orphanage. De Rotz contributed a significant amount of his private funds to save the poverty-stricken Christians in the area, who were considered second-class citizens. Because of more than two hundred years of government proscription of Christianity, the social position of Christians did not improve immediately after the ban was lifted. De Rotz introduced numerous types of machinery and technologies for the production of noodles, shirts, and sheets for sale (Ohta 2004). Christians in the region learned various techniques to manufacture these different products.

On the other hand, outside the Kyushu area, missionaries were gaining converts from the ex-samurai class. Subsequently, a number of female orders became active in the field of education. From 1878 to 1900 alone, three female orders—the Sisters of St. Paul of Chartres, the Société de Marie (Marians), and the Congrégation des Soeurs de l'Instruction charitable du saint Enfant Jésus (Saint Maur)—established more than a dozen primary and secondary educational institutions. Later, German Jesuits joined this effort by founding Japan's first Catholic university in 1913. Many of today's elite Catholic schools, especially in Tokyo, originated in this period. For example, a boys' school, Gyōsei, was founded in 1888, followed by one for girls, Futaba, in the same year; another girls' school, Shirayuri, followed in 1910 (Sophia School Corporation Editorial Committee for New Catholic Encyclopedia, 2002). As Karen Seat (2003) notes, women's education was significantly neglected by the Meiji government and thus was a niche that the Church could fill to have access to an elite segment of the Japanese population at the time. Many of my research participants attended one of these schools as children and later converted to Roman Catholicism.

Whereas members of Protestant denominations were heavily involved in the debate about whether one could be loyal to both the Japanese emperor and the Christian God, the tension between the state orthodoxy and the Roman Catholic Church did not flare up until an incident that occurred when some students of a Jesuit university refused to bow down properly at the national Yasukuni Shrine[16] in 1932. In response to this incident, the Archbishop of Tokyo and an emissary from the Vatican contacted the Ministry of Education requesting the official meaning of mandatory attendance at the Shrine. The Ministry responded by stating that attendance at the shrine is "based on educational reasons and that the bowing at the Shrine required of students and young people should be considered an expression of one's patriotism and loyalty to the state" (Gonoi 1990, 295). The bishops in Japan took this government response at face value and officially allowed Catholic students to attend Yasukuni Shrine.

As shown by this incident, the Roman Catholic Church in Japan did not confront the nationalistic agenda of the Japanese wartime government; rather, the Church collaborated with the country's imperialistic agenda. When war broke out between Japan and China in 1937, the priest Taguchi Yoshigorō was dispatched as part of the army and aided Japan's invasion of northern China. Later in 1941, when Japan's imperial armies invaded southern Indochina, the government requested ten priests and 150 lay members from the Roman Catholic Church in Japan as part of a team responsible for war propaganda. The Church responded to this request by dispatching a "Catholic religious army" (*katorikku shūkyō butai*, Gonoi 1990, 302–3). The Church's collaboration with Japan's imperial armies contrasts markedly with the stance taken by some other Protestant denominations such as the Holiness groups, whose pastors were arrested and members disbanded (Gonoi 1990, 303).

As briefly sketched above, the history of Roman Catholicism in Japan is rich and significantly different from that of Catholic traditions in other nations. The history of the Church in Japan reflects Japan's political history, in which the state, through its control of ideologies, international trade, and popular practices, succeeded in maintaining tight control over its subjects. With the exception of the earliest period, the Catholic Church in Japan has always been "an underdog" in society. Unlike its European counterparts, the Catholic Church in Japan has never assumed a venerable position at any time in its history. To further trace the background of today's Church, I now present another broad-brush portrait of Japanese religious life after WWII.

Postwar Religious Landscape in Japan

The end of WWII clearly marked the beginning of a different era for religious life in Japan. The postwar occupation regime, the US-led Allied Forces, issued the State Shinto Directive in 1945, dismantling the major components of State Shinto. To publicize the demise of State Shinto throughout the Japanese population, the reigning emperor made the Declaration of Humanity on January 1, 1946. Finally, the new Constitution of 1947 instituted the principle of separation of state and religion in Article 20 and the prohibition of state sponsorship of any religion in Article 89 (Hardacre 2006; Shimazono 2006). The 1947 Constitution was the first time that the ruling regime in Japan guaranteed the freedom of religion in practice. The freedom of religion mentioned in the Meiji Constitution was limited in scope, and many leaders of new religious movements as well as Christian groups were arrested and detained on charges of *lèse majesté* when their doctrines contradicted Shinto mythology (cf. Hardacre 2006, 284).

The new changes incorporated in the postwar Constitution gave rise to the development of numerous new religious movements, which led one scholar to refer to this period as the "rush hour of the gods" (McFarland 1967). The Catholic Church in Japan too had its own share of increased converts during this period. In 1941, there were twenty-one churches in the Archdiocese of Tokyo, of which fourteen were destroyed during the war. By 1963, this number had risen to sixty-six. The number of converts also increased. There were 8,455 Catholics in 1941, but this number increased to 54,575 in 1967 (Drummond 1971, 329). With the help of missionaries who needed to leave China after the war, the Catholic Church in Japan underwent a significant expansion during this period.

A prominent scholar of Japan's new religious movements, Susumu Shimazono, proposes 1926 to the mid-1970s as the period of rapid growth for such groups as Reiyū-kai, Seichō no ie, Risshō Kōseikai, and Sōka Gakkai. This period coincides with the rapid urbanization and economic growth of the nation. Shimazono characterizes the founders of these groups as "men or women without high social standing" (1993, 222) and suggests that they were typically this-worldly oriented. Shimazono further characterizes these groups as highly syncretic in their teachings, incorporating elements from Buddhism, Shinto, folk religion, and various other religions. Unlike these earlier movements, Shimazono further argues, the groups that developed from the 1970s onward are otherworldly in their orientation and are concerned with the problems of meaning and fulfillment in life. Examples of these later groups are Aum Shinrikyō, Kōfuku no kagaku, and the Unification Church. These groups particularly attracted the younger generation. Further, there are numerous "spirituality movements" that do not necessarily take the form of religious institutions. Writing in 1993,

Shimazono predicted that this trend would continue throughout the rest of the 1990s (Shimazono 1993).

As predicted by Shimazono, I saw ample evidence for the continuing growth of new religious movements such as Sōka Gakkai and spirituality movements in Tokyo. It became a common sight toward the end of my twelve-month stay to see a commuter train filled with advertisements promoting products of Sōka Gakkai, for example. Sōka Gakkai publishes a number of popular magazines, and it has enough financial and publication resources to provide readers with a variety of magazine advertisements. A relative of mine, a Sōka Gakkai member, also bought me a few months' subscription to *Seikyō Shinbun*, the daily newspaper published by Sōka Gakkai. The popularity of spirituality movements is also apparent through the media. One of the most-discussed TV programs is the weekly talk show *Ōra no izumi* (literally translated as "the spring of aura"), which is hosted by two renowned spiritual mediums, Ehara Hiroyuki and Miwa Akihiro. These two mediums receive a different guest each week, and the hosts and the celebrity of the week talk about the guest's life with "spiritual" commentaries interjected by the mediums.

In contrast to these new religious movements and the "world of spirituality" (*seishin sekai*), it is perhaps fair to state that traditional religious groups such as Buddhist temples and Shinto shrines entered a long period of stagnation after WWII. For most parishioners, Buddhist temples became a place to visit during the summer week of *bon*, or the week of the dead, and on a few other liturgical occasions prescribed by the tradition to perform rituals for deceased family members. Temples derive the majority of their income by performing funeral rites for parishioners (Covell 2005), and in general, Buddhist temples have not made many efforts to change their passive character. There are, however, several exceptions, and some Buddhist clergy are putting forward innovative plans to challenge the dominant idea of "funeral Buddhism." For example, Setouchi Jakuchō, a celebrity writer who became a Buddhist nun, continues to attract audiences of thousands to her monthly sermons at her resident temple. Also, Mark Rowe's recent study documents innovation at a Buddhist temple in Tokyo, where alternative funeral arrangements have been created for those who do not wish to burden their sons and daughters for their memorials (Rowe 2011). This temple has also become a site for various community activities, providing an active social life for its members. Recently, several bars run by Buddhist monks in Tokyo and Kyoto are attracting some people. These examples are, however, rare and not well-known. The majority of local temples rely on existing parishioners' liturgical occasions such as funerals to generate income, and tend not to strive to gain new members or to create opportunities to educate the general public on Buddhism. Shinto shrines, too, are inclined to maintain the status quo, providing minimum contact with general public. This situation is highlighted by ethnographic works conducted at some Shinto shrines (e.g., Nelson 2000; Smyers 1999).

This nominal and weakened affiliation with traditional religious institutions can be discerned in the lives of those whom I met during my fieldwork. Here, I introduce two young recent converts to Catholicism. I start with the story of Kaji-san, a woman in her early forties. When I asked her about her family's religious background, she said: "Ordinary, let's see, Buddhism! Kawasaki Daishi [a famous Buddhist temple]? Well, I don't know! We used to go to Kawasaki Daishi for New Year's. I'm not sure what our denomination is." I asked several further questions to find out her family's nominal affiliation to Buddhism. Often religious ties become much more relevant when a family member dies and the need arises for a memorial rite for the deceased. When Kaji-san's mother passed away, she said the family had the funeral rite conducted at "some ordinary Buddhist place, at something like a 'ceremony center' (*seremonī sentā*)." This term refers to the large halls run by funeral companies that have become popular in recent years. These funeral companies usually do not have exclusive ties to any particular denomination. Her mother's funeral was held there, and Kaji-san did not pay too much attention to which temple the priest came from to chant the Buddhist sutras.

Another research participant, Yabe-san, told me how upsetting it was when his grandfather passed away several years previously. When his grandfather became ill and died within a week from a rapidly progressing illness, the lack of religious ties within the household became evident through a strange course of events. He said:

> It turned out that the cemetery plot that we purchased earlier belonged to the wrong denomination [of Buddhism]. So, the priest from our [Buddhist] temple was considerably upset. So, we discussed what to do, and decided to do a non-religious funeral [without involving the family temple]; the funeral company also agreed to conduct a non-religious rite. [And every process was completed without the family temple's involvement.] But my parents must have felt bad about the entire thing. . . . For a while, [grandfather's] ashes were

placed in the alcove in our house, but soon they [the parents] purchased another cemetery plot, and received a brand-new Buddhist posthumous name [for the deceased grandfather] and everything [from the family temple]. It's a very strange story, isn't it? I believe our household belongs to the Zen or Sōtō Sect, but we mistakenly bought a plot in the Jōdo Shin Sect or something like that. I don't remember exactly, but isn't it a bizarre story?

These two stories came from people in their thirties and forties. They were both born and raised in the metropolitan Tokyo Area. I am not certain how many generations of their families have lived in the same area, but nevertheless, it is obvious that members of the current generation have significantly weak ties to their parish temples. While Shimazono states that the relationship between Buddhist temples and their parishioners has "gradually become formalistic" (Shimazono 2006, 226), my research participants' stories quoted above suggest that the relationship is indeed not alive.

Another element that needs to be mentioned in the religious life of postwar Japan is general mistrust in "religion" (*shūkyō*). As Robert Kisala details in his article on Japanese religions (2006), the popular image of religion, especially that of religious institutions, suffers from severely negative connotations. According to *Yomiuri Newspaper*'s survey conducted in 1995, 40 percent of respondents believe that religious groups "are just out to make money," and 37 percent believe that they "prey on people's fears" (Kisala 2006, 5). According to a different survey conducted by the Nanzan Institute for Religion and Culture, religious institutions were poorly regarded in terms of trustworthiness by the public. Whereas the police (69 percent) and legal system (63 percent) procured a fair level of trust from respondents, religion was rated as the least trustworthy institution, gaining the approval of a mere 13 percent of respondents. This percentage is lower than that for politicians in the national parliament (20 percent). These figures indicate severe mistrust of religious institutions in contemporary Japan (Kisala 2006, 6).

Despite the fact that the Roman Catholic Church is considered one of the most conservative and traditional religious institutions in the Western world, situated in the context of Japan's post-WWII religious scene, the Roman Catholic Church may fall into a different category. From my observations during the fieldwork, the Church is in many ways in competition with new religious movements and spirituality movements in Japan. Some of the converts to Catholicism arrive at the Church as a result of spiritual quests that often entail new religious movements as well as spirituality movements. Although not all converts share this experience, many have tried out these other spiritual paths, and some retain their ties to these movements even after their conversion. Keeping the particularity of the Japanese context in mind, now I turn to today's Catholic Church in Japan.

The Catholic Church in Japan at the Beginning of the Twenty-First Century

It is reasonable to say that the Catholic Church in Japan stands at a critical moment of change at the end of the first decade of the twenty-first century. On the one hand, Japanese members in the Church are in decline. On the other hand, there are significant influxes of migrant Catholics to many dioceses (Quero and Shoji 2014), increasing the total Catholic population in Japan (Mullins 2011). The annual official statistics released by the Catholic Bishops' Conference of Japan reports that the total number of Roman Catholics in Japan in 2007 was 447,720 (Catholic Bishops' Conference of Japan 2008). This figure represents less than 0.4 percent of Japan's total population of approximately 127 million. The Church divides Japan into sixteen dioceses (figure 1.1), including the three Archdioceses of Tokyo, Nagasaki, and Osaka. It is not surprising that the two biggest cities of Japan, Tokyo and Osaka, have received the status of archdiocese.

Some background information on the Archdiocese of Nagasaki is in order. The Archdiocese of Nagasaki holds the second-largest population of Roman Catholics (64,654) following that of Tokyo. Although this is the second largest in number in terms of the percentage of the Catholic population living within the diocese, Nagasaki ranks as the top in Japan. While the Archdiocese of Tokyo claims only 0.5 percent of its area's population as Catholics, the Archdiocese of Nagasaki claims more than 4 percent of its population as Catholic (Catholic Bishops' Conference of Japan 2008). This situation is due to Nagasaki's historical ties to Roman Catholicism, described in the previous section. Because of the special position that the city of Nagasaki occupies in Japanese Roman Catholic history, some call Nagasaki "the Rome of Japan."

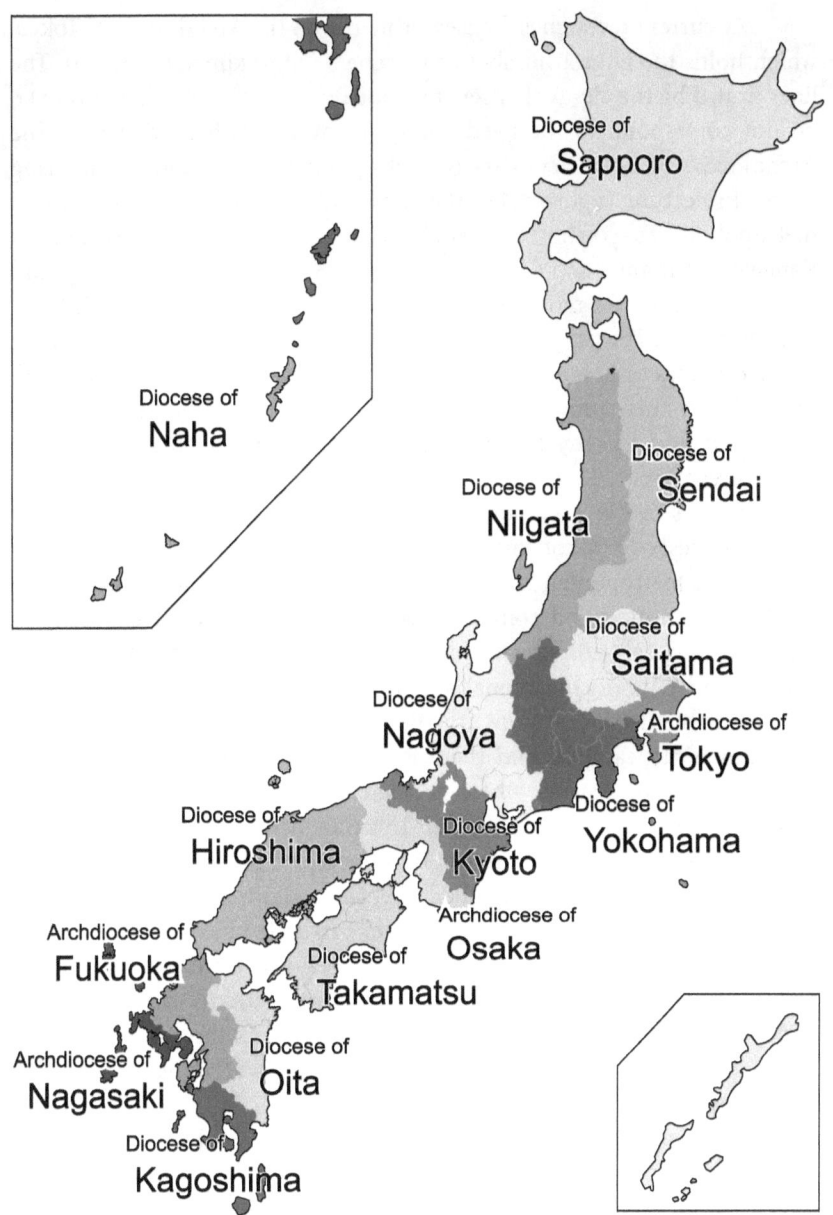

Figure 1.1. Map of Sixteen Dioceses in Japan.

My current research is focused primarily on the Archdiocese of Tokyo, which holds the largest number of members (approximately 93,000). The lines drawn by the clergy that separate one diocese from another, however, do not correspond to the lived reality of my research participants. The Archdiocese of Tokyo consists of metropolitan Tokyo and neighboring Chiba Prefecture (figure 1.1). The area within commuting distance to metropolitan Tokyo, however, includes the neighboring prefectures of Kanagawa, Saitama, and Chiba. Well-developed networks of subways and Japan Railways (JR) move massive numbers of people within this large area effectively. The prefectures of Kanagawa and Saitama, however, belong to the dioceses of Yokohama and Saitama, respectively. As the reader will find later in this study, two parishes within the Archdiocese of Tokyo where I conducted my fieldwork attract people from all four of these prefectures: Tokyo, Kanagawa, Saitama, and Chiba. In other word, these two churches in the Archdiocese of Tokyo had parishioners who resided in the Dioceses of Yokohama and Saitama.

In the metropolitan Tokyo area, I encountered various "unorthodox" practices permitted and conducted by the Church. For catechumens in search of spiritual truth, the Catholic Church provides abundant resources backed up by its organizational strength. For example, there are weekly Zen sitting meditation sessions organized and overseen by a Catholic priest on a university campus, and there is a "Catholic bar" in the middle of Tokyo's "red light district" where people can congregate and discuss their faith over beer imported from Israel. This establishment was sponsored by several high-ranking priests in the Archdiocese of Tokyo. On First Fridays (called *hatsukin* in Japanese by the laity), lay Catholics can attend a prayer meeting led by a Taizé community, attend a mass led by a group of people who want to canonize all aborted babies, or go to a church community hall where the youth congregate to drink, sing, and talk throughout the night with a resident priest and fellow Catholics. As the reader will find throughout this study, Catholics in Tokyo enjoy a wide range of activities offered by the Church and its lay communities.

Last, but not least important, throughout my fieldwork in Tokyo, I had minimal contact with non-Japanese communities within the Church. This situation is odd, considering that the number of Roman Catholics has supposedly doubled with the influx of migrants from overseas. The fact that I was insulated from non-Japanese Catholic communities, however, most likely reflects the segregated reality of Japanese and non-Japanese ethnic communities within the Roman Catholic Church in Tokyo. My encounters with non-Japanese Catholics were mostly through academic researchers who study these migrant communities. Through the different faith groups that I followed closely, the only non-Japanese members with whom I came into direct contact were Koreans and other nationals who spoke the Japanese language. I met a few Koreans in all the faith groups that I attended and an American in a charismatic group, but I only encountered other ethnic groups through the work of my colleagues in Tokyo or indirectly in groups on Sundays at a large church.

Fieldwork Sites

The field data that constitute this research are drawn primarily from my observations at two parishes and one charismatic group, all located within the Archdiocese of Tokyo. These two parishes rank number one and two in producing Japanese converts within the Archdiocese.[17] In other words, these parishes are the most successful in evangelizing to the Japanese populace. One is run by a male religious order. This parish, which I call Our Lady of the Assumption Church, is located in the center of downtown Tokyo. The other parish, which I call the Terada Catholic Church, is run by the Archdiocese of Tokyo and is located in the residential area of Tokyo. In total, the Tokyo Archdiocese produces close to 1,800 converts a year.[18] Whereas most of the local parishes each produces fewer than 50 converts a year, these two parishes combined baptize more than 300 people each year. In 2005, more than 200 people were baptized at Our Lady of the Assumption, and close to 100 were baptized by the Terada Catholic Church. This latter figure is remarkable considering that the Terada Catholic Church only had two resident priests in 2005 compared to ten at Our Lady of the Assumption. The number of converts produced at the Terada Catholic Church is noteworthy and was constantly discussed in Catholic circles in Japan. I attended activities at Our Lady of the Assumption during weekdays, and Sunday masses and other activities at the Terada Catholic Church on weekends. I then rushed to a charismatic weekly meeting on Sunday nights throughout my fieldwork.

I should note, however, that my field research was not confined to those in the process of conversion to the Catholic faith. At the beginning of my fieldwork, I started talking to those who were in positions of power—lay leaders, priests, and nuns—because it was relatively easy to talk to these people. While talking with parishioners, priests, and nuns, I learned that these two parishes were particularly active churches. Through one of the classes that I was attending at Our Lady of the Assumption, I was led to the weekly charismatic group. Similarly, several of my research participants go back and forth between the two parishes or attend both Our Lady of the Assumption and the charismatic meeting. These three sites were all located in central Tokyo, where people can travel by subway and the JR system so it is easy to participate in worship in more than one venue. I interacted with both longtime Catholics and those who were new to the Church throughout my fieldwork at these three venues. Now I turn to a discussion of each venue.

Our Lady of the Assumption

When I slowly pushed open the heavy wooden door to the main sanctuary of Our Lady of the Assumption Church, I saw approximately forty to fifty people quietly sitting in the sanctuary. The sanctuary of this church, whose membership exceeded 14,000, was fairly large. The building was relatively new—construction was completed in 1999—and made of concrete and stained glass. Cool air surrounded my senses. The oval sanctuary was a large, modern structure. There was natural light coming in from the ceiling, and the oval-shaped hall was surrounded and supported by twelve columns, each bearing the name of one of the twelve apostles. There were also twelve long, beautiful stained-glass windows equally spaced around the sanctuary, and each window depicted a different biblical motif, such as fire, grape branches, wheat fields, and sheep. Many people in the church seemed to be in deep prayer. Frankly, I have never seen Japanese people praying, except for the short prayers that many people offer on visits to Shinto shrines at the New Year or for a particular occasion such as for a petition for one's success in an entrance exam (cf. Reader 1991; Reader and Tanabe 1998). Unlike the people I had seen at shrines on New Year's Day, these people who were praying at the sanctuary stayed there motionless for a long period of time. The floor seemed to be made of polished stone, and I had to walk carefully so that my footsteps did not make any noise. The place was meticulously clean and quiet enough to hear a pin drop. The majority were Japanese women of middle age. There were a few Japanese men and a few foreigners.

Our Lady of the Assumption Church is an exceptionally resourceful parish. It is centrally located, offers numerous free classes throughout the year, and is ministered to by a dozen full-time priests. Geographically, this parish is located literally in the center of Tokyo. It takes only a few minutes to walk to the church from the nearest JR station. This geographical convenience attracts people who do not necessarily live in this neighborhood. Many who came to this church said that it is far easier to come to Our Lady of the Assumption than their neighborhood parish because of its proximity to the major train and subway stations. Frequently, after taking the train, one has to take a bus or walk more than ten minutes to travel to the nearest parish church. I learned that many people who came to this church were attracted to its convenience, anonymity, and the variety of classes that it offers newcomers to explore.

The resourcefulness of Our Lady of the Assumption is apparent in the broad array of classes that it offers throughout the year. For the "beginners," there are more than twenty different kinds of classes offered per week. These classes are designed and led by the parish priests, a brother, affiliated nuns, and other priests who work at this parish. At a glance, one cannot discern the differences between these classes; most are focused on reading the Bible and "aim to deepen participants' familiarity with Christianity." There is no mention of catechism, but many class descriptions say that "the class helps to prepare one to receive baptism." It is all the more impressive that there is a separate list of classes for those who are already familiar with the faith. As I gradually learned over the course of fieldwork, however, these classes for "beginners" were mostly attended by people who had in fact already converted to Roman Catholicism. Potential converts attend these classes first, and then, when they are ready to receive baptism, the instructor of the course provides them with separate catechism classes in addition to these classes.

Another aspect of resourcefulness at Our Lady of the Assumption is the church's willingness to make the sanctuary and liturgical opportunities available to the laity. There are a large number of masses offered both on weekdays and for the Lord's Day.[19] On weekdays, the parish offers five masses (6:00, 7:00, 7:30, 12:00, and 18:00) in Japanese. For the Lord's Day, it offers six masses (6:00 p.m. on Saturdays; 6:00 a.m., 7:30 a.m., 9:00 a.m., 10:30 a.m., and 6:00 p.m. on Sundays) in Japanese, and six other masses in foreign languages (English, Portuguese, Spanish, Indonesian, Vietnamese, and Polish).[20] As one housewife said to me, the church offers masses so that "one can accommodate faith according to one's lifestyle." She appreciated that she could go shopping in a nearby district and then drop by for a mass at noon. Similarly, while most churches close the doors to their sanctuary during the day except during mass, Our Lady of the Assumption is open to the public most of the day. The main sanctuary and two other chapels are open to anybody for quiet time, providing a rare "sanctuary" for those who are tired of stress in the busiest part of metropolitan Tokyo.

Physically, Our Lady of the Assumption houses a major sanctuary, two other chapels of a significant size, a large crypt directly beneath the main sanctuary, and an office building that also houses priests' offices and meeting rooms for the congregation. Right next to the main gate, there is a bookstore run by a female order. The store sells books, rosaries, incense, and other religious items. While I was conducting fieldwork, a new building for the order's headquarters in Japan was under construction. The church is adjacent to a university that is also run by the same order. Many priests teach at this university, and the campus also accommodates a residential building for ordained priests who are not necessarily part of Our Lady of the Assumption. The priests' residence, located on the university campus, also has a garden and a historical building, which has a small but handsome chapel. Graduates of this university often choose this chapel as a wedding venue.

"Catholic Village" and Charismatic Meeting

Before turning to the other parish, Terada Church, I would like to describe the area where Our Lady of the Assumption is located together with a rough sketch of a charismatic meeting. There is no nickname for this area other than the official name used by the city administration, but I would personally name this area the "Catholic Village" of Tokyo. Although the degree to which the area contained organizations and schools that were related to the Catholic Church is probably not apparent to those who have no interest in Catholicism, as I proceeded with my fieldwork, I was surprised by how densely Catholic venues are situated in this area of downtown Tokyo. From the major JR and subway station closest to Our Lady of the Assumption, one can easily access four different stores that deal with things Catholic, such as books, rosaries, holy water, and various talismans.[21] Within walking distance, several religious orders are located. Some of these orders run educational institutions such as primary schools and the university, and the presence of these institutions further deepens the degree to which this area is inhabited by those who are related to the Catholic Church. It is not unusual to see nuns walking in their habits when you set foot in this area.

Weekly meetings of one of the Catholic Charismatic Renewal groups in this area take place on the sixth floor of a building owned by a different Catholic male order from the one that runs Our Lady of the Assumption Church. This building is located within a ten-minute walk of Our Lady of the Assumption, and the entire building is dedicated to the sale of Catholic books, cards, altars, and other religious items. Every Sunday, thirty to forty people congregate in a small room on the sixth floor. In the front area of the room, several volunteers play musical instruments; a keyboard player, a percussionist, a guitar player, and a violinist are some of the regulars. Interestingly, this Sunday night meeting has more male participants than other daytime activities sponsored by the Catholic Church. Both men and women take turns leading the charismatic group, and there is a smaller gender gap within this group than in regular parish activities. This group is also attended by people of different age groups. From Korean university students to Japanese retired couples, this group includes a mixture of different types of people. As in other Catholic groups, there are a few participants from other Christian denominations, including an Episcopalian seminarian from the United States.

A few minutes before 5:00 p.m., one of the "core group" members invites participants to come toward the front and join him or her to pray for the prayer leader of the week. Almost all who arrive early, usually about ten to fifteen, surround the appointed prayer leader. The person who would be prayed over sits on a chair, and others may sit or stand, lightly touching a shoulder or a thigh of the prayer leader. Most of the people praying for him or her are closing their eyes. People who stand farther away are stretching their arms and putting their palms toward the person who is being prayed over. Following the "core group" leader's prayer asking God to bless the weekly prayer leader and the night's gathering, almost all participants start praying "in tongues." Shortly after, people stop their prayer and go back to their seats to start the gathering.

The prayer leader begins the session by greeting people. He then announces the hymn book, the page number, and the title of the song to be sung. There are two hymn books on a chair, and the leader has to point out which book to use before he announces the page number. The keyboard player begins her prelude, and the congregation starts singing. Singing is also a form of prayer for this group. Many close their eyes while singing, and some raise their hands up toward the ceiling as gestures of worship. It is common to see people putting their palms up on their laps or raising their arms slightly higher with their palms up. This is also a typical gesture of worship among this group. At the end of the song, some participants may start their glossolalia or speak in tongues. This may hint at other participants to start their glossolalia. Usually, the keyboard person also plays her tunes to accompany glossolalia, and the room is filled with musical tunes that are similar to the sound from an orchestra box when the orchestra begins tuning up the instruments. There are a few people whose glossolalia resembles a song-like melody, and there are those who repeat the word "Hallelujah" rapidly in a set tone. Yet there are those whose glossolalia has a mixture of both characteristics. After a while, without any suggestion, the glossolalia is taken over by a moment of silence. This is as if the area has been cleansed after a rainfall. There is a heightened sense in the air; this is when participants may prophesy. If there is no prophecy, people spontaneously thank Jesus, the Holy Spirit, or God for his kindness, love, blood, sacrifice, heart, and other things that came to their minds. Some people may also thank Mary for her care and protection, and praise her as the mother and the queen. The congregation responds to these phrases by saying, "I thank you" (*kansha itashimasu*), "I praise and thank you" (*sanbi shite kansha itashimasu*), or "Amen" (*āmen*) in unison.

As the meeting continues, latecomers walk into the room. Volunteers at the entrance greet them, and each participant leaves 300 yen (approx. $3.75 US) as a fee to cover the cost of renting a room. All of this may be done without exchanging any words; the receptionist may be singing a hymn while stretching her hands up and may greet the latecomer just by bowing gently. The latecomer would pay the fee, find a seat, and start singing or praying in silence. At about 5:50 p.m., the first section wraps up. The congregation makes announcements, the participants greet each other, and the group may take a five-minute break in which some participants leave for the nearby Our Lady of the Assumption Church for an evening mass. After a short break, the second half begins. The second part is often a talk by a priest or a layperson about faith or the theme of the week. The gathering ends with a collective prayer.

When the meeting concludes at about 7:00 p.m., several group members walk to a "Catholic" café nearby whose owner is a devout supporter of the Church. Often there are priests from the nearby order eating dinner at the café, and here one can talk to a priest in a casual setting. This after-hours session would provide the participants with further occasions to do "faith sharing" in a less formal fashion. Clearly, this area provides a strikingly "Catholic" environment for Japanese members of the church who otherwise live in a completely non-Catholic cultural milieu in Japan.

Terada Catholic Church

The Terada Catholic Church is a typical neighborhood church located in a residential area. From central Tokyo, one can travel on either a JR line or one of the subway lines for ten minutes and then walk for about another ten to fifteen minutes to arrive at the church. The area where the Terada Church is located is known for its reasonable rents, so-called "ethnic food" restaurants, and alternative youth culture, which manifests itself in various casual and hip clothing stores. After exiting the nearest subway station, one walks to the church along one of the major highways in Tokyo. Relative to the major commercial centers of Tokyo, people in this neighborhood dress casually, and there is a feeling of less formality. A neighborhood park hosts a flea market on Sundays, a secondhand furniture store sells refrigerators, and an old, rundown, family-owned tea store still does business. Soon one approaches a major intersection; there is a huge highway running overhead, and there is a convenience store at the opposite side of the road. After crossing the intersection twice—first toward the north side, and then toward the east side, one walks for yet another thirty seconds to a small corner, where one turns toward the Terada Church. From here, it is a middle-class residential area, and on both sides of the narrow road there are apartment buildings and houses. The roads are so narrow that one has to stand on the side of the road whenever a car or truck passes.

The physical appearance of the Terada Catholic Church is typical of a neighborhood parish, yet there are a few additional features that the current pastor added after he became responsible for this church. Like most churches, it has a main sanctuary, a separate building used as a residence and office for the two priests, and some communal spaces for the congregation to hold gatherings. The little replica of the Grotto at Lourdes with a statue of the Virgin Mary located just beside the priests' residence is also typical of Japanese parishes that were evangelized by the Paris Mission for many decades after the proscription on Christianity ended. However, a few unusual physical features of this church attest to the ingenuity of the priest, who is mainly responsible for producing so many converts. Right beside the main entrance, there is a small shop run by the parish. This store, called Angel's Forest, sells books on faith, rosaries, cookies made by Trappist monasteries, and other Catholic items. The designated shelf held several books authored by the main priest (figure 1.2). The priest's sermons are so popular that they are published in several collected volumes. When visitors enter the store, volunteer staff talk to them and serve tea so that they can sit together at the round table in the middle of the store, talking about faith or about the reasons for their visit. Another unusual feature of this church can be found within the office building. The priest decided to make part of the first floor into a "Japanese-style living room" (*ochanoma*) for anybody to enter. In an ordinary Japanese household, the *ochanoma* is a family room where members of the family spend time together, eating dinner, watching TV, and talking about their day. The *ochanoma* has no specific function; it is a

Figure 1.2. Items for Sale at the Angel's Forest Shop.

place where family members eat, relax, receive guests, and sometime take a nap. Often, youths visiting this church end up sleeping overnight in this "family living room." Talking about this phenomenon during a sermon, the main priest jokingly told the congregation: "So, I had to set a new rule: you can sleep over for up to two nights, and no more."

What distinguishes the Terada Catholic Church from other neighborhood parishes in Tokyo relates largely to the main priest. The church is staffed by two resident priests. While both priests were attractive and known for their own unique character, the main priest is well-known for his sermons. Many Catholics and non-Catholics come from different parts of Japan to listen to his sermons every Sunday. For example, I was introduced to a woman who came every other Sunday from Hiroshima Prefecture, which is roughly 800 kilometers from Tokyo. A group of volunteers transcribe his Sunday sermon, and this text is delivered through the Internet within a few days. In this way, his sermons take on a life of their own and are read by people who forward the link to others. His popular sermons have also been collected and edited into a book; so far four volumes have been published. In addition to the bookstore and the *ochanoma* living room, the main priest devised several unique groups within the church. There is a group called the "Fathers' Club" (*Oyajino kai*) for people in their thirties and forties, a "Heaven's Movie Village" (*Tengoku eiga mura*) for people who love to discuss movies from a Christian perspective, and a "Cram School for Discernment of Calling" (*Shōmei juku*) for those who are interested in becoming a priest. The church also hosts a First Friday drinking party for youth in the basement once a month.

The history of the Terada Catholic Church is similar to that of many other neighborhood churches in the Tokyo archdiocese. This parish dates to 1923, when the area was still called Terada village;[22] it was the tenth church to be established in the Tokyo archdiocese. A young French priest from the Paris Mission was appointed as the priest and, along with a congregation of 298 members, started the parish in a temporary sanctuary. Nine years later, a Spanish female order began educating young women next to the Terada Church by starting a women's high school. From its inception, the parish and this female order have continued to maintain close ties. The order expanded its school, and the Terada Church itself also accommodated a different kindergarten and a vocational school for early childhood educators within its precincts in the course of its history. At the time of my fieldwork, the parish had approximately 1,800 registered parishioners.

Every Sunday, almost all the seats at the 9:30 a.m. mass are filled. In addition to the Terada parishioners, a few nuns from neighborhood female orders attend the mass, and there are visitors from all over Japan. A few minutes past 9:30 a.m., the church organ starts a hymn, and the procession of eight or so young altar attendants enters the sanctuary, followed by the priest. When this mass is over at about 10:45 a.m., many people go downstairs to listen to the weekly speaker series, and catechumens go to a part of the *ochanoma* to talk with a nun who conducts the catechism class. After lunch, depending on the week, some people go to a different meeting room to join "Heaven's Movie Village," and children may attend the "Angel's Club." Meanwhile, there is a group of Boy Scouts doing activities outside, making the church a lively place all day.

None of the three venues where I conducted fieldwork can be called a typical Japanese parish or a typical congregation in Tokyo. Rather, they are all atypical in several ways. While each site offers a different brand of Catholicism, I found that many people would visit all of them for various reasons. Many catechumens spend time in several groups to decide which faith group (*shinkō kyōdōtai*) is most appropriate to become their "home" faith group.

Who Are the Parishioners?

What kind of people become Roman Catholics in Tokyo? According the official statistics released by the Catholic Bishops' Conference of Japan (2014), women occupy roughly 60 percent of the Catholic population in Japan. During the daytime, however, women dominate the church activities. At Our Lady of the Assumption, there are often approximately ten times more women than men. Usually, in a class of forty, I would count four to five men. I discuss the topic of gender and Catholicism in Japan additionally in chapter 4, but here I introduce five Catholic people I met in Tokyo, four women and one man. Most of them are in their retirement, in their sixties to eighties, with the exception of one woman in her thirties. It is not an accident that older people dominate this depiction of five parishioners. As I briefly mentioned earlier, the majority of Roman Catholic laypeople I met through this research were in their sixties to eighties. There were children, youth, and those who were middle-aged, but women of advanced age dominate congregations, and these women are the main supporters of many church activities.

The Roman Catholic Church in Tokyo attracts a variety of people, and it is difficult to select any as being typical. Instead, I have chosen five people to be representative of their separate backgrounds and the different paths that led them to Catholicism. The first, Oda-san, is a graduate of Catholic women's schools. Female Catholic school graduates are numerous, and they are quietly but firmly supporting various activities of the Catholic Church. The next is Ogawa-san, the sole man in this sketch of representatives. It is hard to pick a representative male, as there are few of them in the church. Ogawa-san acts as a lay leader in his parish. The third is Fujimi-san, a housewife introduced to Christianity through her own reading, with no previous Catholic contact. Next I introduce Sekiguchi-san, a younger woman who arrived at the church as a result of an ongoing spiritual quest. I end this sketch with a portrait of Kaneta-san, a woman from a remote island located to the south of Kyushu; she is the only one of the five who received an infant baptism. The reader will encounter most of these people again in later chapters.

Oda-san said that she was born in the seventh year of Shōwa (1932) at her mother's summer villa. Her maternal grandfather was a wealthy businessman, and Oda-san acknowledges that her mother had a privileged upbringing. Oda-san and most of her female relatives—including her mother—are graduates of Shirayuri Gakuen, the Catholic women's schools run by the Sisters of St. Paul of Chartres, a female religious order from France. I present her here as an example of Tokyo Catholics, as I met quite a few of these women who are the graduates of the several female Catholic schools in the city. These women are typically married, have grown children, and came to acquire religious faith at various stages in their lives. All of them encountered Roman Catholicism through their education at private Catholic schools run by religious orders from overseas.

Dressed in a casual but elegantly knitted sweater, Oda-san walks slowly as she enters the Terada Catholic Church. Her hair is gray, as she does not dye it. She refers to herself as "watakushi," one of the most polite of the various Japanese forms of the first-person pronoun. All of her maternal aunts are graduates of Shirayuri Gakuen. According to Oda-san, her mother lived in Shirayuri Gakuen's dormitory from the age of fourteen to the age of eighteen under the supervision of the order's French nuns. Oda-san's mother was married to a bureaucrat who spent two years studying in Europe before the Pacific War. Because of his European experiences, Oda-san surmises, her father harbored amicable sentiments toward Christianity. Reflecting her fondness for the Shirayuri Catholic schools with which most of her female family members were affiliated, Oda-san reminisces: "Before I even entered kindergarten, I knew I was supposed to say, 'Bonjour, ma sœur' when I went into the class." Nuns were called "ma sœur" by children at this school.

Despite her constant exposure to things Catholic, her family did not allow Oda-san to receive baptism while she was young. Back then, she says, being Christian could pose enormous challenges in looking for a suitor. She was, however, able to convince her parents to consent to her baptism when she turned twenty, the year of majority in Japan. She chose the sanctuary of the Sisters of St. Paul as her place of baptism. She later married a non-Christian man from a wealthy household from a city outside Tokyo. She convinced the husband-to-be to undergo a Catholic wedding rite at Our Lady of the Assumption Church, a few days before the "official" family wedding that took place in front of all of his relatives from his hometown. She said she was married properly in front of God.

Although she was able to convince her husband to have a Catholic wedding, he did not consent to sign a document that would allow Catholic baptism of their children. The priest married the young couple despite this. In the face of her husband's adamant refusal to allow infant baptism to be given to their two sons, Oda-san took it to heart that it was her task to teach and give the young boys faith. She taught prayers to her two boys and made sure they took time to reflect on the events of the day and talk to the Christian God before going to bed. Both of her sons told their mother that they would like to receive baptism when they were in university. Her husband, who never showed any interest in Christianity but showed respect for his wife's faith, received baptism on his deathbed.

The only male in this selection of five parishioners is Ogawa-san. His case is both unusual and typical: unusual because of his background as a son of a devout Christian from the prewar era, and typical in that he encountered Catholicism through his children's education at a kindergarten run by a Catholic organization. When I saw Ogawa-san in 2006, he was more than eighty years old. When I asked him about his relationship with Catholicism, he began to tell stories of his father: "My father was a devout disciple of Uchimura Kanzō. So, he belonged to the Mukyōkai-ha. He spent six or eight hours commuting to Tokyo every week to listen to Uchimura-sensei's sermon." Mukyokai-ha, or Non-church Movement, is a Japanese Christian group founded by Uchimura Kanzō (1861–1930). This Non-church Movement attracted many young people who later became influential figures in Japan. Uchimura emphasized the centrality of the Bible and individual conscience and renounced the role of the church and the sacrament. From his home in the city of Nagoya, some 360 kilometers from Tokyo, Ogawa-san's father took a night train every Saturday to attend Uchimura's sermon on Sunday mornings in Tokyo. He was such a close disciple of Uchimura that when his wife died when Ogawa-san was very young, Uchimura himself chose a suitable second wife for Ogawa-san's father from Uchimura's congregation.

Describing his faith in the Non-church Movement, Oda-san uses the metaphor of "hanging tightly to a rope so that one will not fall." He has to use his muscles and willpower to hold onto the rope. If he lets go, he will fall. By contrast, he said that the faith of the Catholic Church is like having a security net underneath him. If he falls, the net will catch him and save his life. He encountered Catholic teachings when his children were at a kindergarten located in the precinct of the parish. In response to an invitation from religious sisters to attend Bible classes for parents, he took weekly classes for two years. He received his baptism in 1964 with his wife and two children. He is a graduate of the University of Tokyo (one of the most prestigious universities in Japan), receiving a doctorate in natural science. He later spent two years in the United States for his postdoctoral fellowship. As an independent thinker, he has formed his opinions by reading books, having intellectual interactions with others, and pursuing his questions about God. He is an anomaly in that he was able to afford such a quest while working full-time.

Fujimi-san is a housewife who lives in Saitama Prefecture. She looked as though she were in her sixties when I met her in 2006. She was married with two children, both of whom were working. Born of a mother who was inclined to spiritual practices, Fujimi-san reminisces about how her mother used to belong to different religious groups, one after another.

> She first joined Sōka Gakkai, and then withdrew from it. She then got into the worship of many deities such as Amaterasu-Ōmikami, Hachiman-jin, and other Shinto deities. She used to set up an altar and placed first water and freshly cooked first rice of the day for those gods. I know some people would say that it is strange, but she then read the Heart Sutra (a Buddhist scripture) every single day. I was forced to recite it with her when I was young.

Feeling resentment toward her mother's religious practices, Fujimi-san gradually became attracted to Christianity through the reading of books written by Christian writers. She said the process was gradual; there was no dramatic incident. She did not have any Christian friends who influenced her, nor did she go to any schools run by Catholic orders. She said that one day she simply realized that she was attracted to Christianity. Her mother and father were a cousin-marriage, and all of her relatives belonged to the Nichiren Sect of Buddhism. Her mother continued her spiritual quest and later joined another new religious movement called Reiha no hikari (or the Light of Spiritual Wave) headquartered in Chiba Prefecture when Fujimi-san herself was on her quest to know more about Christianity.

Fujimi-san is not from a particularly privileged background. Her daughter, for example, delivered newspapers every morning as a part-time job to supplement her own educational expenses. Fujimi-san's natal and married families are both rooted in non-Christian religious practices. In addition to conducting Buddhist seasonal rites, her natal family also subscribed to a practice of rubbing a piece of paper cut out in a human form against one's own body on December 31. This is to transfer one's sins and illness to the human-shaped paper (called *hitogata*). Fujimi-san and her brother were assigned the role of bringing these pieces of paper to a nearby river to send them off. In this way, one's ailment and misfortunes would be assumed by the human figurine. I discuss the ways in which Fujimi-san has developed her own ideas of the spiritual role women have in the household later in the book.

Sekiguchi-san was thirty-seven years old when I met her in 2006, but, like so many other women of her generation in Tokyo, she hardly looked her age. Wearing her hair short and clad in a trendy outfit, she stood out as "young" in a church filled with other women in their seventies and eighties. She confided to me that she had married twice and divorced both husbands. She is a "spiritual seeker" interested in visiting fortune-tellers and spiritual seers (*reinōsha*). She came to the Catholic Church as a result of her spiritual quest, which she began in the late 1980s by reading New Age books such as Shirley MacLaine's *Out on a Limb*, which had been translated into Japanese as early as 1986 (MacLaine 1986).

Sekiguchi-san had a female spiritual mentor with whom she traveled, visiting many spiritual places together. She described one of these pilgrimages. "When I sat in the main sanctuary of Ōura Roman Catholic Church in Nagasaki, all of a sudden, tears swelled in my eyes for no reason. I could not stop crying." Through this experience, she told me that she realized that she has been Roman Catholic through all her past reincarnations. According to some New Age groups, humans reincarnate to this world over and over (cf. MacLaine 1986). I had heard about this experience from Sekiguchi-san prior to her baptism. She would later gradually change her discourse on the unseen after going through the catechism with a priest. She took me to different spiritual places in downtown Tokyo, including the Catholic bar, which was created by Fr. Nayland in 1980. I discuss this bar further in chapter 3. Similar to Sekiguchi-san, there are those who are attracted to the Catholic Church for various mysteries that the Catholic Church has to offer.

Kaneta-san is perhaps the most unusual in this group of representative portraits, as she is from a remote island of Amami Ōshima belonging to Kagoshima Prefecture, located more than 1,000 kilometers south of Tokyo. She is from a Catholic family and received infant baptism when she was born on the island immediately after the war in the mid-1940s. According to her, Catholic girls on the island usually receive the name Mary as their baptismal name, and boys receive the name Joseph. Kaneta-san too had Mary as her baptismal name. Her family on the island was a target of severe religious persecution during the early years of Shōwa when the country was increasingly taking its course of ultra-nationalism. I turn her family stories of persecution in chapter 5.

Kaneta-san is short, modestly dressed, and eager to talk about her faith with strangers. This is an unusual trait among lay Tokyo Catholics; few are willing to talk about their faith in Catholicism with strangers. Kaneta-san is an eager evangelist within Our Lady of the Assumption. She takes care of many newcomers to the church, telling them what to do and what not to do. Right after the noon mass during weekdays, in which she wears a veil and sits toward the back of the sanctuary to take care of any newcomers, she leads a rosary group in the crypt downstairs where her mother rests. Kaneta-san is single, living alone, and coping with her illness and the loneliness of old age. She knows many priests and retreats, as she has lived in various places.

After being a parishioner at other churches, Kaneta-san ended up with Our Lady of the Assumption as her parish. She is among those who prefer Our Lady of the Assumption to other parishes for its anonymity. It is such a large parish that even if one does not get along with some of the other parishioners, one can still participate without too much friction. She takes part in the funerary rite choir, a group of women who sing for funerals. Kaneta-san attended Our Lady of the Assumption for many days a week. She became a baptismal sponsor to several of the people that I know, and she seems at home in this parish.

As a result of features of the urban environment that I have discussed in this chapter—such as population density, mobility, and anonymity—many parishioners and catechumens do not observe the traditional notions of the geographically bound parish. Both mobility, supported by well-developed subway and train systems, and anonymity, the result of extremely high population density, lead people to visit parishes and faith communities of their own choice. In addition, the Internet disseminates popular sermons outside Tokyo and throughout Japan, bringing in eager audiences to the archdiocese from hundreds of kilometers away from Tokyo.

In this characteristically urban context of Tokyo, spiritual seekers have many opportunities to explore their spirituality. The postwar era in Japan has witnessed the rise of new religious movements and spirituality movements. Partly because of a general apathy toward traditional religious institutions such as Buddhist temples and Shinto shrines, people are eager to look for alternative opportunities to experience their versions of spiritual truth. The Roman Catholic Church is also eager to provide venues for these spiritual seekers. Catholic Zen meditation classes, weekend retreats, and a Catholic bar are only a few examples of many the venues that one can explore. In this Japanese context, the social location of the Roman Catholic Church is quite dissimilar to its Western counterpart. Many approach the Church for its novelty. I do not intend to downplay the number of converts who come to the Church through their exposure to Roman Catholicism or Christianity through their education at Christian schools; nevertheless, for the majority of the Japanese, Roman Catholicism continues to be something unknown and new.

Roman Catholicism, however, was one of the most severely persecuted religious practices in Japanese history. This particular historical trajectory also influences the status of today's Roman Catholic Church in Japan. Historically speaking, the Church never attained dominant power in Japan. Rather, it has always suffered from being in the position of the oppressed. The implications of these historical discursive processes are discussed in later chapters, especially in chapter 5 on historical consciousness.

In the next chapter, to depict the transformation that Catholics undergo by participating in activities offered by the Church, I begin with a discussion of the major values inculcated by Japanese society.

Chapter 2

Propriety, Virtues, and Social Obligations

"Harmony is to be valued, and contentiousness avoided."
—From the Seventeen-Article Constitution
attributed to Prince Shōtoku

"A human life is truly as frail and fleeting as the morning dew. What a shame that his should end this way."
—*Rashōmon*

One day, at a noon mass at Our Lady of the Assumption, the issue of the *seken*, or society, and its authority was discussed in the sermon. I was sitting in the main sanctuary and waiting for the celebrant for the mass. By this time, I was familiar with the ten priests who regularly celebrated masses at this mega-church. When the bell in the tower outside signaled the beginning of the mass, a stocky Japanese priest came in, following two older laywomen. One of these women was the altar server, and the other did the scripture reading as well as acting as a sort of Master of Ceremonies. The mass was celebrated by Fr. Murata, who was from the Kansai area. This relatively young priest did not conceal his native Kansai accent. For people like me who are not from the region, a Kansai dialect, especially an accent from the city of Osaka, brings to mind comedians and merchants. Whenever I heard this priest speak, I felt like laughing because I associated his accent with the friendly image of Kansai merchants or comedians, and those images were at odds with the image of the pristine Catholic altar at Our Lady of the Assumption. After the gospel reading, he began his sermon. He said, "You know, we often see that kind of press conference called the 'apology conference (*shazai kaiken*).' The other day, I was watching television and there was one by Fujiya. Did you all see it? What do we make out of it? Don't you think that it is strange? The president and executive officers all lowered their heads and apologized to the *seken*. Do you wonder to whom they are apologizing?"

The event that Fr. Murata was describing had taken place on January 15, 2007. The senior management of the confectionary company Fujiya, including its president, Fujiya Rintarō, all lowered their heads at their main office in Tokyo in front of the media. The clicking of countless camera shutters resounded in the room, while the management personnel kept their heads low. The president of the company said: "We are very sorry for becoming a nuisance to the citizens of Japan." This scene was broadcasted all over Japan in the evening news as one of the top stories of the day, and the same footage was repeatedly used in daytime talk shows for the next few months. Fujiya is one of the oldest and most well-known confectionary companies in Japan. It has been manufacturing Western-style sweets since the early 1910s. The company's mascots, Peko-chan and Poko-chan, have been national figures for decades. Toward the end of 2006, a former confectionary factory worker reported extremely unhygienic conditions at one of the Fujiya factories as well as unsanitary practices encouraged by senior factory workers at the manufacturing sites. There were a number of media reports about these unsanitary conditions and unhygienic practices, such as mice running around in the factory, the use of expired dairy products to "save" materials that would otherwise be "wasted," and allowing workers to package products accidentally dropped on the floor as long as they were picked up in "three seconds." The entire country was horrified by this news, which revealed the unreliable nature of Fujiya and the unsafe character of the food they were producing.[1]

This practice of "apologizing to society" is a standard act of contrition in Japan. A Mongolian sumo wrestler grudgingly apologized for the fake illness that allowed him to visit his home country,[2] and the parents of a random street killer held an "apology conference" and stated that they were sorry for their son's crime and apologized for the fact that he had created anxiety within society.[3] This apology is precisely directed to the *seken*, the collective living entity, the public.

In his sermon, Fr. Murata was taking issue with this practice of apologizing to the *seken*. He ended his sermon by saying: "Let's not be bewildered by the idol called seken (*seken toiu gūzō ni madowasarezuni ikimashou*) and let us continue to live our lives righteously in the eyes of God." Through his sermon, Fr. Murata suggested that *seken* is a false god for those who believe in Roman Catholic teachings. Roman Catholics should be afraid of God, the almighty power described in the Bible, and not *seken*, the collective aggregate of human judgment.

This notion of *seken* is one of the major factors in many of my research participants' narratives. In what sense does *seken* interact with people? Does *seken* hold something against individuals? In this chapter, I tease out various ways in which *seken* works as a depository of conventional moral values against which many feel that their behaviors are measured. I also discuss these values themselves. I illustrate that the ethics embedded in the notion of *seken* are often described using Neo-Confucian values, which Japan's political elites have historically mobilized in governing its people. I further show that these values have shaped and (re)shaped the sense of self among Japanese individuals.

Society as God

After attending mass at noon on a Thursday in February, Hirota-san suggested to Kitami-san and me: "Shall we have lunch somewhere?" Right across the street from Our Lady of the Assumption, there were a few restaurants that were popular with those who come to the parish. We slowly walked to the other side of the street while chatting. Once we entered the building, we took an elevator to the seventh-floor restaurant, a smoky establishment with lots of Japanese businessmen clad in dark-colored suits. It was a drawback that we had to eat in the smoky atmosphere, but the restaurant served a bowl of rice with fresh sashimi on top for a reasonable price, which also included coffee after the meal. I was thankful that the custom of having coffee after a meal is so common in Tokyo now. We managed to sit at a long, tall table that was facing the window, where we could see Our Lady of the Assumption from above.

As we sat sipping our coffee together after the meal, Kitami-san started touching her waist, rubbing her back as if to ease back pain. She told us that she had an operation about one year ago, and she was still suffering from the surgery.

> KITAMI-SAN: My husband sometimes tells me that I am . . . how can I say this . . . at an "aseptic condition"?
>
> ME: Does he mean growing up wrapped in cotton wool (*onshitsu sodachi*, "growing up in the green house")?
>
> KITAMI-SAN: No, I don't think he means that. He means that I am not used to dealing with troubles . . . May I say . . . too pure? So, when I read the Bible, I feel vindicated because I feel that it is okay to be pure (*junsui*). How can I express this? You know people often think that one cannot be pure (*junsui*) in order to deal with the real world (*seken*).

I was intrigued by her view of the benefits of Christian teachings and the Bible. What one can detect underneath Kitami-san's discourse is an uneasy relationship between social values typically upheld in Japan and some moral teachings encouraged in biblical traditions. The differences between the two were already pointed out by Japanese Christians of earlier generations, such as Uchimura Kanzō, a prominent Christian and the founder of the Non-church movement in Japan. Writing about Japan's modernization and religion, Sakamoto Takao points out, taking the "God-centered" position, that Uchimura understood Christianity as standing in opposition to many secular values in Japan (Sakamoto 1997, 71). Sakamoto also discusses that, in the processes of acceptance of Christianity, it often served as a symbol of "moral purity" in Japan (50–51). So, while a devout and rigorous Christian such as Uchimura understood Christianity as existing with tension in Japanese society, many earlier converts to Christianity during the Meiji Period were attracted to Christianity and understood it as encapsulating "moral purity" (Sakamoto 1997).

Kitami-san's sense of vindication was, therefore, not unfounded. And what she was feeling resonated with many earlier converts to Christianity in Japan. As a woman who had been brought up as an *ojō-san*, or a daughter from a good family,[4] learning music and getting married into a well-to-do family, Kitami-san was often treated as *seken-shirazu*, literally "somebody who does not know the (real) world." This treatment must have undermined her confidence as an adult. Conservative families encourage their young daughters to avoid learning about negative aspects of society. However, as the proprietor of a business establishment, Kitami-san needs to know both the positive and negative sides of the real world.

In Japanese society, the concept of *seken* can be overwhelmingly powerful. According to *Kenkyusha's New Japanese-English Dictionary*, the word *seken* can be translated as "the world, society, life, people, and the public." The two characters that constitute the word, however, do not connote any sense of individuality that the English words "people" or "life" might hold. The first character, *se*, means "the world" or "society," and the second character, *ken*, means "within." If you survey the usages of this word, the word *seken* emerges essentially as a collectivity. To some extent, the term connotes a living entity, with a sense of powerful authority. In Japanese society, collective judgement is often the most severe form of punishment. I suggest that this observation is not unrelated to the Japanese tendency to view human beings as the ultimate moral authority, a topic to which I turn later.

The usage of the word *seken* reveals some of the power that this collectivity holds. In some cases, the concept is treated almost as a living being. For example, the dictionary cited above provides us with examples such as *seken no omowaku* as "what people may think of [one]"; and (*akuji nadoga*) *seken ni shireru* as "(one's misdeeds) come to light," "become public." The literal translation of the first expression is "the thought of *seken*." The second example literally means "[one's misdeeds] came to be known by society." In the first example, the entity *seken* is portrayed as having the ability to think, and in the second one, we learn that the *seken* is capable of knowing something.

The *seken* is also used as a yardstick to measure people's behaviors. Such expressions as *seken-nami*, *seken-banare*, and *seken-tei* all point to the *seken* as a standard for evaluating those who are in a social group. For example, the literal translation of *seken-nami* is "at the level of *seken*" or "on a par with the *seken*." Therefore, this expression is often translated as "average," "ordinary," and "common." The usage of the *seken-banare* is similar; the only difference is that it points in exactly the opposite direction. The literal translation of the expression is "apart from the *seken*" or "far removed from the *seken*," thereby meaning "strange," "queer," "uncommon," "extraordinary," or "unworldly."

The expression *seken-tei* is an interesting one and also often used. One can convince someone to do something for the sake of "appearing to be decent" (for the sake of *seken-tei*) even if the person is unwilling.

For example, parents may plead with their high school dropout son to go back to high school so that their household "be looked upon as decent by society" (*seken-tei ga warui kara*). That summer, the Japanese media carried reports about a young couple whose baby died of heatstroke after being left in their car. The couple made a false statement to the police, claiming that they were out shopping. Later, it became apparent that they were out playing *pachinko* (a popular pinball machine game), but they had lied to maintain their *seken-tei* (i.e., for the sake of appearing to be decent). It seems ironic that people who leave an infant in a car without a caretaker would still try to appear decent, but it indeed does sound worse to have gone out to play *pachinko* than to have gone shopping. Through the usages of *seken-tei*, we can trace the authority that *seken* imposes on people. The young couple lied because they were afraid of being judged by others. Similarly, the parents of a dropout son would feel social pressure to keep up the standards of *seken*.

In this worldview, the *seken* is an authority that exerts considerable power. This authority derives its legitimacy from its collective status. This authority is not derived from, or embodied in symbols of, such supernatural authorities as the Islamic or Christian notions of God or such elite powers as those of monarchies or political parties (see Geertz 1973; Kertzer 1988; Mahmood 2005; Verdery 1999). The idea of *seken* can be better understood using the Durkheimian notion of society as the origin of religion, or a repository of moral authority. In his celebrated work *The Elementary Forms of Religious Life* (1974 [1915]), Émile Durkheim studies the Australian tribal worship of totems. Durkheim calls what is represented in the totems (which take the form of animals or plants) the "totemic principle" or god and argues that this principle is a representation of the tribal society that produces it. In other words, people are worshipping their own society or collective consciousness in the name of totems or gods. He uses this idea as a premise for further discussion of religion in Western society, but his analysis is also useful for explaining the power that the *seken* exerts on the people I encountered in Tokyo.

In this social and cultural context, "disturbing the tranquility of society" (*seken wo sawagasu*) is something to be avoided. In the course of my fieldwork, a news story illustrating this point unfolded on television one day. During the daytime, the majority of TV stations broadcast so-called "wide shows" (*waidoshō*), live talk shows hosted by famous TV figures, that discuss current news events as well as recent gossip about celebrities in Japan, from singers to Sumo wrestlers. I was not paying too much attention to the show until the host mentioned: "The man who is making a standoff inside this building is saying that he is sorry for causing this trouble. He says he wants to apologize by killing himself. The police continue persuading this man not to kill himself." I dropped what I was doing and looked at the TV screen. The show was broadcasting the standoff scene in a Tokyo suburb.[5] I was intrigued, and then a moment later, I felt sorry for this man. I was intrigued because this discourse of apology by death was so alien from the Catholic worldview that I was encountering through my fieldwork. Moreover, the man was clearly afraid of the consequences that his action caused for the *seken*, in this case, the public. I was saddened, however, because I also understood the cultural logic behind his fear of causing public disturbance as well as the concept of suicide as a legitimate way to make amends for what he had done. The scholarly part of me was fascinated by the stark contrast between the conventional and Catholic worldviews in front of me.

According to the TV show, the man, who was a gang member, shot his colleague dead on the street and then fled to his own apartment in the Tokyo suburbs. His apartment building was soon surrounded by the police, however, and the desperate man started retaliating by shooting at them. As this incident progressed, the special police forces were able to contact the man through his cell phone. His remorseful utterance, "I want to apologize to people by killing myself," was heard in this context. The incident ended with a forced entrance to the apartment by the special police forces. The man was found lying on the ground, his face covered in blood. He had attempted suicide by shooting himself in the head.

Although this incident does not have any direct relationship to the life of my research participants in Tokyo, the cultural logic at work in the gang member's story is relevant to many Japanese. The *seken* is an authority that should not be disturbed, but once you do cause a problem, you must beg pardon from this same authority. Yet the *seken* does not have a central figurehead or a legitimate structure on which to exercise its authority. As the *seken* is a repository of conventions, some people claim that they "know how to deal with the *seken*" (*yowatari ga umai*), and others are considered unskilled at dealing with the *seken*, as they do "not know well how the *seken* works" (*seken shirazu*). Often, one's death is offered to this authority as the ultimate apology. The pattern of viewing oneself primarily within the context of the collective has been discussed by many scholars of Japanese society (Benedict 1974 [1947]; Cave 2007; Inoue 1977; Smith 1983). Although ideas similar to *seken* may be the source of authority in other societies, the Japanese emphasis on *seken* may have repeatedly used, and have maintained its vitality by, drawing idioms from Neo-Confucianism. To further dissect this idea of *seken*, I now turn to the study of Neo-Confucian traditions in Japan.

Neo-Confucianism, Social Order, and Human Hierarchy

David J. Lu states, "Neo-Confucianism as propagated by Zhu Xi (1130–1200, in Japanese, Shushi) of Song China became the most influential doctrine in shaping the thought and behavior of Japanese people" (1997, 243). The values central to Neo-Confucian ideologies were accepted, modified, and formulated by Japanese scholars, and one can see strong influences of Confucian ideas even to this day. Among various values that continue to be influential in Japanese society, I would like to highlight three themes. They are: 1) the primacy of human relationships, especially the effort to maintain "orderly" relationships; 2) the utmost importance of fulfilling one's social role; and 3) the importance of subordinating one's will to that of the group. These values are carefully maintained by participants in different social contexts. Before looking into the ways in which these ideals govern the daily lives of people I encountered, I turn to the historical construction of these ideas.

How did these types of virtues and moralities come to be prominent? In the manner of the French *Annales* school of history, which introduced the idea of the *longue durée*, and various shorter periods that give rise to particular events in the making of history, I attempt here to identify a particular *longue durée* that has a strong tie to a specific *mentalité* (Burke 1990). Below, I describe the Japanese adaptation of Neo-Confucian ideologies that were used by successive governments from the early 1600s to the end of the Pacific War in 1945. Specifically, I discuss two major periods: the Edo Period (1603–1867) and time dating from the succeeding Meiji Period to the end of the Pacific War (1868–1945). During these periods, Neo-Confucian ideas were liberally developed and used by scholars who were willing to serve the government. These ideas were sometimes mixed with Shinto ideas in the government's effort to control the populace. I suggest that the *mentalité* that was nurtured over a long period of time continues to exert an influence over behavior and the sense of self in today's Japan. To begin, we examine how this *mentalité* was formulated in the early period as well as its usages.

In the relative peace of the Edo Period (1603–1867), we can trace many of the foundations on which the modern infrastructure of contemporary Japan was built. At the level of base structure, to borrow Marxist terminology, we can find the roots of the large family corporations that dominate today's Japanese economy—such as the Mitsui Group and the Sumitomo Group. In the political sphere, a Tokyo-centered political infrastructure was carefully designed, and various administrative measures to maintain that structure were implemented rigorously by successive shoguns' regimes (Varley 2000). At a more super-structural level, many forms of popular entertainments, including food and restaurant culture, began to emerge during this period, especially in the urban center of Edo. The quintessentially Japanese contemporary arts and entertainment, such as *kabuki* theater and *rakugo* (i.e., comedic storytelling), or such well-known Japanese dishes as sushi and tempura, all trace their rise in popularity to the Edo Period. Although I am inclined to think that a broad-ranging discussion of history—one that includes such themes as political centralization, taxation, and the rise of popular culture during this period—can support my overall argument, I confine my attention to the *mentalité* that became prominent during this period and continues to influence today's Japan.

Neo-Confucianism during the Edo Period constituted one of the intellectual currents that formed various discourses that were used to legitimize the newly implemented power structure of the Tokugawa government. This was the time when the country as we know it today came under one centralized power held by the single administration of the shogun. According to Herman Ooms, contrary to a long-held scholarly assumption that the Tokugawa administration officially sanctioned Neo-Confucianism as its state orthodox teachings, no single tradition enjoyed such an exclusive privilege (1984, 59). Neo-Confucianism was used, along with other religious symbolism such as Shinto gods and mythology, as a form of persuasion to explain why the samurai class was located at the top of the social hierarchy and dominated the rest of the population (Ooms 1984).

One of the most well-known Neo-Confucian scholars who served the Tokugawa administration well was Hayashi Razan (1583–1657). Writing in the seventeenth century, Razan eloquently describes the "natural and social order" of the rigid class system of Tokugawa, which divided the population into four classes of samurai, farmers, artisans, and merchants and forbade social mobility.[6]

> Heaven is above and earth is below. This is the order of heaven and earth. If we can understand the meaning of the order existing between heaven and earth, we can also perceive that in everything there is an order separating those who are above and those who are below. When we extend this understanding between heaven and earth, we cannot allow disorder in the relations between the ruler and the subject, and between those who are above and below. The separation into four classes of samurai, farmers, artisans and merchants, like the five relationships is part of the principles of heaven and is the Way which was taught by the Sage (Confucius). . . . (Lu 1997, 246)

The five relationships that the writer is referring to is one of the basic components of Confucianism. Razan explains the worth of a person in these terms:

> The five relationships governing the ruler and the subject, father and son, husband and wife, older brother and younger brother, and friend and friend have been in existence from olden days to the present time. There has been no change in these basic relations, and they are thus called the supreme way. In judging the worth of a person, one needs only to use these five relationships as the criteria, and teachings which try to implement the ideals of these five relationships are those of the sage and of the wise men . . . (Lu 1997, 246)

Note the expression "the worth of a person" in this passage. Razan clearly states that the worth of a person can be measured using the scale of the five relationships. Here we can see a seed of what Bachnik later called the "sliding scale" of the self and others in Japanese social contexts.[7] Before turning to contemporary scenarios, let me examine how the worth of a person was actually measured by the Tokugawa administration.

Lu introduces a fascinating legal case from the Edo Period in which we can glimpse how these Neo-Confucian–derived texts were actually used by the government and affected individuals' lives. The case dates from 1711 and is recorded in the autobiography of a famous Confucian advisor to the shogunate, Arai Hakuseki (Lu 1997). A woman from Kawagoe district was called by her father and brother to come home while her husband was away on business. While staying with her father and brother, she became anxious when her husband did not return as planned. When a man was discovered drowned in the river, she insisted on seeing his face despite the advice of her father and brother not to do so. She asked the village head and managed to discern that the corpse was indeed her husband's. After some searching, government officials uncovered the fact that the man had been murdered by his father-in-law and brother-in-law, the very people who had invited the woman to stay with them. Yet the contentious point in this case was the ruling about the wife of the drowned man. According to the law, "anyone who informs on the wrongdoing of his father and mother shall be banished." This meant death by hanging, according to the specification for this particular clause (Lu 1997, 256).

It was a complicated case, as the woman in question was both a daughter (of the murderer) and a wife (of the murdered), thereby touching on the two major relationships of Confucian precepts. First, the government had to decide whether she should have obeyed her husband or her father, as there was a conflict of interest. After a careful search of Chinese authoritative documents that recorded previous cases, Hakuseki managed to locate the passage that states the priority of a woman's duty to her husband over that to her father.[8] Nevertheless, many observers thought she should be condemned for this incident. The councilors recommended that she undergo one year of incarceration and then be condemned to slavery. Some argued that she should have committed suicide immediately after she discovered the wrongdoing of her father and brother; in that way, she could have satisfied her filial and sisterly obedience and loyalty to her husband. Hakuseki, on the other hand, tried to rescue this woman. He recommended to the shogunate that she enter a Buddhist nunnery, thereby avoiding incarceration and slavery and securing her means of survival by donating all the property that had belonged to her husband to the convent (Lu 1997, 257–8).

This case demonstrates that the maintenance of orderly existence was of utmost concern to the people involved. As Hakuseki clearly states: "First, the case must be dealt with in accordance with the fundamental principles governing human relations" (256). From this autobiography of a legal advisor, we can see that human order was indeed paramount and also that suicide was an accepted solution for such a dilemma of entangled human relationships and social disorder.

Tokugawa Japan is also known for its emphasis on education. During this period, children were trained and disciplined in a human hierarchy from an early age. The ethos is evident in one of the teacher's manuals that has survived from the Edo Period. The document is taken from the *Common Sense Teachings for Japanese Children (Wazoku Dōjikun)*.[9] At the age of six,

> Children must be taught by those who are close to them the virtues of filial piety and obedience. To serve the parents well is called filial piety (*kō*), and to serve one's seniors well is called obedience (*tei*). The one who lives close to the children and who is able to teach must instruct the children in the early years of their life that the first obligation of a human being is to revere the parents and serve them well. Then comes the next lesson, which includes respect for one's seniors, listening to their commands and not holding them in contempt. One's senior includes elder brothers, elder sisters, uncles, aunts, and cousins who are older and worthy of respect. The way of man is to observe the virtues of filial piety and obedience, and children must be taught that all goodness in life emanates from these two fundamental values. (Lu 1997, 259)

As the basis for the virtues of filial piety and obedience, the hierarchy of relationships in the social order is clearly articulated for children.

This pattern of human hierarchy, with parents at the top of the ladder, an elder brother at the next rung, a younger brother lower down, and a younger sister at the bottom, was at a later time further adapted and extended to the level of the nation-state in the modern government starting in the Meiji Period. The new Meiji nation-state "family" was to have the emperor as the head of the state/family to whom all the subjects/children were to pledge their loyalty. And this loyalty was expected to go far. The new modern nation-state of Japan was otherwise modeled after the Western nations, particularly the constitutional monarchy of the United Kingdom and the German legal model that influenced the formation of the Japanese constitution. The Meiji government managed to set up a centralized state equipped with a diet, political parties, and a modern, conscript army. However, in contrast to Western nations, starting with the Meiji emperor (1852–1912), the Japanese head of state was at the same time a living deity. This system was maintained until Japan's defeat in WWII in 1945, at which time State Shinto was dismantled by the US-led occupation forces (Hardacre 1989).

One of the most sacred and influential texts in Japanese modern history is the Imperial Rescript on Education (*kyōiku chokugo*) promulgated in 1890 in the early Meiji Period. This document, which Smith describes as "representing the final victory of the conservative elements in the new Japanese government" (Smith 1983, 11), was introduced to implement the moral education of the newly conceived "citizens of the Empire." The school systems in Japan, as Peter Cave rightly notes, "have long been entrusted with a major role in the production of a 'desirable human being'" (Cave 2007, 1). This policy was initiated in the most systematic manner by the Meiji government using the Imperial Rescript on Education. The newly born modern government effectively used the universal education system as the site for inculcating state-sponsored morality and ethics. The actual full text reads:

> Know ye, Our subjects:
>
> Our Imperial Ancestors have founded Our Empire on a basis broad and everlasting, and have deeply and firmly implanted virtue; Our subjects ever united in loyalty and filial piety have from generation to generation illustrated the beauty thereof. This is the glory of the fundamental character of Our Empire, and herein also lies the source of Our education.
>
> Ye, Our subjects, be filial to your parents, affectionate to your brothers and sisters; as husbands and wives be harmonious, as friends true; bear yourselves in modesty and moderation; extend your benevolence to all; pursue learning and cultivate arts, and thereby develop intellectual faculties and perfect moral powers; furthermore advance public good and promote common interests; always respect the Constitution and observe the laws; should emergency arise, offer yourselves courageously to the State; and thus guard and maintain the prosperity of Our Imperial Throne coeval with heaven and earth.
>
> So shall ye not only be Our good and faithful subjects, but render illustrious the best traditions of your forefathers. The Way here set forth is indeed the teaching bequeathed by Our Imperial Ancestors, to be observed alike by Their Descendants and the subjects, infallible for all ages and true in all places. It

is Our wish to lay it to heart in all reverence, in common with you, Our subjects, that we may thus attain to the same virtue.

October 30, 1890
(Tsunoda et al. 1958, 139–40)

Helen Hardacre (1989) tells us how these ideas were disseminated through the rites conducted at schools nationwide. As she observes, distribution of the portrait of Emperor Meiji began in approximately 1882, and by 1888 nearly all the nation's schools had the royal portrait (Hardacre 1989). The Imperial Rescript on Education was added as part of a liturgical set to this portrait, and this Rescript was treated as a holy writ. Along with the portrait of Emperor Meiji, the scroll on which this text was written was housed in newly built shrines or specially designated rooms in the nation's schools (Hardacre 1989, 108). Quoting Furukawa, Robert J. Smith notes that the Rescript "came to be worshipped as 'a document of absolute infallibility'" (Smith 1983, 29). Hardacre further describes the pompous ritual occasion of the first reading of this scroll at schools. There was a parade of the scroll participated in by teachers, students, the mayor, the post office head, local government officials, and the area's senior residents. The text was recited in a special tone by the school principal, who had to be in the most formal attire complete with white gloves. As Hardacre points out, the principal was taking on the role of a priest in this sacred rite. The reading of this text was taken seriously to the point that there were occasions on which school principals committed suicide for mispronouncing some syllables (Hardacre 1989, 108–9). It was a shrewd strategy by the Meiji government to instill the ideologies of loyalty to the state among impressionistic schoolchildren who were to sacrifice their lives for the state in the coming war years in the first half of the twentieth century.

Last, another Confucian teaching called the "rectification of the names" merits some discussion. This is one of the fundamental teachings advocated by Confucius himself, who expressed it in the following terms: "Ruler, ruler, minister, minister, father, father, son, son." The message embedded in these eight words is that the individual who is given the title should live up to the role that is assigned to that name (Amore and Ching 2007, 446). In other words, this teaching emphasizes that the name should reflect the reality. According to Yao, Confucius in his own historical setting was concerned with the discrepancy between names and reality, between language and action, and between rights and duties (Yao 2000, 35). The ultimate goal of Confucius was to actualize order and peace in the world. Yao emphasizes that, in formulating various ways to achieve this goal, "Confucius seldom emphasized the one-way loyalty of the subject or minister to the ruler" (Yao 2000, 35). Rather, he insisted on reciprocity between ruler and subject, and in minister and subject relationships (Yao 2000, 35). In the Japanese adaptation of Confucian teachings, especially from the Meiji to early Shōwa Periods, the emphasis was more on the duty of the subjects than on that of ministers.[10] As we see in the following ethnographic discussions, striving hard to live up to the roles of ideal wife, mother, and daughter-in-law is still important in twenty-first-century Tokyo.

Discussing the conflict between one's sense of duty (*giri*) and human emotion (*ninjō*) seen in literature from the Edo Period, Donald Keene says: "Obedience to Confucian principles does not necessarily bring happiness" (Keene 1984, 135). Keene brings up numerous examples of stories in which one's official role prevents one from acting out of love and caring for loved ones (Keene 1984). In response to Keene's observation, Nosco states:

> The peculiar moral and political dilemma of leading activist figures in the last years of the Tokugawa and the early years of the Meiji suggest that taking one's role in the broader environment seriously,—and of course, all Neo-Confucians were in some sense devoted practitioners of seriousness—involved confronting the fundamental contradiction that arose at that time between the bakufu's professed ideals and the interests of the bakufu itself [. . .]. (Nosco 1984, 24)

It seems that the teaching of the rectification of the names embraces an inherent rigidity—be it for the government's official during the Tokugawa Period or the twenty-first-century housewife. And this rigidity, as Keene boldly suggests, may not necessarily lead one to a state of happiness.

As briefly reviewed, through the Edo Period (1603–1867) and the subsequent Meiji Period to the end of the Pacific War (1868–1945), Neo-Confucian idioms were frequently used by government officials, scholars, or the military as they saw fit to legitimize rule in order to control the population. In the Japanese adaption of Neo-Confucianism, the importance of human relations and loyalty to fathers, to husbands, and, ultimately, to the state is emphasized. In this politico-cultural milieu,

Neo-Confucian idioms were fully mobilized to reinforce hierarchies, and knowing one's status in society, as well as living one's lot in the world, became a preoccupation and one of the important virtues in Japanese popular conceptions of a human being.[11] In addition, performing one's social role well was also emphasized through teaching the importance of fulfilling one's duties. While this is a short and rough sketch of important discursive processes that Japanese elites used to control the populace over centuries, I hope it serves my current purpose of pointing to a cluster of ideals that Japanese society had been upholding for a long period of time. I suggest that this long process has nurtured a kind of *mentalité* that we see in various studies of contemporary Japanese society. Keeping these historically nurtured social ideals in mind, I turn to the topic of the Japanese sense of self in contemporary society. As we shall see, there is a lingering legacy of these state-endorsed teachings about the appropriate ways of being human.

"Relational" Selves

Since the inception of Japanese Studies, the Japanese sense of self has been an important issue of scholarly debate. The most prominent and influential discussion of the Japanese sense of self in English to date stresses its "relational" character, especially when compared with the sense of self in the United States. Kondo (1990) says: "contextually constructed, relationally defined selves are particularly resonant in Japan." In her seminal work *Crafting Selves* (1990), Kondo skillfully captures various ways in which Japanese people are embedded in, caught up in, and dictated by social obligations and webs of relationships. In other words, the self is not separable from its contexts and relationships to others, and an "I" that is independent of context hardly exists. This idea is also explained by Kondo using examples from the Japanese language. The Japanese language includes multiple forms of the pronoun "I," and the proper selection of which pronoun to use presents a challenge to many non-native students of Japanese. The speaker needs to decide which pronoun to use based on her or his gender, class, region, and the power relationships between the people who are involved in the social situation. This constantly shifting "I" requires the speaker's ability to judge the contexts; therefore, the use of the correct pronoun can present challenges to Japanese people as well. Also, the pronoun can disappear altogether from the sentence, and this requires the listener to decide who is actually the subject of the sentence. In this case, again, one would be able to discern the subject based on the contextual clues that are given in the conversation.

Kondo further elaborates on the expressions that relational selves take by pointing out the ways in which people refer to themselves. A wide variety of terms can serve as so-called personal pronouns; these include kinship terms, titles of positions in a company, and sometimes the seniority of the relationships. Most mothers and fathers refer to themselves as "father" or "mother" when they are speaking to their children. A similar practice may be found in North America when mothers and fathers to talk to their infants. However, in Japan, this practice of using kinship terms as personal pronouns can be seen beyond the parent-child relationship. For example, a six-year-old girl may refer to herself as "elder sister" (*onēchan*) if she has a younger sibling, and one can refer to himself as "uncle" (*ojichan* or *ojisan*) when he talks to his nephews and nieces. At the company where Kondo conducted her fieldwork, the president of the company was called *shachō*, the Japanese word for president. Further, even in grade schools, senior students can be called *senpai* or senior by junior students. As a result, social and familial obligations appear prominently in social interactions. As Kondo points out, relationally defined selves in Japan challenge assumptions about distinct identities that stand in opposition to society or culture. Kondo develops the theme of multiple selves that constantly shift in the discursive field of power in Japanese contexts.

The Japanese sense of selves Kondo describes bears a striking resemblance to Samoan personhood, which Bradd Shore depicted in the 1980s. In the section titled "The Samoan Concept of Person," Shore uses a famous Samoan saying, *teu le vā* (take care of the relationship), as a clue for understanding a different conceptualization of a person in Samoa (1982, 136). In this section, Shore emphasizes what seems to me a relational subjectivity of the Samoans (although he does not use the expression "relational subjectivity"). Juxtaposing it with the "European concept of the integrated, coherent, and 'rounded' personality" (141), Shore depicts a relational, multidimensional way of being a person in Samoa using the image of a diamond-shaped, multifaceted gem. Like a gem, an individual is enriched by the many dimensions or sides he or she maintains.

Similarly, Shore introduces an ethnographic vignette in which a person's different sides are brought up and emphasized based on the story's context. The person in question is described as "father," "pastor," and a "man of such and such village" as the story progresses in a short passage.

As I read, my reaction to this passage was one of familiarity as a Japanese person. By contrast, Shore takes a constant shift in one's identification as "remarkable" (138). It is noteworthy that both Kondo (1990) and Shore (1982) choose to juxtapose a foreign conceptualization of a person with that of the European (in the case of Shore) or the American (in the case of Kondo). They characterize this type of personhood using such adjectives as "integrated," "coherent," "round," or "whole." The underlying assumption is an "autonomous, freely operating 'individual'" (Kondo 1990, 26).

The prominence of social and familial obligations to the Japanese sense of self is also a central theme in Hamabata's *Crested Kimono: Power and Love in the Japanese Business Family* (1990). Hamabata worked closely with wealthy families possessing old capital from the pre-Meiji Era, whose enterprises still constitute a major fraction of the Japanese economy. Through Hamabata's work, we see the dynamics of the "interplay of marital and filial relations in the attainment of power and the transmission of resources in a world in which families are also businesses" (Hamabata 1990). By following different actors involved in the succession game, Hamabata illustrates how personal gratification is perceived to come from fulfilling one's expected social and familial roles. This could result in marriage for the sake of maintaining various social and public roles—but in this context, the family is the business and thus obscures the oft-discussed dichotomy of public versus private. Here, social and familial role-playing takes precedence over individual compatibility with the marital partner.

In various anthropological works on contemporary Japanese society, we see that Neo-Confucian values underpin multiple aspects of Japanese lives. The values discussed in the earlier section, considered part of the "natural and social order" that is made up of various pairs of human relationships, are repeatedly reproduced in numerous forms. One is always required to determine where he or she is socially located in a given context. At a moment's notice, for example, one needs to choose a proper mode of speech according to one's social location (Kondo 1990). In his ethnography of a city in Western Japan, Scott Schnell describes his experience of improper seating. In proper Japanese settings, seating is also regulated by a prescribed order. Analogous to one's mode of speech, when attending a social situation that requires sitting, one is expected to discern his or her own social position among the group of people so that he or she can choose a proper spot to seat him- or herself. Space also needs to reproduce the "natural and social order" as a Japanese microcosmos. When Schnell attended a meeting of local villagers, he seated himself in an inappropriate spot. At the next moment, to the embarrassment of the ethnographer, the entire group of people who were almost seated stood up and rearranged themselves so that the seating could resume the proper order (Schnell 1999; see also Moeran 1998).[12]

Among Hamabata's upper-class, wealthy business families, personal preference for a marriage partner, sexual orientation, and other personal choices relating to the family may be sacrificed for the continuity of the family enterprise. The same discourse is played out in Kondo's work as well, although less conspicuously. While Kondo was in the field, teaching English to the son of a small business owner, she witnessed the struggle of a young man who was torn between the expectations of his family that he would take over the business and his desire to follow his personal dreams. In such a context, conforming to family expectations and, by extension, society, and sacrificing individual preferences is often viewed as a sign of maturity.

Even if values derived from Neo-Confucian idioms are less overtly visible in contemporary Japan than during the Edo and Meiji Periods, when they were part of official governmental codes regulating people's lives, in reality, the values embedded in these idioms continue to be upheld as social ideals. These values were also at play in my research participants' life in Tokyo, affecting their identities in their particular social contexts. As I discuss later, the relational sense of self gradually changes as converts acquire a Catholic worldview. Here I confine my discussions to the life of my respondents before they turned to the Church. For example, Hashimoto-san looked back and told me about the time when she turned to the act of praying. She was perhaps in her eighties when I first met her in 2006. She was brought up by an exceedingly liberal father and attended one of the Catholic women's schools in her youth. On this occasion, she talked about her difficult time during her marriage. As we will see, she was expected to be, and therefore struggled to become, a "good daughter-in-law":

> Gradually I turned to Catholicism, although I was still holding some resentful feelings towards the spirit of Sacred Heart. I started the act of praying on my own; perhaps because my married life was extremely difficult. The household that I married into was that of an army officer. It was the household from Kagaoshima Prefecture . . . and everything was extremely strict. There, I had to undergo feelings of sadness, hardships, etc. [. . .]

> I was living with my parents-in-law, [. . .] and it was my mother-in-law's philosophy that the daughter-in-law must do all the housework. So she trained me in all kinds of housework. I had no time of my own other than sleeping and when my children were asleep. In fact, I would hate to say this . . . because I feel miserable about myself . . . but I woke up at 4:30 a.m. every day. Back then, my house was so large, about 200-tsubo.[13] And it was not like nowadays . . . the yard was not covered by concrete. So, naturally, the weeds grew, and I had to weed to keep the area pristine. The area had to be swept, and cleansed so that neighbors would think that the House of Hashimoto was always kept well, setting a kind of a boundary.

The young Hashimoto-san, as the daughter-in-law, served this household day in, day out. From her interview, we can date this situation to the period before or during World War II, as she mentions her father-in-law's occupation as an army officer. (All military organizations were ostensibly dismantled after World War II.) At that time, the country was officially ruled under the discourse of Shinto-Confucian ideologies, of which the Imperial Rescript on Education that we saw earlier served as a primary ethical guideline. We can also see that Hashimoto-san was the *yome*, a woman who was married into the household,[14] and her mother-in-law, a senior *yome*, was on her mission to train the newcomer, a junior *yome*.

Hashimoto-san's own unique character was not important in this training. She recalls how she was corrected by her mother-in-law and sister-in-law about her laughing. "See, my married-household was from Kagoshima." She repeated this point several times, emphasizing that Kagoshima Prefecture is especially known for its appreciation of conservative values. "And my sister-in-law had also agreed with her parents, and told me that it was strange that a woman would laugh loudly in front of others. I was criticized." She also related to me another episode in which we learn how much her behavior was constantly under the surveillance of her in-laws. "It was my mistake to sing in the bathroom. Did you know that you are not supposed to?" Hashimoto-san's playful tone indicated that she was tacitly retaliating for her mother-in-law's opposition to such a trifling gesture. She continued: "When I came out from a bath singing, my mother-in-law told me: 'Kinue-san, you sounded like you had enjoyed bathtime or something, but your stew has all burned and turned black.' She did not turn off the stove for me!" As a daughter-in-law, Hashimoto-san was not to speak back to her in-laws and was to obey the words of the mother-in-law, who had presumably been trained by her own mother-in-law when she was younger. The fact that Hashimoto-san remembers this small incident from forty or fifty years earlier indicates the extent to which she felt attacked and hurt by these interactions.

Raising the question of individuality in the Japanese cultural context of orderly relations, Smith quotes Miyoshi Masao:

> "Miyoshi (1974, 78–79), ever the Cassandra, believes that the Japanese are left without a personality: 'The young Japanese studies his assigned role until he perfects it. His worth will be measured by his approximation to the ideal of his type . . .' The judgment is no doubt too severe, but in fact one hears on every hand characterizations of persons by the extent to which they do approximate an ideal role type." (Smith 1983, 86)

He then explains about those who fail to conform to the ideal type. They are often dismissed as "he or she has too strong a personality (*kosei ga tsuyoi*)" (Smith 1983, 86). Smith's discussion resonates with Hashimoto-san's episode of singing in the bath. Hashimoto-san is a bright, charming, and captivating individual, yet these qualities were not appreciated as the ideal type for a *yome* or a daughter-in-law in the House of Hashimoto.

Okada-san is a woman in her mid-forties. She is a tall, slim, and active woman with a dry sense of humor. When I talked to her in 2007, she was forty-four years old. She was born in the 1960s and therefore roughly one generation younger than Hashimoto-san. Okada-san was married and she had two children who were twelve and fifteen years old. In the beginning of her interview, she referred to her marriage as "where all the troubles began" (*sorega koto no hajimari*). These troubles, however, later worked as the catalyst led her to knock at the door of the church. Looking back to her decision to get married, Okada-san said:

> Although I got married, I did not date him for a long time. I knew him from work. . . . I wonder when did I marry? At age twenty-something. . . . I felt as if I must be married. He worked for the same company, and I sort of knew him. And somehow things turned out so that I married him.

She recalled how she felt that she *must* get married at the time for no specific reason. She herself was trained as a chemist and was working for a well-known company at the time. There was no financial reason for her to get married. After her marriage, she continued her professional life on a part-time basis. Just as she saw getting married as a necessity, she said that she "must stay with the husband for the children's sake."

Her problems with her husband started not long after their marriage. Okada-san gradually became aware of her husband's inability to interact with other people including his wife. In time, this problem emerged as a clinical one, resulting in a number of hospitalizations in a psychiatric institution. I asked her if she ever thought of divorcing him. She said:

> "I think it would be easier for me if I divorce him. I do not need him anyway on my part. But I am not sure what would happen to him, if I leave, especially when his condition gets worse. His depression is quite severe. I remember in last January, I left the house for a while [to take a break from the house where her husband is]. All of a sudden, I started worrying about him thinking what he would do if I were not around him. So, I returned home."

The way Okada-san conceives of her role has many parallels with the wives of alcoholics and the mothers of substance abusers whom Amy Borovoy (2005) studied. Similar to Borovoy's interviewees, Okada-san is also solidly anchored in her role as nurturer of the household: as a wife and mother, taking care of her ill husband at home, driving her children to school club activities, and, when necessary, shielding her husband's condition from the children, who are preoccupied with their schoolwork. Like women in Borovoy's study, Okada-san is the one who manages to keep the family together. Once, when her husband was in a psychiatric ward, she asked her daughter if she was interested in visiting her father. The daughter said 'no,' and Okada-san did not tell her that the father was actually mentally ill. During our interview, she took a call from her daughter, talking to her in a casual mode of speech, as many young mothers do today. By contrast, she did not emphasize any aspect of her professional life as a chemist during the interview. She constantly talked about her husband and children.

Many readers may think of the Roman Catholic Church's negative views on divorce when reading about Okada-san's decision to remain in her marriage. For those who practice Roman Catholicism in metropolitan Tokyo, however, negative sanctions associated with divorce are almost invisible. During my fieldwork, I encountered a large number of female divorcees who had converted to Catholicism in their thirties and forties. Most of them had divorced before coming to the church, and there was no criticism of the fact that, despite their status as divorcees, they received church sacraments, including the Eucharist. As most of these women had been married to non-Christians, the issue rarely comes up. During my twelve months of fieldwork, I did not encounter any Catholics who refrained from taking sacraments because they were divorced. Therefore, even if Okada-san decides to divorce her husband, her life in the church can be continued without restriction. Okada-san, however, interprets her marital situation as her cross—the suffering that she carries with Jesus—and plans to continue her life married to her husband.

Unlike the case of Hashimoto-san, Okada-san lives far away from her in-laws. In addition, her natal home is outside the Tokyo area, and thus she did not have much help from her parents or parents-in-law during her husband's recurring psychiatric episodes. The formation of neolocal households has become common in the metropolitan Tokyo area during the postwar era (Smith 1974). Okada-san had been concealing the hospitalization of her husband from her mother-in-law. One day, when his day of discharge from the hospital was approaching, Okada-san received a phone call from her mother-in-law. She felt that her mother-in-law realized that her son was not living at home, so Okada-san decided to tell her about his illness. To Okada-san's surprise, the mother-in-law related to her that he had suffered a similar episode when he was completing his final degree. Yet Okada-san's position as sole caregiver for her husband did not change after that phone call. She said: "Wouldn't a regular mother-in-law say, 'How are you?' or 'Were you okay?' or something caring when you are back [to the in-laws' house], right? She talked nothing about her son. She talked about anything else . . . it is almost like she was avoiding [the topic]. And then, she [the mother-in-law] said that such illness is like having the flu." Okada-san interpreted these reactions as indicating that her mother-in-law wished to pretend that her son was healthy. By contrast, her father-in-law acknowledged his daughter-in-law's ordeal, and she was comforted by his caring words. Okada-san honestly told me with a sigh, "Most recently, he [her husband] had to take a week off from work, and it was okay at the end . . . but, it is *very* tiring (*honto tsukareru*)!" She was also careful about speaking of her husband's illness to her own natal family. She first consulted her sister who lived close to their parents. Upon hearing the plight of Okada-san, the sister pointed out that it had been Okada-san's own decision to marry this man. In many ways, Okada-san was expected to persevere in this situation because she was married to this man and was the mother of his two children. The idea of perseverance is an important theme in Japanese society, and I turn now to that topic.

Cult of *Ganbaru* or Perseverance

Striving as hard as one can to achieve one's goal is a celebrated theme in contemporary Japanese society. This virtue is often expressed as *ganbaru*. The verb *ganbaru* can be translated as "to persevere," "to strive hard," and "to hang on." Perseverance is another facet of the Japanese *mentalité* in the modern period. Amanuma Kaoru, a Japanese historical anthropologist, claims that *ganbaru* is the ethos of Japan's modernity (1987). When babies start walking, they are encouraged to *ganbaru* ("strive hard"), and when they become schoolchildren, they are told to *ganbaru* ("to persevere") in their studies to achieve better grades. Once young adults enter the workforce, family members and friends encourage the youth so that they will *ganbaru* ("strive as hard as they can") at new workplaces. When a woman is married for several years and has not been successful in conceiving a child, she may say jokingly to her friend that she is *ganbatteru* ("striving hard") at night yet not successful in conceiving (Amanuma 1987). Not surprisingly, the catchphrase "*Ganbare* Nippon!" (Go Japan!) became one of the most sought-after slogans in Japan's competitive advertisement industry. The battle over this slogan evolved into a legal suit involving the Japan Olympic Committee, which insisted on its long-standing usage of the phrase (Kyodo News Agency, October 16, 2003).

The virtue of pushing one's boundaries and limitations to go further is identified with different labels but nevertheless discussed by many scholars (Amanuma 1987; Benedict 1974; Cave 2007; Smith 1983). Amanuma argues, perhaps erroneously, that the concept of *ganbaru* is not found in neighboring Asian countries (1987, 49) and emphasizes the uniqueness of the concept itself as much as the extreme popularity of this notion within Japan.[15] Benedict, for her part, uses the metaphor of a sword in discussing the virtue of honing one's skills in perfecting one's social role. She identifies this behavior with the word *shūyō* and states that it "polishes away 'the rust of the body'" (Benedict 1974, 234); hence the metaphor of the sword. Smith takes up the idea of *seishin* or spirit to discuss this aspect of discipline in Japanese contexts. He states that Japanese "society provides a number of ways in which the individual can acquire the recommended fortitude" (Smith 1983, 98). After noting the example of the "Japanese spirit" (*yamato damashī*), the concept mobilized by the ultranationalist state of Japan during the Pacific War in opposition to "Western materialism," Smith admonishes naive readers: "They were so utterly wrong that this specifically jingoistic embodiment of *seishin* doctrine today appeals only to tiny but clamorous groups on the far political right. In its contemporary form, [. . .] *seishin* training is thought to lead to the attainment of purely practical rather than transcendental ends, such as better performance in school or at work or a happier family life" (Smith 1983, 99). In everyday life in Tokyo, this push to perfection and self-mastery is often expressed as *ganbaru*.[16] This notion also figures largely in many stories my interviewees related, particularly about their pre-conversion lives.[17] Now I turn to some of these narratives from my fieldwork.

It was my first day at Fr. Massey's class at Our Lady of the Assumption Church. At the end of the class, the priest assigned everybody in the class into separate small groups. This is a time of "sharing" (*wakachiai*), meaning that people are expected to share their experiences of faith. Fr. Massey himself participates in one of the groups. I was assigned to a group with three other women aged between fifty and seventy. They were curious about who I was. They also seemed to be happy that they were able to help me with my research. After an appointed leader led a short prayer for that day's sharing, instead of sharing faith experiences, we started chatting.

I began asking questions about whether the majority of people in the class were adult converts. Akiyama-san, who commuted to this church from neighboring Saitama Prefecture, answered: "I think so. The majority anyway are adult converts." This prompted each member to start telling me about the ways in which she had come to this church. Akiyama-san continued: "When I was young, I had been living with my aunt, who was Catholic. Perhaps because my father passed away early, my mother and her sister [who was Catholic] lived with us [to help the family]. So, I was used to having hymns in the house, and I think my aunt was also going to a Protestant church nearby. I remember having a cross and [religious] pictures at home." Akiyama-san was looking back at her youth nostalgically. She is a woman in her late fifties or early sixties with short gray hair. Like many other women in the room, she wore a knee-length skirt, her legs pressed tightly together and her hands placed politely on her lap. Her culturally disciplined body signaled me that I should do the same to maintain a respectable position in this classroom.

Akiyama-san continued: "I am not sure whether this background affected me or not, but when I came to the point that I could no longer carry the burden of taking care of my ill family members, two sayings came to my mind. One is that God does not give you burdens that you cannot carry, and the other is that God did not create anything wasteful." In other words, she interpreted her suffering as something that she could withstand, and this seemingly useless toil as something meaningful with a purpose. This experience led Akiyama-san to knock at the door of a nearby Catholic church. As we see from the work of Rosenberger (2001), the Japanese health care system has continued to rely on women as free caretakers, and many housewives take on the role of caretaker for ill family members in addition to taking care of their children. Like Okada-san, whom we encountered earlier, Akiyama-san also took on the role of nurturer and caretaker (cf. Borovoy 2005). This narrative of working hard to take care of family members to the point of self-exhaustion and sense of loss is a relatively common narrative among Catholic women in Tokyo. As we have seen, however, if one's sense of self is strongly rooted in one's social role (Kondo 1990) as a mother and wife (Allison 1991; Borovoy 2005), and the cultural ideal celebrates one's perfection of that role as articulated by Miyoshi earlier (quoted in Smith 1983, 86), it is not surprising that women strive hard as caretakers and exhaust themselves.

Hashimoto-san, whom we met earlier, revealed a similar sentiment during her personal interview. She was married to a son of an army officer in the prewar period. She explained to me how she had understood the situation back then. Prior to turning to Catholicism: "I believed that, if I'd work as hard as I can (*hisshini hataraite*), by my own effort, I could somehow overcome the sadness that I embraced in my daily life." In explaining her determination to work hard to overcome her sadness, she used the expression *hisshi*, an adverb modifying the verb "work" in this context. My translation, "as hard as I can," hardly renders the desperate feelings that accompany the expression. The two *kanji* characters used in this expression are "necessary" and "death." The conventional expression *hisshi* presupposes one's determination, and a solemn feeling always accompanies this expression.

Amanuma's (1987) meta-historical review claiming the centrality of *ganbaru* throughout Japanese history requires further evidence to support

Propriety, Virtues, and Social Obligations 79

his claim, but I appreciate his appraisal that the ethos of *ganbaru* is central to Japan's modernization. Much of the material he draws on supports the centrality of this notion in the modern period. Amanuma reviews the semantic transformation of this term. He traces two possible predecessors for the term: one is *gawoharu* ("to insist on one's opinion"), and, according to Amanuma, this usage was seen through the Meiji, Taisho, and early Shōwa Periods. This expression entails a negative judgement about the person who insists on his or her opinion, as doing so may contradict the priority often given to the collective in Japanese social contexts. The other semantic predecessor, and older usage, is that of *ganwoharu* ("to keep an eye on something"). This expression connotes the idea that the actor is determined not to move from one spot where he or she keeps his or her eye on something. Amanuma further points out that the contemporary positive usage of *ganbaru* as "to persevere," "to keep going," and "to strive hard" was crystallized in the famous live radio broadcast from the Berlin Olympics in 1936 when the announcer frantically shouted *ganbare* for a Japanese swimmer, Maehata Hideko, who eventually won the event and brought home a gold medal to Japan. The announcer shouted *ganbare* thirty-eight times during this event, that lasted slightly more than three minutes. The nation was intoxicated by this famous broadcast, which affirmed not only this swimmer's but also Japan's position vis-à-vis other nations. This historical recording is often aired on TV shows, and even somebody like me who was born in the postwar era would recognize the phrase "Maehata Ganbare!" This usage of *ganbaru* in the Berlin Olympics commentary is representative of today's usage.

Smith (1983), on the other hand, points to yet another discursive process relating to the idea of *ganbaru* that goes back to the Meiji Period (although he does not use the term *ganbaru*). Writing roughly at the same time as Hosbawm and Ranger's important work *The Invention of Tradition* (1983), Smith brings up a curious piece of historical evidence pertaining to the construction of the "Japanese" idea of *ganbaru*. He states that educators in Japan during the Meiji Period were strongly influenced by the works of T. H. Green, an English metaphysical philosopher. In both official and popular commentaries on the Imperial Rescript on Education, Green's argument lay at the heart of these exegeses on the Rescript. According to Smith, the "eminent educator Yoshida Seichi wrote that Green's doctrine of 'self-regulation' recommended itself particularly for adoption by the Japanese" (Smith 1983, 11). One of the prominent propositions often advanced from this doctrine was that " 'Man's worth is judged by the degree of his effort to approximate his existing self to an ideal self' (Smith 1983, 11)." Here, we see the positive valorization of the effort to push oneself to become the ideal self.

When the cultural ideal of *ganbaru* in the modern period is combined with the previously discussed relational sense of self, the resulting model is a tough one to master for individuals. This social model is amply evident in the stories of my research participants. Akiyama-san, striving hard to be a good wife, mother, and caretaker of her family, was exhausted. Hashiomto-san, fifty years ago, was trying to become a good daughter-in-law, waking up at 4:30 a.m. every morning to take care of the household. Okada-san was trying to put all her strength into maintaining her household despite her husband's mental illness without the aid of her in-laws. The same rules of *ganbaru* in one's given social role apply for male members of the society; however, societal expectations for men are different. Despite the implementation of the Equal Employment Opportunity Law in 1986, Japan is still largely a gendered society (Allison 1996, 1991; Borovoy 2005; Goldstein-Gidoni 2012; Kelsky 2001; Lebra 1984; Rosenberger 2001). Men are supposed to *ganbaru* at their workplace, working many hours of overtime. The ways in which male members of society are affected by this notion of *ganbaru*, and how that affects their relationship with the Roman Catholic Church, are discussed in chapter 4 on gender. In the lives of many of my respondents, the extent to which one is "striving hard" (*ganbaru*) is monitored by human authority rather than that of divine.

Knowing one's position in a given context, perfecting one's social roles, and constantly striving for perfection are reinforced in a variety of ways as ideals, and these values constitute an important part of people's experience in living contemporary Japan. I hope that this chapter provides readers with the basis for understanding the social expectations faced by my interlocutors in Tokyo. I have pointed to several discursive processes in which government or political elites used various discourses to produce "desirable human beings." Over the years, however, these discourses have become part of the Japanese construction of the self, both tormenting and comforting the Japanese people. In the next chapter, by depicting the "Catholic ideals" upheld by the Japanese members of the Roman Catholic Church in Tokyo, I portray the sense of liberation and elation that church members feel when they embrace this different worldview according to which the source of moral authority is located completely outside the human realm.

Chapter 3

Breaking the Barrel and Becoming Catholic

"You do not have to persevere anymore!"

(*Mou ganbaranakute iinoyo!*)

—A Catholic woman in Tokyo

In the tearoom attached to a French restaurant in central Tokyo, we sat at the corner table in the late afternoon. This café was nestled in an upscale neighborhood of Tokyo near the Church of Our Lady of the Assumption. The area was occupied by houses, condos, and a few elementary schools. Hashimoto-san was investigating the cakes that had just arrived at the table. She was in her eighties, yet always maintained a strikingly youthful attitude. She was intrigued by the intricate beauty of the pastry and admired its appearance. She was also a meticulous dresser. She dressed in elegant clothes, and her nail polish was always immaculate. From her open shirt collar, I saw a necklace made with crystal that resembled a rosary. Like most people of her generation, she was not very tall. But her high-heeled shoes make her appear slightly taller than she actually was. Hashimoto-san always wore a rather broad smile, and it was hard not to smile back at her because her positive and mischievous facial expression was contagious. Whenever I smiled at her, she chuckled and said, "What, are you laughing at me?" This exchange usually sparked further "girly" and giggly conversation despite our age difference.

In the interview, Hashimoto-san described the changes that her faith had brought to her life:

Once I gained faith, what had changed [in me]? I had been liberated. Yes, I am really liberated. I feel free! This is the most fabulous thing [that resulted from my acquiring faith]." I was married into a strict household. My father[-in-law] was a high ranking officer in the army. My [husband's] family was so strict, and there were so many "do-nots" in the household. But, once I was baptized [she chuckles], do you know the belt that goes around the barrel (*taga*)? As if those barrel hoops had come off! I was free! I was so happy and could not stop smiling. I was so happy that I wanted to talk to even a dog on the street. I would say [to a dog]: "Say bow-wow!" I was so free!

As the reader may recall, I introduced Hashimoto-san in chapter 2. She is the same person who used to get up at 4:30 a.m. to get her household ready for the day as a good daughter-in-law. Her expression here, "the barrel hoops had come off" (*taga ga hazureru*), is an idiomatic expression in the Japanese language used to describe a loose state of being that should be regulated by a proper set of rules. This expression describes a negative condition. For example, many people talk about how they would gain weight once their "barrel hoops had gone," meaning once their determination to avoid fatty food, or to stay slim, was gone. People also talk about indulging themselves with shopping, sex, and even depression once their "barrel hoops had gone." Barrel hoops therefore represent self-imposed regulations and emotional disciplines that help people maintain themselves as properly regulated members of society. In this context, however, Hashimoto-san asked whether I knew about "barrel hoops" (*taga*) and described her liberated feeling "as if those barrel hoops had come off." Here, what is intriguing is that she described her uplifted, liberated feeling using the otherwise negative expression "barrel hoops." As somebody who has mastery over the Japanese language, Hashimoto-san deliberately used this idiomatic expression in a contradictory and playful way.

Reflecting back to the time when she grew exceedingly tired of the household chores that she had to do under the constant vigilance of her in-laws, Hashimoto-san told me that she had started visiting Kyoto, some 600 kilometers west of Tokyo, on a daily basis without telling her in-laws with whom she was living. She said these trips were a coping mechanism that she chose to manage her everyday life back then. "I had a yearning for something immovable at the time," she said. In search of something solid, not affected by time, she frequented Akishino Temple[1] in Kyoto, the former capital of Japan for centuries. Hashimoto-san would tell her family that she had errands to do in downtown Tokyo. By taking the bullet train to Kyoto, she could spend time with the large Buddha statue that looked down on her. She would return home to Tokyo by dinnertime so that she could serve dinner for her immediate family as well as her aging in-laws. She said, "I was longing for something that would not move for hundreds of years. So, during that time, my exploration of Catholicism and my trips to Kyoto went on simultaneously."

Many laypeople in Tokyo mentioned that they had encountered the Roman Catholic Church in their "search for something reliable" in their lives. The large Buddha statue that Hashimoto-san was visiting in Kyoto metaphorically depicts such notions of solidity, constancy, and reliability. Hashimoto-san stated clearly what the Catholic faith means to her:

> Well, we can say that it [faith] is the relationship with God, but it seems to me that I established a clear "coordinate grid" (*zahyōjiku*) in me. Establishing and finalizing this coordinate grid within me had led me, how can I say this . . . I may say . . . to my independence as a human being.

I asked her to elaborate further on this "coordinate grid."

> What is it? It must be God. [. . .] This is something that determines who I am. In other words, you can say that I established my own identity (*aidentitī*).

The image of the horizontal x-axis and vertical y-axis in a coordinate graph gives us a sense of standards against which one can judge things.[2] Also, it is a fixed location in space that anchors a person—the center is the point where the axes intersect. In the previous section, I depicted a Japanese sense of self as that on a sliding scale; one has to assess one's position in a given context—which status one occupies in a group of people based on gender, seniority, and other relational factors. According to Hashimoto-san, however, embracing Roman Catholicism enabled her to find an immovable point from which she can act. Presumably, the point usually called "origin" where the x-axis and y-axis intersect must indicate God. Hashimoto-san calls this center the relationship with God.

In what follows, I describe popular conceptions of Catholicism among the laity in Tokyo and discuss the ways in which they embrace and cherish these values. I argue that many laypeople in Tokyo find that espousing the Catholic worldview is a liberating experience precisely because of its difference from "Japanese" social ideals that dictate appropriate behavior. The significant element that underlies this sense of liberation is the shift of authority from the human world to the Christian deity. As cleverly encapsulated in Hashimoto-san's expression "barrel hoops," Japanese society constantly demands its members to follow the sets of rules and ideals to achieve an orderly society. Continually keeping up with these regulations and ideals, however, could result in emotional and psychological difficulties for some members. In this context, by immersing oneself in the Catholic worldview, these socially sanctioned rules and ideals can assume secondary significance among Japanese members of the Catholic Church. I suspect that this experience explains why Hashimoto-san used the Japanese expression "barrel hoops" to describe the impositions of rules and then described the lack of barrel hoops as liberating.

In this worldview, the Christian God emerges as the new "third person" for these laypeople, who are situated in a society that is governed by human relationships (*ningen kankei*). In Japanese society at large, tight webs of human relationships are repeatedly and constantly reinforced through gift giving (Rupp 2003) and other means, and because of this, the notion of reciprocity is taken seriously to an extent that is unimaginable from the viewpoints of Americans or Canadians. When converts gradually transition into Roman Catholic worldviews, however, they came to embrace such ideas as "entrusting" (*yudaneru*), "God as love," and "rejoice always" as ideals. As they embrace these ideas, they simultaneously place the Christian God at the center of their relational webs. With this shift, the laity's sense of self can shift from a "sliding scale" of self to that of one anchored in a fixed point, that is, the relationship with the divine.

As the laity gradually move into the Roman Catholic worldview, the location of social others shifts in the minds of many laypeople. This reordering of values in social others manifests in various ways, eventually effecting changes in one's sense of self. These changes also affect one's capacity to act. As laity shift their allegiance from the aggregate of humans to the non-human divine, they feel a sense of liberation and eventually are able to rely less on other human beings.

This two-tier model of conversion—juxtaposing historically conceived Japanese traditional values on the one hand and Catholic teachings and values on the other hand—seems to generate harsh criticism from both academic and Catholic audiences. This model appears simplistic and does not provide an immediate answer to a frequently asked question: why are so few Japanese converting to the Christian faith? Many Catholics in Tokyo might disagree with my argument because it does not portray them as part of an "amicable society," also a long-held, conventional Japanese social ideal. I answer some of these questions and respond to these critiques in chapter 4 on gender and chapter 5 on historical consciousness. For now, I note that while the Japanese converts transform their worldview based on Catholic values, for the most part they continue their efforts to be caring wives, good mothers, and hardworking team members of society. What is more, they often conceal their Catholic identity within their social or even familial circles. Nevertheless, their understanding of self and the roles within their given contexts have shifted internally, as we will see in this chapter, and this shift often provides a significant sense of relief. On the surface, however, they remain the same people, performing the roles expected by others in Japanese society.

Although the number of Japanese converts to Catholicism in total is small, Protestant church members represent a significant portion of those who became Catholic in the two parishes where I conducted fieldwork. Those who had entered the Catholic Church from Protestant denominations often understood their conversion to Catholicism as involving a move from a people-centered life to a God-centered life. To describe this major shift in allegiance from the human to the divine is the primary goal of this chapter, and now I begin with the notion of God as the new "third person" in Tokyo.

God as the New "Third Person"

Sekiguchi-san, a hip divorcee in her late thirties, always took me to a new place, often out for drinking. She lived with her parents in a suburb of Tokyo and was pursuing her role as a catechumen on a full-time basis. As somebody who was neither in school nor engaged in family life, her prolonged single adult life was mostly devoted to the world of New Age and spiritual questing when I met her (cf. Rosenberger 2013). It was the second time she had taken me to the bar, Épopée, which was sponsored by some priests from the Archdiocese of Tokyo. The idea for this drinking establishment was conceived by a French priest, Fr. Nayrand, who was a close friend of the late Endo Shūsaku, a famous writer often referred to as *the* Catholic writer of Japan. Fr. Nayrand himself served as bartender at the Épopée for many years. After Fr. Nayrand's retirement, the position was taken over by a Japanese "Master" (*masutā*), Shindō-san, who was also the president of this company. Although Master is not a priest himself, he is able to converse with people about Catholicism and the Christian faith while serving alcohol and light meals. He is immensely knowledgeable about the church, its teachings, and current events outside the church.

The bar is on the fourth floor of a narrow, scruffy-looking building typical of the area. The establishment is located right in the middle of Kabukichō, a famous "red-light district" of Tokyo. As a result of my somewhat conservative upbringing, I had never stepped into the center of this area in Tokyo, even though I spent ten years of my youth in this mega-city. As I had been told over the years, there were many cabarets, men who resemble pimps, and bouncers on the street. Sekiguchi-san and I were somewhat of an oddity here, but we pushed our way through to the building. In many ways, this area was typically "Japanese," filled with tired *sararīman* dressed in suits, completely drunk; and young women, both Japanese and non-Japanese, selling their bodies and youth. I understood why Fr. Nayrand wanted to be here. This area would make an ideal venue for a "Catholic outreach" in downtown Tokyo. While the bouncer from the cabaret on the ground floor threw us a suspicious glance, we took an elevator to the fourth floor.

"*Irasshaimase!*" As we opened the door, the greeting welcomed us from a dimly lit space inside. The bar was simply furnished with only a U-shaped counter. There were always some non-Japanese Asian foreign students working there alongside the Master behind the counter. We sat on two stools. Master remembered from my last visit that I was conducting ethnographic research on Japanese Catholics in central Tokyo. After settling into our conversation with Master, I asked him a question: "What is the benefit for a Japanese person to become Catholic?" With a friendly smile, he answered with conviction: "I think that we can have this new third person in our life called God, the third person authority that is completely divorced from our human relationships." I was struck; his argument made complete sense. The notion of God creates a new space for the Japanese, who are constantly entangled in the webs of human relationships, and provides a rupture in those relationships, making room for fresh perspectives. I looked at Sekiguchi-san with amazement. She did not seem to care what was going on in my mind. She seemed content that I was engaged in an animated conversation with Master.

As discussed in the previous chapter, Japan's discursive processes have emphasized human relationships and the hierarchies associated with them. This Neo-Confucian–inspired order was constantly reproduced through modes of speech, seating arrangements, and other social forms. In the opening story of this chapter, Hashimoto-san describes her liberation from the various "barrel hoops," which I interpret as the social conventions and values that are deeply rooted in the culture of the primacy of human relationships. As converts to Catholicism deepen their familiarity with the notion of God as an almighty authority, they make a gradual departure from the worldview dictated by humans. To understand the ways in which the Christian God is manifested in Japanese cultural contexts, a discussion of the constant reinforcement of human relationships in daily life in Tokyo and the meticulous care that they require is in order. In particular, I review reciprocity and its binding effects that I have traced in the field.

Reciprocity and Vigilance

The primacy of human relationships (*ningen kankei*) within Japanese society is expressed in a variety of forms. In addition to seating arrangements and the modes of speech that constantly reproduce a Neo-Confucian–inspired human hierarchy, strict adherence to the principle of reciprocity is observed in numerous social interactions. I suggest that the emphasis on reciprocity also relates to the marginal position of supernatural authority figures in Japanese society. Strict adherence to the principle of reciprocity is clearly and physically apparent in the practice of gift giving (*zōtō*). "A major avenue for social mobility in Japan is through bribery and patronage," writes Katherine Rupp in her study of gift giving in Japan (2003, 1). As Rupp shows in her study, however, people in Japan carefully avoid the term "bribery" when discussing the money and goods that are given and received in these interactions. Instead, many forms of monetary and material transactions are understood as gratuities, seasonal gifts, and sometimes simply as gifts. Rupp notes that seasonal gifts (summer and winter gifts, *ochūgen* and *oseibo*, respectively) account for 60 percent of the annual profits of most Tokyo department stores (Rupp 2003, 1). As part of social convention, many people keep a record of give-and-take transactions between individuals as well as between households. These records come in handy when determining how much to give to those from whom one received a similar gift before. A highly specialized sensitivity is required for maintaining the conventions of gift giving in Japanese society. As Rupp explains, there are underlying rules governing the value of a gift, to whom it must be given, and how to give. Furthermore, the way in which one handles gift giving is often judged as an expression of one's personality (cf. Rupp 2003, 192–97).

In my interactions with people who attended Our Lady of the Assumption, gift-giving relationships played out in different ways. For example, I often received gifts from people who were new to the church. It seemed to me that these gifts represented a way to initiate and maintain our personal relationships. When I took Kitami-san to a different church that she had never attended, she brought me some of the treats from the "care package" sent by her mother, who lived some distance from Tokyo. I inferred that Kitami-san gave me these gifts as a token of gratitude. Mita-san asked me to participate in family masses from time to time, and I always received gifts to take home after these masses. I was perplexed when I received those gifts, as I was not sure what to do in terms of reciprocity.[3] Gradually, I realized that these gifts were intended to make our social ties stronger. In analyzing the practice of gift giving in Japan, Rupp distinguishes three major factors that determine how much to give. They are the strength of the human relationship, gratitude, and hierarchy (2003, 34). My only consolation when I received gifts was that I was younger than the women who had gifted me, and therefore I was not obligated to return gifts. In a way, their gifts indicated their role as patrons to me as a younger member of the community. Interestingly, however, people who were strongly committed to the Catholic worldview were less inclined to engage in this kind of relation building through gift giving. The two people who gave me gifts most often were new members of the parish. Kitami-san was still a catechumen at the time, and it had been only one year since Mita-san had joined the Catholic Church.

The observance of reciprocity in social interaction extends beyond gift giving. Emotional attachment, which can be expressed as loyalty, is also subject to the rules of reciprocity that govern human relationships in the "traditional" worldview. For example, when I was visiting one of the graveyards located in Yokohama City near Tokyo, I noticed small slits on several stone monuments. The slits are marked with the words "business cards reception" (figures 3.1. and 3.2). Here, even tombstones

Figures 3.1 and 3.2. Business Card Reception Box at Cemetery.

can be accompanied by a business card holder so that the living can keep track of ongoing social ties that are being maintained with the members of the household (or family business).

Although I gave two examples of gift giving in which I was personally involved at Our Lady of the Assumption, in the wider Catholic Church community, gift giving was mentioned as a human relationship that one should treat with caution. Honda-san, a woman I encountered at the very beginning of my fieldwork at the Cathedral located in central Tokyo, told me that she was not involved in many parishioners' activities at the church because she hoped to avoid these webs of human relationships:

> I don't like being involved too much. That would make things too worldly (*sezokuteki*), wouldn't it? When I receive some gifts, then, I have to do my return gifts, you know. I only know a few people here. I saw one, actually today, but [when I come here] there is no guarantee that I see anybody that I know. But I believe this is better suited for me. I can come [to the church] at my own pace.

Honda-san was baptized eighteen years ago and comes to visit the cathedral once a month when she visits her mother, who is living in a retirement home nearby. Honda-san lives in Chiba Prefecture, a prefecture near Tokyo, and also attends a parish church close to her home. While I was talking to her, I sensed her independence, self-confidence, and autonomy. Like most women of her generation, she did not seem to be a professional woman or financially independent. Rather, she gave the impression that she is a housewife who supported her husband's full-time work.[4] Nevertheless, I felt that this woman stood on a solid foundation that had nothing to do with her children, her husband, or her work as a housewife. Her personal strength seemed to result from her dependence on supernatural authority.

The parish, however, is by definition a community. Therefore, forming some human relationships is an inevitable part of the lives of parishioners. Yet some church members were fearful of others in the community. The judgments made by other people can be a source of constant threat to some individuals. During my fieldwork, I heard repeatedly that one individual was contemplating leaving the parish because of troubled human relationships there. One day I was invited to attend Okada-san's father's memorial mass scheduled immediately after the Bible class during the week at Our Lady of the Assumption. Okada-san's father had passed away from illness in her hometown in Kansai area, a few hundred kilometers west of Tokyo. Some time after the funeral, she arranged to have a memorial mass for him in Tokyo. Our Lady of the Assumption has several chapels, and private masses were often conducted in these chapels. For Buddhist memorial rites, it is conventional for invitees to wear black, but this was a Catholic mass, which would be attended by only a few parishioners who were close to Okada-san. I called Kaneta-san, who was the baptismal sponsor of Okada-san and who had been born into a Catholic household, hoping to be able to count on her judgment in terms of social conventions about what clothes to wear to the memorial mass. This assumption proved to be wrong. She said: "I was wondering what to wear too. I would normally wear black for a memorial mass. But I am not sure whether the priest will invite all the class to her memorial mass—because it would be immediately after the class. If so, then, people would realize that I had been invited originally [if I am in black clothes] but they had not been invited personally, you know? I am afraid what others would think of me . . ." The memorial mass was scheduled to take place immediately following the class that Okada-san attended, and the celebrant was the priest who was the instructor of the class. Considering that he was young, non-Japanese, and a welcoming priest, it was likely that he would invite others in the class to the memorial mass without paying too much attention to the dynamics with which Kaneta-san was concerned. After I had hung up, my cell phone rang again. It was Kaneta-san. She had realized that she was also acting as a cantor for the mass and therefore should wear black. I, on the other hand, as a researcher, decided to be ambiguous, and chose to wear a black-and-white checkered skirt with a black summer sweater. I put a white summer cardigan on top of my black sweater so that I did not look completely prepared for a memorial mass. Yet if I took off the cardigan, I would look respectable for the memorial rite.

Kaneta-san's fear of what other people might think about her was not unfounded. Being aware of one's reputation and maintaining one's human relationships are crucial to one's social well-being in Japanese society in general; the Catholic Church cannot be an exception. I heard a great deal of gossip in both parishes where I conducted fieldwork. As I was participating in multiple social circles during fieldwork—two classes at Our Lady of the Assumption during the week; attendance at mass in another parish, Terada Catholic Church, on Sundays; and a Catholic Charismatic Renewal meeting in Sunday evenings—I felt guilty when one of my research participants from one circle saw me with another research participant from a different circle. From a conventional Japanese social point of view, I should stick to one circle of people, making my allegiance explicit. In reality, however, I could not afford to be partial; I needed to collect as much data as possible during the twelve months of my ethnographic research. I felt as if I were "sleeping around," metaphorically speaking, selling my intimacy with others in exchange for information that they would provide me about their experience as Catholics in Tokyo. As an ethnographer, such information would become my academic currency later. For my research participants, forming a close tie with somebody in the church is valuable, especially in these two parishes where there is a constant influx of new people and one can feel lost in a large crowd. In a strategy to negotiate between my culturally informed sense of guilt and the need to facilitate my field research, I attempted to sit alone when I attended mass. In that way, I could appear alone and avoid being caught up in any particular circle of people. This strategy also enabled others to talk to me easily while allowing me the space I needed to approach people I had not yet met within the parishes.

Interestingly, some of my research participants decided to take advantage of my status as temporary and not related to any particular clique. Kimijima-san was attending both Our Lady of the Assumption and Terada Catholic Church in search of faith. She had not yet started the process of the Rite of Christian Initiation of Adults (RCIA) and was shopping around for a faith community to join while I was conducting fieldwork. One day I saw her by chance at a crossroads near the Terada Church. We were delighted to find each other. "I wanted to contact you, Omori-san!" she exclaimed. "I am not sure which faith community to join, and just can't make up my mind. I know you have a better perspective on things, I am sure, as you are a scholar. Do you have any advice for me?" I was perplexed. Her phrasing of the question was full of respect for me on the surface, but I could sense some calculation that lay underneath. I did not know what to say. Instead of giving her any advice, once we arrived at the Terada Church, I introduced Kimijima-san to an experienced Catholic woman who had presumably gone through a similar process. Her advice to Kimijima-san was typical of a devout layperson in the area: it is God who decides which faith community she should join, and therefore the answer to her question would come without Kimijima-san's own effort. I peeked at Kimijima-san's face to discern how she received this message.

After mass, over a late lunch together, Kimijima-san told me the real reason why she thought I would be a good source of advice for her on the pressing issue of selecting a faith community. "I am not sure who to speak to, because I do not want to be caught up in the webs of relations in any of these churches." According to her logic, I was officially "safe" because I would leave the church at the end of summer 2007; in addition, as a researcher, I was not supposed to be part of any of the cliques. Kimijima-san was right. Meanwhile, she was exploring a vast array of Roman Catholic venues as part of her soul searching. Interestingly, she was not the only one who confided in me because I was perceived as "safe." There were several others who decided to make me their confidante for the same reason. In such cases, their stories were often about their difficult relationships with other parishioners.

Over the course of fieldwork, I learned about the centrality of human relationships (*ningen kankei*) in Japanese society, mostly through the eyes of those who were caught up in them, detested them, and were therefore vigilant about them. As I concluded my twelve-month fieldwork in Tokyo, Itsuki Hiroyuki, one of Japan's celebrated contemporary writers, published a book titled *Human Relations* (Itsuki 2007) that made the bestseller lists. As much as human relationships are central to Japanese lives, these relationships are also a constant source of problems. Because people know the power of social relationships and the care that is required for their maintenance—for example, by gift giving—many people I encountered through fieldwork made efforts to avoid social entanglements. While human relationships are formed between, and dictated by, two parties, the notion of the Christian God ruptures this worldview by presenting the "third person" party as the ultimate authority. Now, by narrating the stories associated with some of the popular values among Catholics in Tokyo, I hope to depict some of the outcomes of embracing different and nontraditional worldviews in Japan.

Popular Catholic Values in Central Tokyo

To my question: "What are some of your favorite passages or hymns?" I received surprisingly consistent responses. One day at a Catholic bookstore run by a female order, I picked one of the rolled paper "oracles" from the basket provided by the cashier. An "oracle," or a message of the day, is written on paper that measures approximately one by five inches, and each strip contains a passage from the Bible (figures 3.3 and 3.4). The passage that I received that day was "Rejoice always, pray without ceasing, and give thanks in all circumstances" (1 Thessalonians 5:16–18a). This is the opening line of one of the most popular hymns among those I interviewed. This incident further confirmed my developing assumption that there are several values that are popular among lay Catholics in the area. These values and sayings are also reflected in various Catholic products, such as postcards, paper "oracles," and bookmarks.

In this section, I explore three of these popular Catholic values in an effort to capture the ethos shared by the laity in central Tokyo. However, I would be cautious to extend this claim to people outside this cultural sphere. My limited encounters with Catholics in the Nagasaki and Tohoku areas reminded me that my research findings should be confined to the area where I conducted ethnographic fieldwork. Nevertheless, the values discussed below are the ones that the majority of people I encountered through my fieldwork cherished dearly in their daily lives. These values allowed them to see themselves in a different light, often giving them solace and the building blocks to create and re-create their Catholic worldviews.

Entrusting. One of the most often mentioned and emphasized concepts in the worldview of groups of Catholics that I studied was the notion of "entrusting" (*yudaneru*). In a conversation about translating this term, "*yudaneru*," into English, Fr. Francis Mathy, who is a Jesuit scholar of comparative literature, suggested two words: "to surrender" and "to entrust." Sometimes I heard laypeople use the expression "completely entrusting" (*kanzen ni yudaneru*) God by "emptying oneself" (*jibun wo karappo nishite*). The word, to entrust (*yudaneru*), at least in my understanding retains the subject "I" that gives consent to the almighty power. In either translation, the crux of this notion *yudaneru* is the idea of giving the driver's seat to the divine instead of trying to maneuver things by oneself. This aspect of the Catholic worldview often comes into contradiction with the Japanese popular notion of "perseverance" (*ganbaru*), which I discussed in the previous chapter.

Many people who decide to knock on the door of the church at a time of crisis do so after trying hard to better their lives through their own efforts. This strategy should sound reasonable to readers in the West who are familiar with the virtues of hard work, self-reliance, and, above all, independence. As discussed in the previous chapter, however, hard work often takes place in the context of interdependence in Tokyo. Many women I encountered conceived of who they were in terms of their familial or societal roles. They worked hard to fulfill their roles as good mothers, daughters-in-law, wives, or professionals. This hard work

Figures 3.3 and 3.4. "Paper Oracles."

undertaken to fulfill one's social role, however, is not gender specific. In my limited encounters with male members of the church, I learned that they too must strive hard to achieve cultural ideals or else be forced to do so by peer pressure from their coworkers.

To give up such a culturally celebrated notion of "striving hard and persevering" (*ganbaru*) is a new and foreign endeavor for many Japanese people. When newcomers came to the class at Our Lady of the Assumption, Fr. Massey usually asked them to introduce themselves. Often newcomers might say something like "As I listened to everyone's engagement with the faith, I realized how immature I am. I pledge my perseverance and would like to strive much harder to become a better person (*motto ganbatte iihito ni naritaito omoimashita*)." This type of comment indicates that the newcomer is still in the Japanese cultural mode of striving hard for the ideal. Hearing this, the priest would often say, "Didn't you strive so hard already, though?" with an inquiring smile.

Interestingly enough, the centrality of the discourse of entrusting also came into conflict with that of New Age spirituality in the classroom. One day the priest asked the class, "What is your image of heaven?" Some people mentioned physical and sensory images of heaven, such as gentle breezes and light; others talked about being there with deceased family members and their hope of seeing them in heaven. Sekiguchi-san had this conversation with the priest:

SEKIGUCHI: "This is my own way of thinking. . . ."

PRIEST: "Okay."

SEKIGUCHI: "I think heaven is where I would end up with those who have the same level of consciousness."

PRIEST: "Consciousness. . . ."

SEKIGUCHI: "Yes, therefore, by raising the level of consciousness, I may be able to reach heaven."

PRIEST: "Then, how do you reach that point?"

SEKIGUCHI: "For example, by serving others . . . working hard, by persevering (*ganbatte*) . . . by doing many things, I may reach that point."

PRIEST: "How much is enough, I wonder? Is there such thing as enough hard work [laughter]?"

Sekiguchi-san was a neophyte in the class. At this time, she was undergoing a one-on-one catechism with this priest, hoping to receive baptism in the following month in Christmas 2006. Although Sekiguchi-san presented her "own" idea of heaven as a place where those who possess "higher consciousness" congregate, this idea can be found in many pieces of New Age literature. It is interesting that the New Age picture of heaven includes the idea of *ganbaru*, which requires individuals' efforts to better themselves. In this conversation, the priest did not reprimand Sekiguchi-san's inclination toward New Age thinking, but focused on dismantling her discourse on *ganbaru*, which he must have encountered constantly over his fifty years of pastoral life in Japan. As I illustrate later in the story of Kitami-san, many newcomers to the church make this shift from *ganbaru* to entrusting. In this process, followers learn different values, such as "God is love." I now turn to this other popular notion.

God is Love, God as Parents. "God is love" is a prominent teaching of the Roman Catholic Church in the global arena, but this concept is also popular among the lay Catholics in Tokyo whom I encountered.[5] The concept of love in Japanese society, however, is not necessarily clearly articulated, at least not in the same way it is in the West. The idea of love, which is often taken for granted in Western culture, arguably has its own genealogy in any society. Writing on love, anthropologist Sonia Ryang says:

> Love, therefore, despite all its seriousness and profundity, is not universal. No form of love—including agape, eros, philia, storge, *amour passion*, patriotism, filial piety, and paternalism—is supra-historical. But all love, even infatuation, comes in the guise of eternity, with a force that is beyond oneself, sometimes considered as madness and other times as sickness. Moreover, every love has its own story, structure and history, and its own social and cultural logic. (Ryang 2006, 1)

In today's usage, the Japanese word *ai* denotes the concept of love that is closest to the English word "love." Yet, as Itō Susumu argues, this usage appeared only after the Meiji Restoration of 1868, "primarily as a translation of 'love,' 'liebe,' or 'amour' in order to accommodate encounters with Western literature" (Ryang 2006, 13; the original discussion is found in

Itō 1996, 32, 95). Itō explains that, prior to the advent of the Western conception of love, the word and the character *ai* (love) existed, but it was used to describe a state of attachment that had negative connotations (Itō 1996, 94). Itō is careful in making this point. He speculates that, considering that Japan was under strong cultural influences from Buddhist and Confucian thought for many centuries, it might be difficult to claim that Japanese people were not affected by the Buddhist notion of *jiai* (affection) or the Confucian idea of *jinai* (benevolence). Yet Itō states with confidence that prior to the Meiji Period, the word *ai* was never popularly used to denote love (*aijō*) (1996, 95). Romantic feelings and longing between two adults were often expressed in terms of *koi* (love) by ancients who lived in the Japanese archipelago, and this tradition has been retained over many centuries to the present (93). Although the word *koi* is translated as "love," it is used only between lovers today, and it is not used to denote any type of positive emotion among family, friends, or strangers. Itō, unlike Ryang, traces the indigenous history of the word *koi* to discover the construction of "love in Japanese society." Itō collects many examples of the usage of *koi* from the famous Manyōshū, a collection of poetry compiled in the eighth century.

There is yet another story relating to love in Japanese society closer to our own time, dating from the 1940s. Toda Yūko, who served as an English-Japanese translator and interpreter in the northeast region of Japan during the occupation by the Allied Forces immediately following Japan's defeat in World War II in 1945, reminisces on her own encounter with the Western idea of love. One of the young soldiers, Pierre, asked Yūko to teach him the Japanese language. She agreed, and the classes were to take place on the street, partly because at the time Japanese residences were "off limit" to the US soldiers. One day, Pierre asked Yūko the equivalent of the word "darling." She was perplexed:

> 'Darling' . . . 'my beloved' (*itoshiihito yo*), 'the one that I love' (*aisurumono yo*) or 'my lover' (*aijin yo*), there are a plenty of direct translations, but I could not find any Japanese daily language that is equivalent to 'darling,' the word that people use to call for their beloved; what Americans often use in the parent-child relationship or in the husband-wife relationship. [. . .]
>
> I told Pierre: "There is no equivalent word."

"What? You don't have the word for 'darling'?" He looked startled and stared at me in my face. After a while, he continued:

"Okay, it does not have to be 'darling.' Something equivalent . . . like 'honey,' 'sweetheart,' or how about 'dear'?"

"None of them has an equivalent."

He stopped and stood right in the middle of the road and said:

"I don't want to learn the language that does not have a word for 'darling.' Okay, that's it. I quit." He kicked a pebble. (Toda 1978, 100)

As soon as Yūko arrived at her residence, she asked around among those who were staying in the same residence about their daily expressions of love. One said that his love for his wife was expressed through the act of quarreling, and another man jokingly quoted the saying that "a man would not feed bait to the fish that he caught," suggesting that the expression of love was no longer necessary once a couple was married. Yet another man suggested that his wife knew exactly what he wanted by his subtle gestures such as coughing; hence the word is not necessary. Young Yūko concluded that the Japanese are a people who do not express love in their daily language unless they are in the middle of courtship. She, then, quotes two poems from the nation's distant past to nuance her conclusion:

Koisu chō
Waga na wa madaki
Tachi ni keri
Hito shirezu koso
Omoi someshi ka.

It is true I love,
But the rumor of my love
Had gone far and wide,
When people should not have known
That I had begun to love.[6]

—Mibu no Tadami

Tama no o yo
Taenaba taene
Nagaraeba
Shinoburu koto no
Yowari mo zo suru.

Like a string of gems
Grown weak, my life will break now;
For if I live on,
All I do to hide my love
May at last grow weak and fail.

—Princess Shokushi

The first poem by Mibu no Tadami was composed in the tenth century, and the second one by Princess Shokushi is from the twelfth century. Again, these two poems are concerned with the expression of *koi*, longing between two lovers. The emotion expressed in these two poems is intense, yet, effectively, Toda's writing seems to confirm what Itō has argued about love in Japanese society—there seems to be a lack of vocabulary denoting the idea of a "loving relationship" that goes beyond that between two lovers.

The Christian formulation of love never gained currency in Japanese historical discourses. This situation is not surprising considering the marginal position Christianity has occupied throughout Japanese history. Yet the word love itself came to be used initially to denote conceptions in Western literature, as noted earlier. Taguchi Randy, a contemporary author who writes about the pursuit of spiritual paths, tells of her own uncertainty toward the idea of love (*ai*), which I suggest that many others in Japan may share:

> I have not been able to recognize the concept of love [*ai*]. I do not know what love is. In the way that I recognized "winter," I've never recognized the sound of the word "love" as if I was struck by the thunder and felt that "this is love." Therefore, I do not understand love. I cannot grasp what kind of phenomenon love amounts to. Do those who talk about love anticipate love? Have they experienced the sensation of being cracked opened with the word love becoming one with all of their bodily sensations? I don't. I can imagine it, but I do not feel it. (Taguchi 2007)

Sonia Ryang (2006) presents her version of the genealogy of love in modern Japan through studies of nationalism, the state control of female bodies, and sex education, among other factors. I do not necessarily agree with Ryang's presentation of the genealogy of love in Japanese society in modern times. However, I have to agree with her that, as she demonstrates, Japan has its own genealogy of love that is different from the Western formulation of love. And, as Itō discusses, the idea of love, articulated through the term *koi*, revolves around two lovers. In other words, outside of lovers' love, Japan's genealogy of love is not extensive.

One day at Our Lady of the Assumption, Fr. Massey discussed the passages on love from Corinthians. I was curious to see how the passages were received by a Japanese audience that otherwise would not have encountered this conception of love. After collecting the Bibles from other people's seats, I brought them to the front shelf and was able to talk to two people who were getting ready to go home. When I asked about the passages, they were both animated. "Ah, aren't they wonderful? Let's see, they were from Corinthians, weren't they?" The other woman responded right away. "That was from Paul's First Letter to the Corinthians, Chapter 13." She recited the following verses without looking them up:

> Love is patient; love is kind; love is not envious or boastful or arrogant or rude. It does not insist on its own way; it is not irritable or resentful; it does not rejoice in wrongdoing, but rejoices in the truth. It bears all things, believes all things, hopes all things, endures all things. Love never ends. (1 Corinthians 13:4–8a)

I was impressed that she did not have to look up the verses at all, but had memorized them by heart. The two women looked delighted, as if I had managed to find and admire their secret treasures.

Because the notion of "love" itself is not popular in the conventional worldview, how do Catholics understand the notion of "God's love" in Japan? One of the most popular priests in the Archdiocese of Tokyo, Fr. Haresaku, emphasizes this concept in his teaching and combines it with the idea of God as the parents (*oya*). In the Japanese language, nouns often do not possess gender or number—this is the case with both the words "parents" and "God." The essence of the word "parents" can be "somebody who takes care of you." If you say somebody acts as your *oya-gawari* (literally "acting-parent"), it means that somebody is taking care of you as your primary guardian. Fr. Haresaku has developed the brilliant strategy of using the word "parents' love" (*oyagokoro*; literally "parents' heart" or "parents' mind") to translate the notion of divine love to his Japanese-speaking audience. Pulling many illustrous examples from that of daily life—such as mothers' efforts to make lunch boxes every day for their children (Haresaku 2005, 269–70; cf. Allison 1991) or shedding tears of joy for their children in the graduation ceremony at kindergarten—he relates this "parents' love" (*oyagokoro*) to the intentions of Holy Spirit, Jesus Christ, and God. According to Fr. Haresaku, just as parents genuinely care about their children, seek the best options for them, and prepare everything for their children's well-being, God prepares everything out of love (i.e., "parents' love") for his followers.

Fr. Haresaku delivers sermons comparing God with the father and mother who are always making sure of their children's well-being. God, in his sermons, is a father who embraces his prodigal child, and also a mother who picks up her crying baby for nursing:

> Such "fatherly embracement" and "motherly breastfeeding." From the morning when we wake up till the night when we go to sleep, no, even during our sleep, we never realize that we are embraced and breastfed constantly by God. But the mass is precisely—in a visible form—to be embraced by God and breastfed by God. By becoming an embrace and breast milk, Christ sacrificed himself in the form of Holy Sacrament and we are saved through these experiences [of sacrament]. (Haresaku 2005, 58)

In Fr. Haresaku's popular sermons, to which many people come from hundreds of kilometers away, this theme is prominent. For example, he tells a story of an advertisement that he decided to put in a telephone directory when he was at a different parish some years ago. He said many other churches were listing the times of masses and the names of pastors, but he thought the priority should be given to the Good News instead. There was a space in the ad for only a few lines. In his words:

> On the first line, I decided to put "God is your true parents," on the second line, "God loves every single part of you," and on the third line, "How wonderful that you were born!" When

I boiled down the Good News, and made it into haiku, these three lines came out.[7] (Haresaku 2006, 271)

Although the above quotation does not directly say God is a mother, the implication of the words "parents" (*oya*) necessarily entails mothers (as well as fathers). Using the image of the mother, Fr. Haresaku is successful in expounding the idea of God's love in Japanese cultural contexts. Although the word "love" may initially appear slightly foreign to many Japanese people—as can be seen in the writing of Taguchi Randy—by using the images of caring parents, Fr. Haresaku is successful in depicting the concept of divine love in Japanese terms. Sharing a common thread with Confucian parent-child terminology, this image of parents' love as a higher ethico-moral principle works well with Japanese historical discourses.

"**Rejoice Always.**" When asked about their favorite quotation from the Bible, the majority of people chose "Rejoice always, pray without ceasing, and give thanks in all circumstances" (1 Thess. 5:16–18a). There is a hymn using this passage, which is extremely popular among those women whom I interviewed. For example, Hashimoto-san (whom we encountered earlier) said she sung this hymn continually after baptism. She recalled that she sang while walking, bathing, and cleaning the house. Kōda-san, who received an infant baptism more than seventy years ago, said she still sang this hymn while riding her bicycle to Terada Catholic Church every Sunday. She said: "I start off singing, 'Rejoice always, pray without ceasing, and give thanks in all circumstances,' and then, I change later lyrics so that the altered lyrics would fit what is going on in my life at the time. But I sang this hymn all the time!"

Akiyama-san often mentioned this biblical phrase in her "faith sharing" session at Fr. Massey's class at Our Lady of the Assumption. "When I was first told about this passage, I felt that 'oh, that would be a difficult teaching to keep up!'" But she persistently tried to live up to this ideal. Sitting with her back straight and her neatly ironed handkerchief held tightly in her hand, Akiyama-san told a small group that she had a friend who is suffering from a serious illness. "She does not like to communicate with others much—perhaps because she is very ill and would not want others to pity her . . . who knows. So I often leave her alone, but she is willing to communicate with faxed messages. So I send her messages. I was talking to her the other day, and learned that she is going through so much! I can't tell too many details here, but [. . .] and, then, I realized that what I am [personally] going through, all the things that I am crying over, all of a sudden looked like a cheap melodrama. After that, I feel so much lighter. There are so many things to be thankful for, you know?" Akiyama-san was teary. But she said virtually nothing about what her problems actually were, and nobody in the group asked about them. Apparently, I was not the only one who did not understand the whole story of Akiyama-san's problems. Yet I detected her thankfulness and contented positive feeling. Those who participated in this "faith sharing" shared her processing of the problem and the joy she experienced, and not the problems themselves.

As seen in the opening story of this chapter about Hashimoto-san, a sense of liberation and joy often accompanies the experience of becoming Catholic in Tokyo. Murakami-san received baptism in April 2007 at Terada Catholic Church while she was going through divorce mediation. She was thirty-nine years old, attractive, and had a positive persona. I noticed some of the male members of the church were charmed by her beauty and happy energy. Describing her change after baptism, she said:

> I have absolutely changed! How can I express that feeling? You know, it was like I was squished into a bin sealed with pressure, and all of a sudden I was released in the air or something. It was like I was out in a large field. If I hung in there and continued to persevere, I would have gotten sick with some mental problem.

Murakami-san received baptism when she was separated from her husband of ten years. Her husband, according to her, was a controlling man who never gave her much time for herself. He occupied her as much as he could, accompanying her to do grocery shopping and on other outings so that she would not have much chance to interact with other people. She saw little of her friends, and he even came to pick her up when she went out for cooking classes, one of her rare legitimate outings as a housewife when she could leave her husband behind. When Murakami-san finally left the husband and moved in with her own father, her brother took her to a mass. This event brought her in contact with the priest of the Terada Catholic Church, leading to her baptism. She further described the changes that the baptism brought to her:

> After all, we have to find our own solutions to the problems we have, right? Because I do not have my mother anymore,[8]

> I always cry when I read my diary from one year ago. Help me, mom! Please come back, mom! Stuff like that [occupies my writing].
>
> Now, things have changed. On a practical level, when I come to the church, I get to talk to different kinds of people, regardless of age. Like I am doing it right now. How can I describe this? I am always amazed by the way things are here.

Murakami-san seemed genuinely impressed by the different social setup that existed in the Terada Church. This church attracts not only older women but also many young people, which is rather unusual. As a result, in the day-to-day life of the parish, one can see people from different age and gender groups. One day I was watching one of the videos in the "living room" of the church with two older women. A young teenaged boy walked in and started talking us about whether he should become a priest. Kaneta-san, who was with me at the time, started telling the teenager about the possibility of becoming a deacon, who has the option to marry. Meanwhile, a woman in her sixties asked us if we want to eat apples that she had just peeled. In the next-door office, I knew Yoshida-san, a man in his seventies, was working on the parish budget of the day. There is also a group at the church called the "Fathers' Club" that limits its membership to men in their thirties and forties. As an active volunteer at the church, Murakami-san was constantly in touch with these different groups of people. In a society where maintaining hierarchy is an integral part of ethical behavior, a community like this church that does not place a primary emphasis on generational and gender differences is certainly a rarity. This reality, which contrasts strongly with the Japanese social fabric, provided a sense of liberation for Murakami-san. She explained her sense of liberation in the following terms:

> Really, I became very cheerful. I have no worries or complaints. I don't remember exactly how much he (i.e. her ex-husband) weighed, but it is as if I lost sixty-something kilos! Now, I need a bit more detox?

In interpreting her comments, one needs to take into account the fact that she had just separated from her husband and that her sense of liberation might have come from her separation. Murakami-san, however, was not engaged in any professional employment at this time, and her life did not seem secure in any way. She was living with her retired father, who was suffering from a critical illness.

Natsume-san, who used to work in the publishing industry, used an interesting visual analogy to express the ways in which her world had been transformed when she received baptism. She compared the world before conversion to a typeset with the letters in white and the background in black, while the world after conversion was the exact opposite: a typeset with letters in black and the background in white. The world had turned into shiny white. Many people associate their conversion experience with a leaping feeling of rejoicing, and this emotion is often expressed through reference to the biblical verse "rejoice always."

As these three popular notions—"entrusting," "God is love," and "rejoice always"—suggest, the ethos of these two parishes where I conducted fieldwork is characterized by enthusiasm, warmth, and liberation. As we will see in the discussion of converts from Protestant denominations, the Protestant-derived tradition of scholasticism, secularism, and humanism are not commonly appreciated among Japanese Christians. Philosophical and theological traditions within Catholicism do have their supporters, yet the majority of those whom I interviewed overwhelmingly support the pre-Enlightenment values (cf. Foucault 1984, 32) of depending on God and direct interaction with the divine, as I describe shortly in this chapter.

How Did These People Come to the Church?

When I asked about how people initially approached the Roman Catholic Church, answers varied to a large degree. Each individual had his or her own story, and it certainly was not possible to reduce them into neat categories. Nevertheless, there are some common threads shared in converts' narratives, and here I attempt to introduce three oft-mentioned reasons that prompted some of the people to visit the church. These stories convey some of the ways in which laypeople conceive of the Roman Catholic Church in Tokyo.

In Search of Something Reliable

Nagae-san, who was a fifty-three-year-old divorcee when I met her in 2007, told me what had prompted her to come to the church in the first place. "Well, in the year of Heisei 4 [i.e., 1992] when my daughter was still small, about six years old perhaps, I got divorced and became "one strike" (*batsu-ichi*).⁹ At the time, I was in search of something that could form my core, the center, and ended up at the church." Nagae-san was not baptized in Tokyo, but in the northern city of Sendai after attending one year of a Bible study group led by a Dominican priest. She is the youngest child in her family, and at the time of her divorce, her mother was in her late eighties. Her father had already passed away. Nagae-san's natal family operated a Buddhist temple, yet she said in a matter-of-fact manner that she "was not attracted to Buddhism at all." In a stark contrast to the Western conception of Buddhism, in Japan there is a widely held negative image of Buddhist temples as money-making institutions. Terms such as "funerary Buddhism" (*sōshiki bukkyō*) and "profiteering monks" (*bōzu marumōke*) epitomize these popular conceptions (Covell 2005; Rowe 2011). This negative image partly explains Nagae-san's matter-of-fact dismissal of Buddhism as a potential source of "something reliable." Nevertheless, Nagae-san was struggling to find her home parish in Tokyo. She frequently attended the Terada Church, as she was very enthusiastic about its priest. Yet she was not certain about settling her roots in this parish. The last time I talked to her, she was starting a new class at Our Lady of the Assumption, which was located on the same train line as the Terada Church.

In Search of Something Else in Life

Some other converts arrived at the church in search of alternatives in their lives. Here I present examples of two different orientations. Kuramoto-san, a prominent church committee member at Our Lady of the Assumption, claimed that the "alternative" did not have to be faith. Her case resembles those who are "in search of the self" (*jibun sagashi*) that Nancy Rosenberger has studied over many years (Rosenberger 2013). Using the concept of "long-term resistance," Rosenberger depicts ways in which women of postwar-generation Japan wander about in the space between conformity to societal expectations and their inner desire to go beyond accepted norms (2013, 11). In these processes, these women are looking for enrichment of life and growth from a narrow sense of self to a larger one.

As she made it clear, Kuramoto-san had been looking for "something else" and trying out activities like golf lessons. She was not in a crisis and was not looking for any particular moral values. Her sons were attending an elite high school run by a male Catholic order, and through this school system, she and her entire family encountered Catholicism and converted to the Catholic faith. Once she became part of the church, she became a devout member, serving on committees and organizing many pilgrimages with priests, tour companies, and the laity. As a prominent member of this mega-church, her responsibilities were numerous and the areas in which she worked considerably expanded. In many ways, this is possible because her church membership was supported by her immediate family; they all received baptism at once. As I discuss later, many women parishioners maintain their lone existence as the only Catholic at home, and this condition would make it difficult for them to fully and thoroughly commit themselves to social organizations of the parish. Kuramoto-san, however, was able to fully commit to various duties at the parish because of the conversion to Catholic faith by a family as a unit.

Another orientation that I found was in search of an alternative religious organization. Mito-san exemplifies this pattern. I encountered her when she first visited the church in 2007, and she remained a reluctant catechumen during my fieldwork. Through her experience of organizing her in-law's funeral, she was disgusted by the commercial orientation of the Buddhist clergy and its connection to the funeral industry. Her "grandmother," that is, her mother-in-law, was in a nursing home in Nagano Prefecture, some distance away from Tokyo. When the "grandmother" passed away at around 9:00 p.m. in February 2007, it took a while for the family in Tokyo to arrive at the facility. A staff member at the nursing home asked the family whether it was acceptable to set up an altar for the deceased "grandmother." Mito-san said, "Of course I said yes. Because it would take a while to get to all the way up to Nagano Prefecture, and what else can we do?" But when the family arrived, the body was placed in front of an elaborate altar that would have cost a large sum of money. "That nursing home, the nearby hospital, the funeral company, the Buddhist temple, and even the florist! They all ganged up on me in that place! The Buddhist priest from that temple has nothing to do with our denomination." Mito-san was clearly upset by the systematic way in which her family had been exploited by various institutions in the face of the loss of a loved one. By the time the family arrived, every arrangement had been made, and the family was asked to pay a large sum of money for one of the most unpleasant funerals that they had ever attended. This experience reminded Mito-san of a simple Catholic funeral that she had once witnessed when a neighbor passed away. She said: "There was a bouquet of flowers, not too tacky, and I had a positive impression. I felt that it was a fitting way to see off our loved ones, you know?" Mito-san said she came straight from the grandmother's funeral to Our Lady of the Assumption while the "smell of funeral incense was fresh." Hearing this comment, Fr. Massey responded with a smile: "Jesus uses unexpected tools to invite us to the church."

At the Time of Crisis

Some people were drawn to knock at the door of the church in a time of crisis. A few of these stories have already been noted in chapter 2. As we have seen, Okada-san came to the church when her husband's mental illness was deteriorating and she learned that he needed to have medical attention from a psychiatric hospital. From time to time, she came to visit the church and sat in the sanctuary to pray. Both Hashimoto-san and Nagae-san were experiencing difficulty relating to their marriages when they came to the church. Just before Hashimoto-san turned to the church and to Akishino Temple, a visitor to her house told her that she "would go crazy if she did not 'breathe outside air.'" Using the idiomatic expression "to breathe outside air" (*soto no kūki wo suu*), this visitor suggested that Hashimoto-san go outside the house occasionally. This visitor saw in Hashimoto-san a crisis that she herself could not detect. Nagae-san became a divorcee who needed to look after not only herself but also her young daughter. Both her parents and her siblings were not dependable for a variety of reasons.

Mita-san, whom we encounter later in this chapter, came to Our Lady of the Assumption after her daughter's premature death. Her daughter had become Catholic while she was attending a Catholic university, and Mita-san chose to come to Our Lady of the Assumption, where her daughter had been baptized many years before. As I record later in the chapter, Mita-san had left the Protestant church behind many years earlier. In the face of an unexpected life crisis, her daughter's death, Mita-san chose to be part of the Roman Catholic Church.

In this section, I have loosely categorized the reasons people gave for their initial visits to the church. Overall, however, I did not detect any dominant pattern shared by those who become part of the church. If you asked converts why they had chosen the Catholic Church, as opposed to other religious organizations, the most common answer would be that they "were guided" (*michibikareta*). The noun form of this idea is "*omichibiki*," which can be translated as "guidance." To the interlocutor's eager question "What prompted you to visit the church?" many responded with a perplexed facial expression and presented their situation as a case of "being guided" by the divine. Several people pointed to the following Biblical passage: "You did not choose me but I chose you" (John 15:16) to back up their point. This understanding of conversion is consistent with their Catholic worldview in which humans are the ones who accept the will of God, rather than initiating the relationship with the divine.

On a quite different note, one factor that I have not discussed is the influence of mission schools in the lives of those who appear in this study. Many of my research participants had one connection or another to a mission school. Hashimoto-san herself went to a Catholic school throughout her life, and Kuramoto-san and Mita-san had enrolled their children in the Catholic school system. The laity's relationship with mission schools is further explored in the next chapter on gender and the Roman Catholic Church in Tokyo.

Establishing One's Center

The human collectivity is often referred to as *seken*, as we saw in chapter 2. The scope of *seken*, however, appears flexible. Often *seken* refers to Japanese society in general. Because of mass media and the use of a common language, this extension of concept is not difficult to understand; other times, the concept of *seken* can be confined to one's neighborhood or a social group. Yet *seken* appears to be something of which people are constantly conscious, and simultaneously afraid, and therefore many of my interlocutors referred to this entity as something from which they were liberated by adopting the Catholic faith. A few instances and conversations during fieldwork highlight the ways in which people depart from social conventions—or at least feel liberated from the binding effect of them—and go against the grain of *seken*. In these instances, people explained their ability to flout social conventions with reference to their Catholic faith or linked their actions to a deepening of faith and understanding of the Catholic worldview.

After Fr. Massey's class, several of us walked together to the nearby train station. People from Fr. Massey's class were invited to Hashimoto-san's husband's memorial mass, which was to take place in a week's time. It was the first anniversary of his death. In the midst of the crowded subway station, I asked Suzuki-san if I should bring any "incense money" (*kōden*). It is customary to bring incense money to a Buddhist memorial service, and I wondered what people would do at Our Lady of the Assumption. In a conventional Buddhist memorial, each guest would present an envelope containing cash and would receive a return gift on his or her way home. Looking straight into my eyes, Suzuki-san emphatically said: "Oh no no, we don't have to worry about incense money! Of course, other people outside the class may bring it, but we are different. In addition, Hashimoto-san would not want us to bring any money." I did not reply and looked straight back into Suzuki-san's face. She was short, and her hair was tied a ponytail in the back. Unlike many women in Tokyo who frequent hair salons to keep their hair stylish, Suzuki-san tied hers back with an elastic band. Her simple makeup, clothes, and handbag all pointed to her modesty and middle-class status. Suzuki-san's style contrasted with that of Hashimoto-san, who always paid particular attention to her clothing, makeup, and accessories. Suzuki-san had grown up and was living in a neighboring prefecture outside Tokyo, while Hashimoto-san lived in the central part of Tokyo, where real estate prices were not easily affordable for most Japanese. I could see no commonality between the two women in terms of dress or social standing. In short, Suzuki-san was trying to persuade me that I belong to a special faith community that stands outside "regular" social conventions. She conveyed her sense of privilege at being part of this community. After observing her emotion and logic, I felt it would be offensive to bring incense money to the memorial mass.

On the day of the anniversary, I found Hashimoto-san standing and greeting all the guests at the entrance to the chapel where the memorial rite was to be held. As soon as she saw me, she greeted me with her regular broad smile and squished a fancy paper bag of "return gift" into my hand. It was a package of traditional confectionary from Toraya, a famous store that is known for its *yōkan*, a sweet made of bean paste. I felt slightly awkward, as I had not brought any incense money to "earn" this expensive return gift. However, the manner in which Hashimoto-san smiled and the way she signaled me using body language and facial expressions amply demonstrated that I did not have to be concerned about such "mundane" business. It seemed that the Hashimoto family was receiving the gift envelopes from other guests who insisted on bringing them and distributing the return gifts to everybody who came to the memorial mass regardless of whether they had contributed incense money. In this way, the traditional gift giving practice (Rupp 2003) was maintained, yet the circle of the parish members was exempted. Fr. Massey's class sat together at the mass toward the front, a prominent position according to a Confucian reckoning, and they were the ones who participated actively in the mass, as the majority of the other attendees were non-Catholic. This participation was a different kind of offering, and perhaps a priceless one in the mind of Hashimoto-san. In a country where only 0.5 percent of the Japanese-speaking population is Roman Catholic, the support of fellow parishioners is essential in holding a successful mass.

On yet another occasion, I was attending a different class at Our Lady of the Assumption. I bumped into Kuramoto-san. The reader encountered Kuramoto-san earlier; she was the one who became a convert along with her entire family through her son's attendance at a selective Catholic boys' high school. Whenever she saw me in the parish, she made a point of inquiring about how my research was progressing. One day, while people were dispersing after a weekly Bible class, I had a chance to ask her about the benefits of becoming Roman Catholic. She said: "Before becoming Catholic, I worried about such things as what to wear to school, and so forth. I constantly worried about how other people would think of me!" According to Kuramoto-san, by adopting the Catholic faith, her priorities became clear, and she realized that clothing does not really matter in life. "You know, people would say you have to wear either dark blue or subdued colors when you go to school [as a parent]." But after becoming Catholic, she said, "They did not matter at all. There are other important things, and I was freed from such worries." She laughed carelessly and tapped my back in a friendly way, as if to make her point stronger.

While Kuramoto-san was freed from such worries, she was always nicely dressed whenever I saw her. As a woman in an official capacity in this parish located in the affluent district of Tokyo, she always kept herself presentable. But from the way in which she told me her story, and from her broad smiles and excited tone of voice, I realized that this change had been a tremendous relief for her. As I observed in chapter 2, the human being is the ultimate authority in Japanese society, and enormous energy is spent on maintaining "human relationships." Giving and receiving gifts is one of the major avenues to maintaining these ties (Rupp 2003), and breaking away from these conventions, as Suzuki-san insisted I do by not bringing any incense money to the memorial mass, can mean unimaginable relief for those who are constantly involved in these webs of social obligations (Kondo 1990, 26). Interestingly, on the surface, these converts continue the traditional conservative practices—Hashimoto-san maintained the gift-giving practice with non-Catholics, and Kuramoto-san always dressed nicely—yet they profess tremendous relief from the social pressure by aligning themselves with Catholic values. Internally, therefore, the meaning of a particular dress code and gift-giving practices are transformed. As Catholic values such as love, entrusting, and a prayerful life gradually take on significant positions in the minds of converts, social and emotional pressures to keep up with the *seken* and the psychological need to do so gradually diminish.

Interestingly, among these devout laypeople, as the internal authority shifts from the *seken* to the Christian God, there often occurs a change in their sense of self. By "entrusting" themselves to the hands of the deity, and by being empowered through their association with this new, non-human authority, the laity gain strength to sever mental ties with the traditional authority of the *seken*. To leave societal values behind is a key element in understanding this transformation.

In his essay "A Modified View of Our Origins: The Christian Beginnings of Modern Individualism," Louis Dumont (1985) discusses both Indian society and Hellenistic society to advance his claim. First, he compares two sets of people seen in Indian society over two millennia. One is the majority of people who are imposed a tight interdependence on each other in this world, and the other is the world renouncers who willingly sever ties with the society. Dumont points out that it was the latter kind of people from which all sorts of religious innovation came, and, more relevant to my topic, he suggests that because of the distance from the reality of the world, renouncers were able to discover the self. In other words, leaving the society enables the emergence of the individual. Dumont says the "discovery of the self is for him conterminous, not with salvation in the Christian sense, but with liberation from the fetters of life as commonly experienced in this world" (95). He further states that the "path of liberation is open only to those who leave the world" (95). This is an interesting observation when considering my research participants' "joy" in becoming Roman Catholics in Tokyo.

Dumont then uses this Indian example to introduce his main thesis of the Christian beginning of modern individualism. Mapping out historical developments, Dumont notes a surge of individualism in philosophy and increasing self-sufficiency in the *polis* during the Hellenistic period in which Christianity arose. Turning to a sociological study of Ernst Troeltsch, Dumont introduces the idea that "the Christian is an 'individual-in-relation-to-God'" (98). An underlying principle for this formula is that absolute individualism is only possible on the condition of universalism. Put differently, Christian salvation is predicated on one's individual relationship with the ultimate authority, God. Dumont posits that a negation of worldly values and a tension arising from this negation is a constitutive element of Christianity (98).

While relating the first-century Hellenistic world to twenty-first century Japan seems far-fetched, there are several similarities. First, the negation of this-worldly values embedded in Christianity and a sense of liberation that comes from leaving behind this-worldly values may resonate. From my ethnographic fieldwork, at least, severing ties to this-worldly affairs gives converts a sense of liberation, as we have seen in the opening story of Hashimoto-san. Second, while I avoid using the expression, individualism, a kind of transformation seen in one's sense of self accompanying conversion processes, can be understood as a move toward a subjectivity that outwardly appears as somebody who embraces individualism.

In the present case of Roman Catholics in Tokyo, in the processes of deepening of faith, there seem to occur a subtle yet stable change in one's agency. Here, taking on the formulation of Laura Ahearn, by agency I mean "the socioculturally mediated capacity to act" (2000, 112). As Sherry B. Ortner has articulated, the relationship between subjectivity and power is a fertile ground in which one can investigate the issues of agency (2006). As discussed so far, Japanese Roman Catholics experience the diminishing of human authorities as the source of legitimation while deepening their faith. As this happens, the urge to conform to societal values lessens, as seen in several ethnographic vignettes in this book. Over time, as the result of reliance on the non-human God as the utmost authority, the converts in Japanese society became able to assert themselves more fully compared with their prior non-Catholic selves from which they used to act.

To describe this transformation of one's sense of self and agency among Japanese Roman Catholics as gaining a sense of self that is "analogous to a Western sense of self" is one way to describe these phenomena. Eschewing the expression "Western sense of self," however, I suggest instead understanding this situation as converts establishing a sense of self that is firmly rooted in the relationship with the divine. This newly formed relationship with the divine works as an anchor or inner compass from which one can act, and for those who look from outside, the converts' enhanced capacity to act on one's own appears similar to the notion of "individual."

LOCATION OF THE SOCIAL OTHER

Another noteworthy shift that often accompanies laypeople's transition to the Catholic faith is a change in their understanding of social others. As laypeople deepen their faith in the Catholic worldview, some of them also change their views about the social other and the less privileged in Japanese society. This process was most clearly illustrated in the case of Satō-san, a housewife who married for a second time to a middle-class *sararīman*. In the winter of 2006–2007, Satō-san and her husband decided to become foster parents. This is a practice about which the average Japanese citizen would have only a vague idea. Adoption in Japanese contexts often occurs within a kinship unit to "save" a married couple who could not conceive their own biological children. Raising children of troubled parents for the sake of these children—many children in the welfare system are often from troubled households—is not a common practice. In a society where maintaining human relations (*ningen kankei*) is highly valued as an avenue to social mobility, being acquainted with those who are socially less privileged is often interpreted unfavorably, and adopting or raising underprivileged children could meet with opposition from the family of the adopting parents.

When I met her in 2006, Satō-san was in her early forties. She became interested in Catholicism after marrying her husband, who was from a long-standing Catholic family. She was a petite, modestly dressed woman, but she also had a wild side. Satō-san and her husband, who was a few years younger, met on an online dating site. They both enjoyed drinking and smoking, and I learned about different aspects of this couple at downtown casual restaurants and pubs over many pints of beer. The husband, who was articulate in his own way, gave me his views on Catholic rites using idiosyncratic analogies from horse racing. Although I did not understand many details about horse racing, I learned about this couple through these rather funny conversations in cigarette smoke–filled pubs.

With the distinctive, husky voice of a chain-smoker, Satō-san described the radical change in her view of social others:

> It is kind of strange, but I did not like children at all. And even worse, before I became Catholic, I was disgusted by physically handicapped people. I live close to Kamata, and there are a lot of the handicapped on the train—somehow there are a lot

of facilities [for those handicapped] nearby. Before [becoming Catholic], I felt "how disgusting! I don't even want to see them!" Sometimes, I made real effort to avoid those specific coaches [in which there are handicapped people], right? But now, not at all! I feel that there is God's love [among the handicapped]. It is a tremendous change.

It's not because I made any efforts [in effecting these changes]. Not at all! I made NO effort. Everyday, I prayed, "please change me, please change me so that I may become a better vehicle of your will." Then, that is how this change happened! My siblings [who are not Christians] can't believe what is happening—because they know me from before. [They are thinking] Are YOU becoming a foster parent? You know, I won't blame them. Before, I didn't even care about my relatives' kids.

Satō-san confessed her previously held negative perspectives on the handicapped and children in general without showing any trace of guilt. She made these statements in a matter-of-fact manner and, with excitement, told me about her later transformation. Satō-san described this change as something that was designed and brought about by the divine and not of her own making. According to her, the only thing she did was to pray, asking for change.

To take care of social others, however, is a prominent teaching of Christianity. The Roman Catholic Church constantly emphasizes this value, and the laity in Japan slowly learns the prominence of this teaching. As conventional Japanese ethical values are not articulate about charity toward social others, the lay Catholics I encountered in Tokyo receive these teachings as novel and also noble. Neo-Confucian–based Japanese ethical values place a strong emphasis on the family and senior-junior relationships and provide little explanation for the situation or value of the socially underprivileged and the weak. As a result, some adult converts undergo significant change in their views of social others.

Now I turn to the story of Kitami-san to illustrate various changes that she went through to become a Catholic in Tokyo. These changes includes her view of social others, and also her shift from *ganbaru* to entrusting. Her story is typical of woman converts I encountered in the two parishes in Tokyo.

The Case of Kitami-san

Kitami-san came to the Church of Our Lady of the Assumption when I started fieldwork in the fall of 2006, and she received baptism in the summer of 2007. As I was able to follow her gradual change toward becoming Catholic in Tokyo closely, I describe her life in detail here. Kitami-san was a married woman in her early fifties when I first met her in the fall of 2006. Kitami-san and her husband had just started their business in an affluent part of central Tokyo. She was the oldest daughter of two siblings, and her younger sister also lived in Tokyo, some distance away from their aging parents in another part of Japan.

From her clothes and the way she carried herself, I could tell that Kitami-san had lived a materially stable and privileged life. Her dresses were not fancy, but she wore conservative clothes in subdued colors made of good-quality material. The fact that she and her sister had graduated from a Protestant high school indicates that her parents were wealthy enough to send both their daughters to private school. After finishing high school, Kitami-san went on to study music, and she later became a piano teacher. Her profession, music teacher, is also often considered to be the occupation of a "well-brought-up daughter" (*ojō-san*) in Japanese cultural contexts.

When I first met her at one of the Introduction to Catholicism classes, Kitami-san seemed timid and exhausted, but very eager and attentive. It so happened that this class was her first. It was my second day, however, so I knew that the class was having a special lunch gathering to "get to know your fellow classmates" that day. She sat next to me in the very last row of the class. I explained to her that she could order a lunch box for the later social gathering. After the class, when women and men started moving desks and chairs and getting ready for the lunch gathering, both of us—the two newcomers—rushed to the kitchen to wash our hands so that we could be helpful for the occasion. It is expected in Japanese social settings that newcomers will take the lowest position and work hard in a group. After I washed my hands, I realized that there was no paper towel ready for me, as in North America. Everybody present had a fancy and colorful tiny handkerchief made of terry cloth or a classy cotton handkerchief. "Please use this! It's fresh, because I have two in my bag." Kitami-san offered me a clean handkerchief with a smile on her face. I felt embarrassed. It is a failure for a Japanese person, and especially a grown-up woman, not to have a handkerchief. When I was in grade school, we often had unannounced examinations to check whether we were "properly equipped" with a handkerchief. I thanked Kitami-san and accepted her offer.

I did not see her again in that class. After a few months, she surprised me by showing up in a different class. Unlike the class where we first met, this class was much smaller, and there were many interactions among the members, as the meeting was set up in seminar style. Between the lunch gathering and this second encounter, Kitami-san had gone through a time of difficulty. She told me that she had been in her hometown many kilometers away, looking after her father, who had eventually passed away. But she explained to me that this time was also a respite from her own nervous breakdown in Tokyo. In addition to her emotional pain, she suffered constantly from physical conditions. She had recently undergone an operation on an ovary, and it became her routine to go back to the hospital for an injection every month or so to ease the pain. Simply sitting in one place for a long period of time was not an easy task for her. Despite such physical discomfort, I noticed that she gradually settled into this class and became enthusiastic about Catholic teachings.

As I spent more time with Kitami-san, I gradually learned more about her struggles. Most of her problems related to her marriage. She was having a difficult relationship with her husband of more than twenty years. Now in her early fifties, she had lost all hope of having her own children, as she had hoped to have a child for many years. From our day-to-day conversations, I learned that Kitami-san was also suffering from something else. Her immediate suffering related to a conflict at the business that the Kitamis run. A small business operation, the company was staffed by a few employees and the owners, the Kitamis. As frequently occur in many small Japanese businesses, the Kitamis were asked to hire a young woman who was related to one of their acquaintances. Hiring this person constituted part of the Kitamis' social obligations toward this particular acquaintance. Therefore, the ability and quality of this individual as worker were, on principle, not to be questioned. It turned out that this young woman was incapable of maintaining smooth relationships with other staff members in the office and constantly created troubles that the Kitamis had to deal with as heads of the business. After the opening of the business, Kitami-san, as the wife of the owner, had attempted to be part of daily operations at the office, helping her husband to run the business. Dealing with constant discord among the staff, however, was taxing her emotions. Some employees quit because of this troublesome member. These troubles had to be dealt with by Kitami-san while she also had to take care of a husband who was emotionally dependent. Gradually, Kitami-san became worn out emotionally and physically.

Kitami-san often sat right next to the priest during Fr. Massey's class. The way she took notes, looked at the priest, and talked to the class all pointed to her sincere personality. I could feel that she was thirsty for a release from her pain—the emotional, psychological, and physical suffering that had become part of her life. Although Fr. Massey's weekly class was small, there were different people constantly joining or leaving it. After all, this was a free class. People had nothing to lose by dropping the class. An aging priest, eighty-four at the time, Fr. Massey sometimes seemed to be unable to grasp everything that was going on in the classroom. People in the class were sometimes anxious to find out whether the priest would know if a certain person needed his catechism. It was the first class of the year in January 2007. Fr. Massey went around the table to ask for people's updates. When he came to Kitami-san, she pledged to do her best so that she could be a better human being. She also acknowledged that she had not been striving hard enough. Right away, I noticed that her discourse was not in line with that of the rest of this group. Her words did not match the Roman Catholic ideals in the room. She was not supposed to accuse herself, and she was not supposed to *ganbaru* (i.e., strive hard) by herself. She was supposed to be thankful and happy and entrust the extraordinary to take charge of her life by giving up being in charge herself. Even I could spot right away that she was somebody who had not been baptized yet.

Fr. Massey gently asked her to remind him whether she was baptized or not. She answered in the negative. He then went on to explain what to do while he would be away for a trip to South Asia in the following weeks:

> Please keep fifteen minutes of silence every day. This cannot be too short. It would take roughly fifteen minutes in silence to empty one's mind. Ten minutes is not enough. When you are not sure what is the best course of action in life—to get married or to work for example—just maintain the question in your mind and sit for fifteen minutes every single day. Then, the answer will come. We first have to encounter ourselves; otherwise, we will not understand [the right answer]. If you do this, you will begin to like yourself. This is really mysterious [*fushigi*]. Wasn't that so, Sekiguchi-san [smile]? I have to go away for the next few weeks, but you can do this while I am away.

In this way, the priest spotted a newcomer and guided her so that she could start a Spiritual Exercise.[10] Kitami-san was seriously listening to this instruction and writing notes. Virtually all the members in this class who had been baptized by this priest had undergone this process of fifteen-minute meditation as preparation prior to catechism. Fr. Massey is a strong proponent of Ignatian spirituality.

Two weeks later, it was the first week that Fr. Massey was absent. One of the lay leaders was in charge of the class, but there were only three people attending when I arrived late. Kitami-san was one of them, and she was enthusiastically talking about her recent progress in encountering the divine in her personal life:

> KITAMI: Lately, after I attended this class, my husband sometimes asked me if there was anything good today. He said I looked happy. Or, if anything difficult arose, he surprised me by asking what Jesus would say in this kind of situation.
> I am just buying books at a bookstore and studying on my own, but I started feeling that all I have to do is entrust everything to Jesus. I would be fine. I feel so relieved lately.
>
> MIWA: Wow, you made such fast progress! The last shall be first [laughter]!
>
> KITAMI: Oh, no no. I did not mean that.
>
> LEADER: Oh not to worry. There was a saying in the Bible: "the last shall be first."
>
> MIWA: I feel that the Holy Spirit is working [on Kitami-san].
>
> MIWA: In my case, the Father asked me whether I would like to receive baptism when I was not sure what was really going on. I said "yes" nevertheless and received baptism. I had been coming to this weekly class for almost six months, and still did not understand what other people were saying [laughter]!

I was intrigued by this conversation. Two weeks prior to this, Kitami-san had produced a typical Japanese discourse of *ganbaru* and regretted that she was not working hard enough at things. In a mere two weeks, however, she was able to transform herself and aligned her thought with two of the popular Catholic values that I discussed earlier, entrusting and rejoicing. In addition, she was feeling relieved from her previous state of mind and enjoying this new way of looking at the world. When Kitami-san heard of Miwa-san saying "the last shall be first," she perhaps felt improper about "jumping over the queues" of seniority. The idea of jumping the queues is often criticized in this society that highly values order.

Our Lady of the Assumption was only a few minutes' walk from the main train and subway station. As this stop was so close to the church, most of the people attending class used this station. A homeless man lived between the station and the church. He probably knew about the Christian idea of helping the less privileged and prominently hung a wooden rosary in the tin that he used to collect money, perhaps to provoke Christian compassion among the passersby. One day, Kitami-san told me that she had started wondering about the welfare of this homeless man. "I was a little bit scared at the beginning, but today he was not sitting at the regular spot. So I went to his spot and left rice balls for him." She smiled as if she were a little girl reporting some mischievous and naughty act. "I wonder if he ate them . . . ?" In this way, Kitami-san also exhibited her new concern for social others and the less privileged. I was surprised by this new development. I had seen the homeless man drunk and occasionally violent on the street. For the majority of passersby, he was definitely somebody with whom acquaintance should be avoided.

In the summer of 2007, Kitami-san received both baptism and confirmation from Fr. Massey. Her husband insisted on attending the baptismal rite and briefly entered the sanctuary during the mass in which his wife received the sacrament. One year after her baptism, Kitami-san was still suffering from physical pain, troubled relationships among her employees, and an emotionally dependent husband. However, she reported that she is able to assert herself more toward her husband and that was a significant change. She was still suffering from emotional instability and was taking pills to induce sleep. She told me that she carried a small statue of the Virgin Mary whenever she went far and held tight to this statue when she was suffering from anxiety.

PROTESTANTS AS PEOPLE-CENTERED, CATHOLICS AS GOD-CENTERED

As we have seen so far, in becoming Catholics in Tokyo, many previously non-Christian Japanese make a transition from a worldview that is dictated by people to one dictated by God. Interestingly, this shift of authority from the human to the divine is also seen among those Japanese who convert from Protestant denominations to Roman Catholicism. Two parishes where I conducted fieldwork included a significant number of people converting to Catholicism from Protestant denominations, and I introduce some of these people while describing similar patterns in the shift of authority figures from the human to the divine realm.

Yabe-san was a thirty-year-old man who was exploring the Catholic faith as a member of a Protestant church. Wearing his long hair in a ponytail, he rode his motorcycle to church every time I saw him. His typical Sunday would begin with a Lord's Day service at his home church (Protestant), followed by volunteer work for the same church in the afternoon. He then rode his bike to central Tokyo and had a time of quiet meditation in one of the chapels at Our Lady of the Assumption. He then went on to attend a weekly "Praise Meeting" of the Catholic Charismatic Renewal (CCR) group where I met him. The CCR meeting promptly began at 5:00 p.m. every Sunday with singing of hymns and occasional glossolalia, or speaking in tongues, for one hour. Following a short break at 6:00 p.m., the group listened to a talk given by a different Catholic priest each week and ended the meeting at 7:00 p.m. with prayers. At the short break, some participants would slip away to attend a mass at the nearby Our Lady of the Assumption Church. Most of the time, after the Praise Meeting, some of the participants would go out to eat at a nearby "Catholic" café for a light meal, sometimes accompanied by a glass of wine.

Sitting with a few of the people after the CCR meeting, I somehow managed to convince Professor Ōnishi to have a glass of wine with our meal. He was one of the lay leaders of this group. I used the honorary suffix of "sensei," which means "teacher" in Japanese, when I spoke to him because he was a professor at a well-known university. Yabe-san, however, decided not to "yield to temptation" that night. He said: "Our church is somewhat strict on those things. Both drinking and smoking are prohibited. Well, I drink anyway sometimes, like when I went to Épopée, for example. But today, I will refrain from drinking because I can [laughter]."

Yabe-san, as a member of a Protestant church of Pentecostal derivation, provided me with a different perspective on the Catholic faith in Tokyo. He said:

> I was really surprised with the Roman Catholic Church. I always thought that Catholic people would not be directly connected

to God, but I think they are more connected to God than we [Protestants] are. Think about it; if you think somewhat conservatively, there is God on top of everything else and then us below, and the priest in the middle. That is Catholicism. So, Protestant folks came about to stop that [structure by eliminating the priest's intermediary role], right? But, in truth, it is not so at all. On the contrary, I feel that Catholic people may be in direct conversation with God!

Yabe-san further explained what he saw as his brand of Protestant faith in Tokyo. "From what I see, I feel that Protestant people are connected through the human part of our life—having pastors, or churches as a focal point. It is not exactly God who is in the center—it is more like Rev. Pastor (*bokushi-sama*)." He then went on to tell a story about how he ended up at the Praise Meeting as an illustration of direct communication with the divine among the Catholic faithful. One day he was praying at the sanctuary of Our Lady of the Assumption. A woman who was praying next to him talked to him and told him about the Praise Meeting. Yabe-san later decided to check out the meeting. He said, "So, I went to the Praise Meeting one day. And then, I went back every week ever since! It has been quite a while since I first went to the meeting in November." I was not sure about the point that he was making. I asked: "You mean the woman who was sitting next to you had received a divine message to invite you to the meeting?" "Oh yes." He answered as if I should have known better. He continued to explain that after Sunday service and volunteering at his home church, he would come to Our Lady of the Assumption "to relax." For him, all the community work related to human relationships was part of his Protestant experience, and he was able to shift his focus to his relationship with the divine when he was at Our Lady of the Assumption, where he could be released from social obligations.

Being part of the Roman Catholic faith in central Tokyo often entails experiencing or hearing about mystical things. This type of experience is also considered characteristically Catholic, or at least "unlike Protestant faith" in the discourse of former Protestant members of the Catholic Church. Those who had converted from Protestant denominations tend to regard this mystical aspect of Roman Catholicism as "evidence" that Roman Catholics are more directly connected with the unseen. Yabe-san's comment quoted earlier can be also situated within this discourse. Especially among the members of the CCR, there are many stories of mystical experiences such as becoming aware of the scent of unseen roses, being showered in golden particles, and miraculous healing.

A Japanese researcher, Omoto Kumi, who conducted fieldwork at the CCR National Convention held in Tokyo in 2000 also reports several of these mystical incidents (2006). This convention, attended by approximately 700 people, was led by a guest priest from the United States, and many laypeople as well as priests and nuns participated in this three-day event. Omoto reports that some people gave testimonies about miraculous events experienced during the convention, such as receiving physical healing, renewed faith, gift of prophesy, and being showered in golden dust. However, more interestingly, Omoto reports that many experienced "golden dusts" and were aware of the "scent of roses" during the convention. In particular, she quotes Fr. Itakura, who experienced a golden particle after receiving the "charisma of healing" from the guest priest:

> While feeling the divine presence and being filled with the Holy Spirit, I kept my eyes closed and was putting my hand upward. While heaven is opened for us, I wanted to receive something that would descend from there. I was not thinking of being healed, or somehow my problem being solved, or asking God to show me golden dust or anything like that.
>
> After a while, I felt my body was becoming warm and I slowly opened my eyes. Everybody was in the midst of prayer. I saw a sparkling object on my palm. First I thought it may be sweat, but I could see sweat on my right hand and I could clearly distinguish [this sparkling object] from sweat. I thought this may be the golden dust that the priest was talking about. It was about 2 mm, golden colour, surrounded by a round rainbow, and emanating whitish light. (Omoto 2006)

When I talked about the above article with Professor Ōnishi at our regular café after a weekly meeting of the CCR, he chuckled. As one who is deeply involved in the charismatic movement, Professor Ōnishi knew about these stories and was in contact with many of the people who had attended the CCR National Convention. He told me yet another story. One of his fellow charismatic Catholics had a silver tooth that turned golden during a charismatic meeting! Professor Ōnishi said: "I asked him to show which tooth it was, and I saw it. It was indeed golden." He was laughing, as if this was a funny incident. Professor Ōnishi and other Catholics who were close to this charismatic circle had many stories of this type. They do not treat such phenomena too seriously. As one devout charismatic Catholic told me, "extraordinary phenomena themselves can come from demons; and therefore you should stay focused on faith, and not on a miraculous phenomenon." Nevertheless, the stories of extraordinary incidents were often discussed as a "sign" among devout lay Catholics that I met in Tokyo. Moreover, for many members of Protestant churches, a miraculous experience may be a decisive element leading them to move away from a Protestant denomination that emphasizes a humanistic and demystified tradition that is based on post-Enlightenment theology. The following case illustrates this point.

Ezaki-san came to Our Lady of the Assumption vexed by her troubled marriage. She was a member of a Methodist-derived denomination. She had a friend who went through a significant transformation in her life by coming to Our Lady of the Assumption, and Ezaki-san thought, "this is a church that can make a miracle happen." According to Ezaki-san, the Roman Catholic tradition is more authentic (*honmono*) than the Protestant church precisely because of these mystical experiences. She compared her experience with the two traditions: "When I asked the pastor [of the Protestant church] for advice, what do you think he told me? He said he had been referring people to a psychiatric hospital when he cannot resolve the problem!" Ezaki-san seemed upset just by remembering this conversation. In Ezaki-san's mind, the problem originated in a spiritual sphere, and therefore the solution should come from a religious organization and not from a medical establishment. She then went on to explain how wonderful it was that she was receiving personal spiritual guidance from a Catholic priest. "I can't tell you in detail, but Fr. Toba has been teaching me how to search for light in the darkness, you know?"

She used an interesting metaphor comparing the two traditions in Tokyo:

> The [Japanese] Protestant tradition is as if the pastor is standing right in front of the cross, and he speaks with words. Then, you cannot see God; you cannot feel anything spiritual. Of course there are those who can feel spiritual things, but I cannot go beyond logic. On the other hand, we can be healed through the masses in the Catholic Church.

One day, I happened to be with Ezaki-san when she volunteered her explanation of the concept of sacrament to a Protestant visitor to the church. She said: "The Catholic tradition is centered on experience; not on intellectual understanding" (*katorikku wa ne taiken nandesuyo, atama janaino*). In response to this, Kaneta-san, who was also at the same table, started explaining the seven sacraments of the church. Interestingly, like Mita-san, this newcomer also complained about the Protestant tradition of Bible studies. She said she gradually stopped going to her Protestant church. On the day of Pentecost, however, while she was praying, she was inspired to visit Our Lady of the Assumption. She said: "When I entered there [the sanctuary of Our Lady of the Assumption], I thought 'God is here!'" Her statement seemed to confirm Ezaki-san's point that Catholicism is experience-centered. The newcomer also confirmed the spiritual way in which she was led to this particular Catholic church through prayer.

On another occasion, Ezaki-san described the temporal world as a reflection of the spiritual world. According to this worldview, you can effect changes in this world by manipulating the spiritual world; hence the effectiveness of a prayerful life. Through prayers, one can procure changes that otherwise would not be forthcoming through human endeavors. As seen in both Yabe-san's and Ezaki-san's stories, those who come into the Catholic Church from Protestant denominations often understand the Catholic Church as more spiritual and directly related to the unseen celestial world. As somebody who also knew churches in the United States, Ezaki-san carefully pointed out to me that her experience with Protestant churches in the United States was absolutely different. She insisted that Protestant churches in the United States were "alive," unlike their Japanese counterparts.

As I have attempted to show through this chapter, the ways in which the Catholic worldview is understood, accepted, and practiced by laypeople in Tokyo are strongly influenced by the social fabric of Japanese society. To a society that is primarily focused on strong reciprocal ties between humans, Roman Catholicism can bring a new third-person authority, God. In the process of espousing the Roman Catholic worldview, many laypeople managed to make the transition from the conventional value of "persevering" (*ganbaru*) to the unfamiliar Catholic value of "entrusting" (*yudaneru*). When they were successful in making this transition, they also made a shift from a state of "being watched by people" to a state of "being watched over by the divine." As the dominant Japanese values emphasize human relationships heavily, and tremendous effort is required to maintain those relationships, many converts feel enormous relief when they align themselves with Catholic values. Interestingly enough, this shift from a people-centered world to a God-centered world was also experienced by those who converted from Protestant denominations to Catholicism in Tokyo.

Now we turn our attention to the topic of gender. In the next chapter, we see that the process of shifting the authority figure comes relatively more easily to women than to men. In particular, I depict the ways in which the conventional Japanese value of ideal manhood comes into conflict with some Catholic values. In addition, I show that often women are a catalyst for men's conversion to Catholicism in Tokyo.

Chapter 4

Housewives, *Nippon Danji*, and the Church

"Me? I received baptism, because I did not want to get divorced from my wife. I had heard that you are not allowed to divorce once you become Catholic."

—A male parishioner in Tokyo

Women typically form the majority of the membership in the Catholic churches in contemporary Tokyo. Although this gender imbalance is not unusual, what is perhaps surprising is that these Japanese women often are the only Christians in their households. This situation has multiple implications for their faith experience, as they often are the ones who take care of household altars and the dead in a primarily non-Christian cultural context. Men, on the other hand, typically say that they would like to join the church after their retirement, and many husbands have converted on their deathbed for their Catholic wives. How did these gendered patterns come to dominate the present-day Roman Catholic churches in Tokyo? What are the motivations and cultural reasons behind these contemporary situations? By examining the stories of both women and men using a perspective of gender as a lens,[1] this chapter further unravels the ways in which gender plays out in acquiring and maintaining faith. Although the majority of this book narrates the stories of women, their relationships with the divine, and the resulting changes in their sense of self, this chapter includes several stories of men. Typically, however, I heard the stories of men through the words of women.

Here, to illustrate the complicated picture of gender and the church, I begin by sharing my conversation with three women on the issue of men and faith. This conversation took place during the time of "faith sharing" (*wakachiai*) in one of the classes at Our Lady of the Assumption. On this day, there were two men in attendance in the class of fifteen (although one of the men left in the middle of the class because of his busy schedule). At the end of the class, I was assigned to a small group of three women to share the experience of faith. Instead of talking about their faith, the women discussed the complicated relationship that men have with the church:

> A: For example, Ikuta-san. She first came to this class [at Our Lady of the Assumption] because her husband asked her to come and check it out for him because Mr. Ikuta was interested in having a Catholic funeral for himself!

> B: Men are strange, aren't they? They somehow struggle with the idea of being baptized; as if that is beneath their dignity (*koken ni kakawaru*). I know they are ready [for baptism] at the bottom of their heart, but they somehow cannot cross the threshold [to become Christian/Catholic].

> A: It's the same in my household. My husband's position and your husband's [position] may be similar. Even if he knows he is ready, men have this idea that work has to be an utmost priority. My husband says that he cannot think about it [becoming Christian] while he is working. He would think [about becoming Catholic] after retirement. It [i.e. becoming Catholic] should not have anything to do with his retirement. Nevertheless, we [my household] have already purchased a Catholic burial plot.

> C: Yoshimoto-san was at the church with her husband one day. Then, Fr. Massey told Mr. Yoshimoto that he too can be baptized. He said "yes" on the spot. Then, later, I heard their son was hoping to have the same thing happen to him. Their son also wants to be baptized, but he is too busy [with his schoolwork]. He is saying that "How can I get lucky like Dad [so that I can receive baptism] without any study [i.e. catechism]?"

Everybody in the group laughed at the son's humorous yet seemingly sincere utterance.

> C: But the family in which the man has received baptism is different [from ours]. How can I say? May I call it a "holy family"? Everything is properly done.

I was listening to these stories with a sense of amazement. These three women had received adult baptism in their mid- to later life and only one of them had a husband who became Catholic with her. The other two women were the only Catholics in their immediate family. Yet, from the above-quoted conversation, I could see that there could be potentially more male converts in the future because of these women. These women have considerable influence on their husbands and sons and successfully exert it on the men's lives. I can see these women's covert yet real influence through their ability to convince a husband to buy a family burial plot in the crypt of a Catholic church or to make a son want to convert to the Catholic faith. Through conversations like the one quoted above, I gradually understood that women can become a catalyst for the conversion of male members of the family.

The humorous expression "holy family" (*seikazoku*) calls for some explanation. The phrase in this context denotes a Catholic family in which all immediate family members are baptized; that situation is not common in Tokyo. Although this expression sounds unusual, I heard it used by many people in different parishes across Tokyo. It is used with some humor, as the word should, strictly speaking, refer to the historical holy family of Mary, Joseph, and Jesus. This humorous and odd usage of "holy family" in Tokyo, however, implies that families in which both husband and wife are Catholic are rare and idealized. Although the conversation quoted above implies that the men involved hold positive views on Roman Catholicism, this is not necessarily the norm among the wider population. I heard a plethora of negative portrayals of Roman Catholicism made by men throughout my fieldwork. As I discuss in the next chapter, Japanese society in general may not necessarily harbor positive views of Christianity, and this is often apparent in non-Christian husbands' negative views of Christianity.

The above conversation points to some of the interesting dynamics and differences between men and women in relation to faith and becoming Catholic in Tokyo. Although there are a variety of reasons behind this condition, in this chapter I focus on the difference between the dominant "Japanese" worldview, especially in the form of culturally sanctioned gender ideals, and that of Catholicism. Women have been encouraged to abandon their egos and transform themselves into nurturing wives and mothers in Japanese society (Borovoy 2005, Lebra 1984). This construction of the self parallels many sanctioned qualities within the Church. On the other hand, Japanese men are encouraged to work hard to succeed as part of a larger collective. Abandoning one's ego to surrender to divine will does not have much in common with traditional ideals of manhood in Japan.[2] Societal gendered ideals, therefore, may facilitate or deter one's transition to affiliating with the Roman Catholic Church. The chapter further unravels the ways in which women converts tacitly exercise their agentive power to influence their husbands and sons so that they desire the same faith as their wives or mothers.

I begin my discussion of gender and faith by relating the predominance of women in the Catholic Church to Japan's political economy. In particular, I emphasize various ways in which the government has encouraged women to stay away from full-time professional work. Although they were marginalized in professional settings, the successful implementation of this policy in effect gave women time to explore their spiritual and religious life during the daytime. Then I go on to explain the two distinct gendered ideals that Japanese society hold for women and men. In so doing, I hope to illustrate the ways in which women sometimes become the only Christians in the household and at other times become the conduit for men to convert in their retirement or on their deathbed.

Prominence of Women in the Church and Japan's Political Economy

The majority of participants in weekday classes at Our Lady of the Assumption were middle-aged women and seniors. There were several men with mostly gray hair, but these men never exceeded 10 percent of the total class size. These men are usually retired seniors. Although the official statistics on church membership in Japan (Catholic Bishops' Conference of Japan 2007) tell us that women occupy roughly 60 percent of the membership, women are overrepresented in daytime activities at Our Lady of the Assumption. As this was my sole fieldwork site during weekdays,[3] I do not have comparable field data at other sites. I assume, however, that a similar gender ratio can be observed at other parishes as well because this gender balance, generally speaking, is reflective of a larger societal structure that goes beyond the confines of the parish.

My office work space during fieldwork was situated within the university that is annexed to Our Lady of the Assumption Church, as both institutions were run by the same Catholic order. Whenever I stepped out from the church or the university during my lunch hour, I was intrigued by how the two genders in Tokyo are segregated. I often walked with women from the church to have lunch in the vicinity. Women with whom I went out for lunch ranged between their forties to their eighties; some were married, some divorced, and a few had never married. Most often, they were wives, mothers, and grandmothers without full-time employment. It was not too difficult for me to blend in with this group of people by virtue of being a female (and Japanese). Although my single status was somewhat of an oddity, my female gender was sufficient for me to be accepted as part of the group. On the street, I often noticed that men walked with their male coworkers to lunch and women walked with their female coworkers to lunch; there was a clear gender division. Perhaps this mundane Tokyo scene struck me as "odd" and "new" because of my ten years of absence from the country. Watching groups of men and women on the street, I felt comfortable with this Japanese situation of gender segregation. Back in Canada, I had felt increasingly uncomfortable socializing with girlfriends who were all paired up with their respective future husbands. Oddly enough, gender-segregated Japanese society provided me with a break from the difficulties of being a single person in the "couple culture" of Canada.

During the lunch hour, restaurants in the vicinity of Our Lady of the Assumption were packed with office workers. Although the area is not known for housing giant multinational corporations like some other areas of Tokyo such as Shinjuku and Marunouchi, nevertheless, this is a typical central Tokyo white-collar corporate neighborhood. Interestingly, I could observe that there are three types of restaurants in Tokyo in terms of gender. One type caters to a predominantly male clientele, the second to a predominantly female clientele, and the last to a mixed population. For example, restaurants that feature various kinds of Indian and Japanese curries were typically occupied by *sararīman* (businessmen) clad in dark-colored business suits, whereas fancy Italian and French restaurants offering affordable lunches were typically occupied by uniform-clad "Office Ladies" and other women. Traditional soba noodle restaurants, however, have both female and male customers. I managed to venture to a soba restaurant in the vicinity of Our Lady of the Assumption Church often but I felt intimidated by the large number of male customers. Japanese restaurants often assume that customers will share a table with other customers at the peak lunch hour to facilitate both the business of the restaurants and to save waiting time for customers. Because of this practice, I sometimes ended up sharing a table with a few *sararīman*. Although I classify the soba noodle restaurant as having a "mixed" clientele, men tended to outnumber women. This gender segregation during lunch hour is a reflection of a wider societal practice, as I discuss below.

In the two parishes where I conducted fieldwork, women figured prominently. Here, I do not mean that women took up prominent positions; rather, I mean women took care of many aspects of daily church activities. It is not an overstatement to say that the church could not function without these laywomen volunteers. Nevertheless, "prominent" positions were most often occupied by male members, even if they were a numerical minority. At Our Lady of the Assumption, women cleaned the building, including its many washrooms; made exquisite flower arrangements for the altars of the sanctuaries and each saint's statue; sang hymns for funeral masses; and served as cantors and altar service persons for the noon mass every weekday. Kitami-san, for example, signed up for washroom cleaning duties after she became an official parishioner with her baptism. Kaneta-san, who is a baptismal sponsor of Okada-san and likes to sing, joined a choir specifically formed for the parish's funeral masses. Often, women made flower arrangements during the week; they wore colorful aprons and carefully composed, exquisite, traditional flower arrangements. The main sanctuary's flower arrangement always reflected the season, and the arrangement looked absolutely professional. On the other hand, I did not see many activities taken up by male members at all during weekdays at Our Lady of the Assumption. Men are conspicuously absent from the daytime volunteer work.

At Terada Catholic Church also, women are the ones who make all aspects of church activities run smoothly. Women attend to the bookstore, make weekly flower arrangements on Saturdays for the main sanctuary and each saint's statue, sell coffee and bread on Sundays before and after the mass, work in the kitchen for the resident priests, and help facilitate wedding and funeral arrangements for parishioners and non-parishioners. Kikuchi-san, the mother of a twenty-year-old daughter, for example, sells bread before the mass begins on Sunday mornings, but she also sells coffee to fund-raise for other church activities as soon as the 9:30 mass is over. She also participates in and helps to organize the meetings of the Heaven's Movie Village that meets once a month. Mika-san, a single woman in her forties, literally runs around all day on Sundays. She organizes a speaker series and also is responsible for transcribing the priest's sermon for Internet publication each week. She seems to pick up odd jobs here and there on top of her regular duties to the extent that Kikuchi-san started wondering if Mika-san was working too hard on Sundays.[4] At Terada Church, however, I was able to see more men participating in church activities. For instance, I observed men cleaning the sanctuary (as this duty was assigned to neighborhood groups.)[5] At Terada Church too, men are involved in the weekly management of the church fund and planning special events with the pastor. I observed more male involvement in the Terada Church because I was there on Sundays when there were generally more men in attendance. As seen through activities at these two parishes, however, women are an indispensable part of the life of these churches in Tokyo. At both churches, the head of lay parishioners[6] was male, and perhaps those who were responsible for church budgets also tend to be male. The rest of the positions, however, are mostly assumed by women. They are the ones who serve tea after the "Sunday speaker series" that follows the mass. Women also attend bookstores and sell cookies and bread for fundraising.

Why are women so readily available at the church? Are men not as interested in volunteering at the church as women? Is there any correlation between these gendered patterns of church involvement and the fact that women and men workers eat lunch separately in Tokyo? Anthropological literature on the Japanese sense of self suggests that gender is one of the most salient factors in Japanese identity construction. Gender is embedded in the "relational" sense of self in which familial and societal roles emerge as prominent—such as the self as the mother, the president, or the employee of a company. Japanese constructions of gender have been shaped through historical discursive processes, but even in contemporary contexts, gender is one of the primary elements that dictates the life course in Japan. For women, the ideal of being a "good wife and wise mother" (*ryōsai kenbo*) enshrined by thinkers during the Meiji Era (1868–1912) still lingers as the ideal in the twenty-first century. For a man, to work as a company employee and devote his full energy to work is still held as an ideal, although some men are deprived of such opportunities in recent years (Allison 2013). Nevertheless, at the time of my fieldwork, the clear gendered division of labor is reflected in the male and female groups of lunch-goers (cf. Ogasawara 1998) near Our Lady of the Assumption as well as in the predominantly female character of church activities, especially during weekdays.

The works of Nancy Rosenberger (2001), Helen Hardacre (1997), and Anne Allison (1991) provide us with insight into political power and public discourses, including those of the mass media, that have impacted the spheres of family, sexuality, and gender in Japan. Rosenberger's *Gambling with Virtues* (2001) traces the shifting of the female sense of self from the 1970s to the 1990s, and in particular contextualizes the shift by looking at changing governments' discourses on the female role in society. During the 1960s, when Japan's yearly economic growth was 9 percent to 10 percent, gender difference, morality, and disciplines were reinforced. Soon, the nuclear family became a new unit of family, and the home became the "place for the reproduction of energy" that would fuel the nation's economic growth (Rosenberger 2001). Reproductive life was standardized—women married before twenty-five, men in their thirties, and they typically produced two children a year or so apart (Rosenberger 2001, Hardacre 1997). By 1973, Rosenberger points out that social policies held "family" responsible for the care of sick siblings or parents (2001, 19). This policy was implemented simultaneously with that of pension plans that favored corporate and government employees. Using the cutoff line of 1,030,000 Yen (approximately 9,000 U.S. dollars) as the maximum that one can earn to be eligible for the tax benefit as a spouse, the government has encouraged wives to take on part-time jobs with no benefits and no overtime.[7] As Rosenberger has shown, the government kept inventing a "new sense of self" for women. In the 1980s, women were encouraged to be avid consumers, and in the 1990s, to explore their sense of individuality in tastes in shopping and vacations. Nevertheless, keeping women out of full-time management jobs with promotions was a consistent policy throughout these postwar years. In line with this policy, the home was envisaged as the domain of women from which they could venture for part-time work and shopping for high-end consumer goods. However, their primary responsibility was childcare and the care of the sick (Rosenberger 2001; cf. Kondo 1990).

Japan has seen decades of economic stagnation since the early 1990s, and the suffering of both male and female workers from larger structural forces has been increasingly discussed in recent scholarship (Allison 2013). The majority of women I encountered through this fieldwork, however, were older, and their life stories often resonate with earlier studies of Japanese women who made themselves available as the backstage supporters of their family members. For example, Hirota-san was working as an office worker when she met her future husband. She quit her job for marriage and as a *sengyō shufu* (housewife) brought up two daughters (cf. Brinton 1994; Ogasawara 1998). The couple managed the household of four with mostly the income of her husband, who worked for a municipal government office as a civil servant. Hirota-san helped her friend's company when she was available, but this remained a casual position to supplement her husband's income. Akiyama-san too was a *sengyō shufu*. She had a husband, a son who is now a medical doctor with his own family, and a daughter who had been sick but had just gotten engaged when I was in Akiyama-san's class at Our Lady of the Assumption. She was the one who sought help in faith when she could not bear being the sole caretaker for the sick members of her family.

In general, at Our Lady of the Assumption, the majority of participants during weekdays were housewives who were either married or widowed. Many women that I met had two children, and a number of women were taking care of sick members of their households. Over recent decades, government policies have encouraged women not to earn more than 1,030,000 yen and to remain nurturing and caring figures who run the home. Making the most of their daytime hours before they have to go home to prepare the evening meal, women come to visit the church for a variety of reasons. Men, on the contrary, are struggling to carve out the time to attend church. Many manage to visit the church in their retirement. As such, the predominance of women at the church is intimately related to the political economy of Japan as a nation.

Christian Meekness vs. *Nippon Danji*

On our way to Tokyo, Kikuchi-san, Mika-san, and I managed to find a table in a busy café in Kamakura City on one sunny day in May. It is a historic city that once was the political capital of Japan during the Kamakura Period (1192–1333). The city is located less than an hour's train ride from Tokyo, and the area is known for its many Buddhist temples, greenery and beaches. That day, there was a group of us from Terada Church visiting Kamakura City, as we had all attended the ordination mass for a young priest who had spent two years in training at Terada

Catholic Church. Because the young priest belonged to the Yokohama Diocese, we all traveled to this neighboring prefecture for the ordination. I heard that the young priest had asked for Terada Catholic Church as the parish for his training even though this parish was located outside his diocese. The resident priest at Terada Church is extremely popular. The young priest-to-be must have hoped to learn how to run his future parish successfully. On that day in Kamakura City, the rite of ordination was very well attended despite the fact that only one priest was being ordained. The site, an elementary Catholic school gym, was packed with people, and during the mass, organizers had to run around to collect communion hosts from nearby chapels. The organizers had prepared for 1,800 attendees, but there must have been more people in attendance, as the hosts had all been distributed by the middle of the holy sacrament. Those people toward the end of the lines to take communion received only wine from the chalice. Noting the large crowd, Mika-san exclaimed: "Wow, this is also a form of blessing! The hosts have run out."

When the ordination mass ended, a number of us walked together toward a nearby Japan Railways station, but one by one, the group dispersed and, in the end, only three of us were left. When we reached a popular tourist destination, a street called Komachi-dōri that led to a famous Shinto shrine, we decided to rest in a crowded café for tea and cake before we headed back to Tokyo. After all, it had been a long service, and we had to take another hour-long train ride. Kikuchi-san recounted her husband's experience of baptism:

> Oh, when my husband received baptism, we had not decided on who would be his baptismal sponsor; back then, things were less organized than nowadays. On the very day, Fr. Kimura told Mr. Hattori, "Hattori-san, this is Kikuchi-san who is going to be baptized today. Would you mind becoming his sponsor?"; that was how we decided [on the sponsor]. On Hattori-san's part, he was also pretty easygoing about the entire thing. He went like, "Oh, no problem."
>
> Then the first thing that this Hattori-san told my husband was that "See, Kikuchi-san, you do not have to worry about telling anybody [about baptism]. You need not talk [about this] to your coworkers at all." Then, my husband said he was so relieved! It looked like he was anxious about it [being recognized as a Christian]. At his work, if he was thought of as a

Christian, when he wanted to fire somebody, for example, or when he wanted to negotiate with other firms, he said he was not sure whether he could be tough. It looked like he was worrying about that kind of things [about becoming a Christian].

Soon our orders arrived and we started eating our cake. Kikuchi-san continued: "But, that kind of makes sense. Aren't those [men] who are at the church all similar? Kind of gentle looking. Sudō-san, for example. Don't you think?" Being asked for her opinion, Mika-san strongly agreed, saying "Yes, yes. They do!"

I was rather surprised to see these women validate the view of Christian men as meek. However, their views resonate with another story that I heard from a priest. Fr. Shimoda was a guest speaker for the charismatic group that met every Sunday night in central Tokyo. After one hour of singing and speaking in tongues, the last hour of the meeting was devoted to a sermon by a different priest each week. Fr. Shimoda belongs to the Archdiocese of Tokyo. He started telling the congregation about his own infant baptism. His mother went to Sacred Heart School, a well-known women's school in Tokyo, and became Catholic through the Catholic education she received there. The young woman wanted to become a nun and talked to the Mother Superior of the convent about her wish. The Mother Superior said to her, "You were born of a distinguished house (*yangotonaki ouchi*) as the only daughter. If you entered the convent, it would be unbearable for your parents, and I do not believe that it is the Lord's intention. You could serve our Lord in a different way by marrying a certain qualified individual, giving birth to many children, and then offering up those children to the Lord. That is also one way to serve our Lord." The young woman accepted this suggestion, and her parents began to search for a suitor. Everything was arranged and she married a promising, but poor, diplomat. Soon, the couple had a daughter, and another daughter, and eventually they had four daughters.

When the husband was stationed in Switzerland for his diplomatic duties, the couple finally had a baby boy, who was to become Fr. Shimoda. The young Japanese parents in Europe wavered over their decision about whether to have their baby boy baptized. In the words of Fr. Shimoda:

> My parents thought that they wanted to raise this child as an excellent *Nippon danji* [lit. Japanese man]. They worried that if they had me baptized, whether Japanese society [*seken*] would

accept me as *Nippon danji*. But [in the end] they decided that they wanted to baptize me in order for me to become an excellent *Nippon danji*.

While telling us this story from his past, Fr. Shimoda began to cry. Fr. Shimoda was looking back with nostalgia to his parents' difficult decision made many decades previously. It is noteworthy that Fr. Shimoda did not mention anything about whether his parents had decided to baptize their daughters. Some of these daughters, however, became nuns later in life, making their mother's dream true that she was not able to realize for herself.

The phrase *Nippon danji* can be literally translated as "Japanese man," but this concept entails more than gender and country of origin. The concept of *Nippon danji* embodies ideal manhood in Japan. This concept of ideal Japanese manhood has constantly shifted over time according to both official governmental and popular discourses. However, in the context of Fr. Shimoda's story, this concept generally entails such adjectives as strong, brave, masculine, and decisive. By contrast, the concept does not include the ideas represented by such adjectives as meek, gentle, and submissive. Contemporary views on the ideal Japanese man are inclined to masculinity. Unlike the court gentlemen of the Heian Period (794–1192), whose excellence was measured by their ability to compose poetry and sing, or the kabuki actors of the Edo Period (1603–1868), who were praised for their beauty when they were playing female characters, the "manly" requirements for Japanese men in the modern period have tended to focus on the ability to work hard, exert authority, and conform to group norms to achieve goals set by those in positions of leadership.

Two common themes unite the two narratives cited above on male conversion. One is the perception of Christianity, or Catholicism in particular, as somewhat feminine and meek, and the other is that images of Christianity or Catholicism are not appropriate for men, who should strive for culturally sanctioned ideals of manhood in Japan. I should note that I do not know to what extent this opposition between masculinity and Christianity was observed by those who belong to Protestant denominations or even by those who belong to Catholic churches in other parts of Japan such as Nagasaki. Among those whom I encountered in Tokyo, however, this opposition was consistently expressed. For example, the husband of Kikuchi-san owned and ran a construction company. Although he wished to become Catholic and was about to undergo baptism, he was not sure how to reconcile his identity as Catholic with his position as president of a construction company. He worried about whether he would still be considered "manly enough" with his new Catholic identity, especially when he is required to fire an employee or to be tough in negotiating a business deal. Just as Kikuchi-san's husband was anxious in the twenty-first century about the compatibility of Japanese manhood and being Christian, the parents of Fr. Shimoda in the early twentieth century had also been anxious about the implications of baptism for their son's success in Japanese society. Fr. Shimoda was born in the 1930s before the Pacific War. The ideals of Japanese manhood would have been strongly influenced by the Japanese militarism of the time.

Meekness was repeatedly included in men's explanations of their uneasiness about being affiliated with Christianity. Some men pointed to passages in the Bible with which they were uncomfortable, and others explained their view that Christianity comes into conflict with the "manly qualities required" in the Japanese business world. During her period of spiritual quest, Fujimi-san—a woman with whom we met earlier at the end of chapter 1—went to visit a Christmas gathering organized by a nearby Protestant church. She decided to go to the event on her own and did not consult her husband. When her husband found out that his wife had been to a Christian church, he became exceedingly angry. He broke the red candle that she had been given at the church and tore up her newly purchased Bible. Fujimi-san recalled him saying: "My father hates Christianity. I would have to try you in the family assembly (*kazoku kaigi*). This could mean divorce, do you understand?" Although he had an emotional reaction to her attempt to go to church, he also had a rational reason to support his dismissal of Christianity.

> I asked my husband why he did not like [Christianity]. He said because his father hated it. Then he said this. When he was a child, he was invited to a Sunday school. When he said this to his father, the father became infuriated. [. . .] And then he also said this. Christianity asks to offer the left cheek when one is hit on the right cheek. That is hypocritical. [He said] "I don't like that." [He said] "I find it is difficult to accept that kind of teaching."

It is noteworthy that these men do know about the characteristics of Christianity.[8] To be fair to these men, among the many teachings of Christianity, the idea of meekness is a strange and difficult one to understand. Both from a modern secular perspective and from a Confucian-based perspective, the Christian valorization of meekness appears illogical, even "weird" and nonsensical. From a modern secular perspective, to respond to the powerful by complete submission means defeat, most likely accompanied by a sense of humiliation on the part of those being defeated. According to contemporary secular logic, it would be better to retaliate to the best of one's ability, in order at least to strike a balance of power to deter the opponent's next attack. From a Confucian-based perspective, which respects an orderly hierarchy, turning the other cheek makes no sense. If Christ is a god in a Confucian world, he should reign over any others in the world. Why would he have to offer his other cheek in response to an insulting blow? As Fujimi-san's husband has pointed out, the teaching of meekness, in particular, appears enigmatic both to secular sensitivities and Confucian-based mainstream Japanese worldviews.

Semantically speaking, the concept of meekness is something that does not have a historical root in the Japanese language. The *Collins Cobuild English Dictionary*, which is designed for non-native speakers of English to facilitate their practical understanding of English words, describes the word "meekness" as "If you describe a person as meek, you think that they are gentle and quiet, and likely to do what other people say." The same dictionary gives "The meek shall inherit the earth," as a sample sentence. The *Kenkyusha's Middle English-Japanese Dictionary* translates meekness as *sunao* and *nyūwa*. *Sunao* can be translated as obedient, tame, docile, submissive, meek, gentle, and mild. *Nyūwa* can be translated as gentle, tender, and mild. *Sunao* is most often an ideal attribute of a child and often mentioned as a desirable quality for a young woman in Japanese contexts. Children are often told repeatedly to be *sunao* by parents and teachers and are praised for being *sunao*. Both children and young women are in need of protection in a Confucian-based human social hierarchy, and both children and women in general are expected to be submissive, docile, and tame to maintain hierarchy. *Nyūwa*, on the other hand, can be used to describe gentle-mannered women and men, and often the word is used to modify the noun "smile." This usage does not seem to limit gender or age. Generally speaking, however, the idea that "the meek shall inherit the earth" would be unthinkable in the popular mainstream Japanese worldview. As we can see in the usage of *sunao*, meekness is expected to be found among the socially weak, namely children and young women. According to the traditional Confucian-inspired hierarchy, the powerful rather than the weak should inherit the earth.

As seen through these three ethnographic vignettes and discussion of the concept of "meekness," Christianity, especially its teaching about meekness, presents a stumbling block for many Japanese men. Modern views of ideal Japanese manhood do not support the Christian ideal of meekness, and potential candidates for conversion to Catholicism have to deal with the tension between Japanese manhood and the concept of meekness.

Feminine Catholicism in Tokyo

Although dealing with the Christian ideal of meekness deters the conversion of Japanese men, there is another side to the overrepresentation of women in the Catholic Church in Tokyo. There is an image of Catholicism in Tokyo as essentially "feminine." To begin my discussion, I start with a scene that I encountered while I was staying in Tokyo. At an academic study group in Japan, one of the participants described a Roman Catholic follower as "somebody who looks stuck up, as if to be proud of her colleagueship with Empress Michiko at the Sacred Heart." Although this image was his personal view, he also considered it to be widely shared. This unfriendly image of Roman Catholicism in Tokyo is a relatively common stereotype. It is expressed here as embodied in a person: feminine, proud, and somehow connected with elite social classes in Japan. This image of Roman Catholics in Tokyo is radically different from North American ideas. In Canada, for example, a typical image of Catholics might be an immigrant elderly Italian woman of modest means. She may be short and clad in black dresses. She lives in a small house in an Italian neighborhood where you find grapevines in the backyard and images of Catholic saints in the front yard. For the majority of the population in Tokyo, however, the schools operated by various Catholic religious orders provide people with their most immediate reference point for the Roman Catholic Church. As the population of Roman Catholics in Japan is fewer than 1 percent, it is rare to have many friends and colleagues who are actually practicing Catholics. One may know, however, somebody who went to the Sacred Heart Elementary or Junior High School, for example. Several of the women's schools, such as the Seishin Joshi Gakuin (Sacred Heart) and Futaba Gakuen, are known as established traditional schools for the daughters of wealthy families in metropolitan Tokyo. It is not an accident that two successive crown princesses, Empress Emerita Michiko and

Empress Masako, went to these women's schools run by Catholic orders in Tokyo. These private Catholic schools are known to cater to the "sons and daughters from wealthy families" (*ryōke no shijo*). For better or worse, over time, the students that these schools have produced have come to represent a popular image of Catholicism in Tokyo. The majority of the Catholic orders in Japan originated in France, and the schools established by these orders were run by French nuns who taught classes along with some Japanese teachers. To further understand the contemporary popular image of Tokyo Catholics as embodying femininity, sophistication, and a degree of exotic foreignness, I explore some historical background.

As previously stated in chapter 1, Roman Catholicism reentered the Tokyo area after the official ban on Christianity was lifted in the Meiji Era. Unlike the initial evangelization period of the sixteenth and seventeenth centuries, the Vatican entrusted the evangelization of Japan to the Société des Missions Etrangères (the Paris Foreign Missions Society, or Paris Mission). This organization consisted of parish priests from France who worked under the direct leadership of the Vatican. Until 1904, when the Shikoku Diocese was separated from the Osaka Archdiocese and was entrusted to the Spanish Dominicans, the initial re-evangelization of Japan for half a century was single-handedly accomplished by the Paris Mission (Ohta 2004, 178). As a result, most of the clergy, brothers, and nuns who arrived in Japan before 1904 were French nationals or worked in the French language. In this way, as Ohta correctly states, modern Japan's Catholic Church has had distinctively nineteenth-century French influences (Ohta 2004, 178).

The Tokyo Archdiocese was not an exception to these dominant French influences. A number of female orders became active in the area of education. From 1878 to 1900 alone, more than a dozen primary and secondary educational institutions were created and run by three female orders—the Sisters of St. Paul of Chartres, the Société de Marie (Marians), and the Congrégation des Sœurs de l'Instruction charitable du saint Enfant Jésus (Saint-Maur). These female orders were instrumental in establishing today's privileged female Catholic schools, such as Futaba (Enfant Jesus), Seishin (Sacred Hearts), and Shirayuri (Sisters of St. Paul of Chartres). As Karen Seat (2003) notes, the late nineteenth century and early twentieth century were times when women's public education was significantly limited because of government policies. Before World War II, women were trained to become "good wives and wise mothers" who would serve the family-state. At public schools, women were taught Confucian ethics and domestic arts so that they would fulfill the feminine ideal. Female students were not allowed to attend public universities. Men, on the other hand, were encouraged to study sciences, law, medicine, and other subjects. In this cultural and political milieu, private missionary schools offered the highest education available for women until the end of the Pacific War. For example, some missionary schools offered classes in literature, philosophy, and Latin. As Seat points out, in the cultural milieu of prewar Japan, missionary schools appeared exceedingly liberal in comparison to the rest of the options available to female students. At this time, women's education was a niche that the Church could fill, and this role led to the Church's contact with an elite segment of the Japanese population in Tokyo.

After WWII, however, this situation was reversed. Postwar reforms introduced a coeducational system to Japan, and public schools had to allow female students to participate in higher education. As a result, private missionary schools lost many promising talented students to the public system. To survive this structural change, missionary schools needed to innovate. Paradoxically, they achieved this goal by reforming their curriculum so that their schools would prepare women to become "good wives and wise mothers." Many missionary schools reorganized themselves into junior colleges to serve this goal (Seat 2003, 322). Even in contemporary society, ideal womanhood in Japan still requires a modest education so that a woman's educational training does not surpass that of her husband (cf. Ogasawara 1998). Catholic schools, as well as other Christian junior colleges, therefore produce many "ideal" marital candidates who work for a short period of time as OLs ("Office Ladies") and then become mothers and wives of "corporate soldiers" in postwar Japan.

Many of my research participants were graduates of these women's Catholic schools. Hashimoto-san, for example, went to the Sacred Heart School. She transferred to Sacred Heart Elementary School in the fifth year of her primary education. This was before the Pacific War, and in Hashimoto's case, her father was captivated by the new idea that women should also be educated. Her family relocated to Tokyo from Ibaraki Prefecture for the sake of their daughters' education. Their exceedingly liberal young father decided, instead of giving expensive kimonos for his daughters' weddings, to give them an education. The father, who was studying literature at the time, heard an excellent review of the school and decided to send his first daughter to one of Sacred Heart's schools.

Hashimoto-san was to continue her education at Sacred Heart, and she remained there until she obtained her associate degree in history. To have a degree from a junior college is unusual for a woman of her generation.

The story of Kubo-san, a married working woman in her early fifties, reflects the situation of missionary schools after the postwar period. The way she speaks in an extremely polite form of Japanese indicates her high social status. Hashimoto-san also speaks in this manner. Coming from a middle-class household, I would not use some of the expressions that these women use because I would feel out of place. Kubo-san also went to one of Sacred Heart's schools in Tokyo. Unlike the majority of my research participants, she was born into a Catholic family and therefore was baptized as an infant. According to Kubo-san, her natal family has a tradition of sending daughters to Sacred Heart and sons to Keio Gijuku. Keio is another prestigious private school that runs from kindergarten to university, but it is not connected to a Catholic order. The graduates of Keio are often assured well-paid jobs at big corporations and government offices. Because the name of the university from which one graduates affects one's job prospects to a significant degree—to the extent that is unthinkable in North America—the entrance competition to Keio is fierce. Kubo-san reminisced about how her mother advised her friend's mother, who presumably also was Catholic:

> When my friend was deciding on his selection of schools, my mother told his mother something like boys can go to church but they may not have to go to Catholic schools necessarily. [She said] something like that. He was also my junior at the company. He told me later that his mother got advice from my mother, and that was how he ended up going to Keio.

In a quintessential way, these two gendered tracks—boys to Keio Gijuku and girls to Sacred Heart—reflect societal gender norms. Men are expected to climb a social ladder, whereas women are expected to be groomed for a "good marriage." Catholic women's schools came to be known as places where women are segregated and protected from outside negative influences, hence an ideal setting for unmarried young women.

Contrary to the stereotype of "Tokyo Catholics" as affluent, proud, and belonging to high social strata, there are a wide range of people within the Archdiocese of Tokyo. Graduates of privileged Catholic schools in Tokyo can definitely be found within each congregation, but they do not even constitute a majority. Some new converts had sent their children to a nearby kindergarten run by a Catholic order and had been introduced to the faith; others just came to visit the church as a result of personal spiritual quests. There are a variety of routes that have led people to contact with the Church. Yet the image of "affluent Tokyo Catholics" and their relationship to privileged Catholic schools is influential among the general public. Another woman in her seventies, Oda-san, was a graduate of Shirayuri Gakuen and therefore belonged to a graduate class that experienced a prewar Catholic school. I introduced her earlier in chapter 1. She explained to me why some affluent people in Tokyo became Catholic:

> Generally speaking, they [affluent converts in Tokyo] are all graduates of Catholic schools. A lot of us [who became Catholic] went to Catholic schools from kindergarten to high schools where there were brothers and fathers, whom we addressed as Musshū [Monsieur] and female ones whom we addressed Sisutā [Sister] or Masūru [Ma Soeur]. Why did those [affluent] people become Catholic . . . this sounds like self-aggrandizing, but that was because those religious people were truly good people. They truly loved us, students. That was so apparent even to us children. They came from far away to a place where everything was completely different. And they abandoned themselves [to the faith] and taught us the love of Christ for 24 hours a day, enthusiastically. Because they were the religious, they were unmarried. We were their sisters, sons and daughters.

She attended schools run by the Sisters of St. Paul of Chartres before, during, and after the war. Confirming Oda-san's observation, there are large numbers of converts from these schools from her generation. There are, however, fewer converts from later generations of alumni from these schools.

Despite the actual number of converts from these schools, it is still the case that these schools and their graduates are often associated with, and bear the image of, "Catholics in Tokyo." A Polish priest who regularly visits one of the convents of the Sisters of St. Paul of Chartres told me that he would feel that his table manners are "barbarian" when compared to those of the Japanese Mother Superior there. He made the point that the sisters there are trained in more sophisticated European manners than those of an actual European: himself. The most famous graduates of these schools, Empress Emerita Michiko and Empress Masako, are also known for their ties to "sophisticated Western" culture. Empress Emerita Michiko often gives speeches in fluent English, and Empress Masako's upbringing in foreign countries as well as her degree from Harvard are widely discussed. Although they are not Catholics themselves, their images certainly parallel that of Roman Catholicism in Tokyo. They are feminine, sophisticated, and somewhat foreign.

It is probably correct to state that Roman Catholicism, when compared with its counterpart Protestant denominations, has taken on an even more feminine image in Tokyo. My limited encounter with people from Protestant denominations also supports this conclusion. As Ikuo Abe has discussed in his contribution to *Muscular Christianity in Colonial and Post-colonial Worlds* (2008), some Protestant denominations in Japan historically have taken on more masculine images than feminine ones.[9] According to Abe, early Protestant missionaries, Japanese Christians, and Western foreign teachers were responsible for establishing "sportsmanship" in modern Japan. This Japanese sportsmanship, invented in the Meiji Period, was heavily influenced by Euro-American ethics, and Japanese Christians introduced these sporting ethical ideals. During the Meiji Period, nationalistic sentiment ran high, and the Japanese ideal of sportsmanship was formulated through the hybridization of *Bushido*[10] and Christianity.

The masculine images of Christianity among Protestant denominations were also discernable among the former and current members of Protestant churches I encountered through my fieldwork. Here, I introduce the stories told by one of my research participants, Yabe-san. The reader has encountered him earlier in chapter 3 as the biker who was dealing with his grandfather's cemetery problem. As a motorbike rider and spiritual seeker, Yabe-san came across a Christian missionary riding a Harley Davidson. He recalled this charismatic figure fondly. This pastor is known as Arthur Hollands,[11] but he looks ethnically Japanese and speaks Japanese as his native tongue. One day, Yabe-san joined Hollands's bike team, known as "the Road Angels," and toured around the base of Mount Fuji. Yabe-san recalled this experience warmly, saying he was also able to participate in a baptismal rite conducted at Lake Kawaguchi near Mount Fuji on that day. According to Yabe-san, the Road Angels had members who included:

> A former *yakuza* (i.e., a member of an organized gang group), a former swindler, a motorbike test driver, a pastor of another

church, and a Buddhist monk, etc. There is always somebody leaving and somebody coming in [to the group], but those who cannot find their places in a regular church are able to follow Christ through the Teacher Arthur. Indeed, he is a missionary for masculine Christianity.[12]

On Hollands's professionally produced website, we can see the performance of this unusual Japanese missionary. Clad in a leather jacket and with his hair in a ponytail, the missionary looks like a biker gang member more than anything else. His shoulders and half his chest are covered by tattoos, a hallmark of somebody who resides outside "normal" power structures in Japan.[13] A short movie clip introduces his sermon, in which he talks to his audience in rough and casual Japanese. He says: "I understand being passionate, but [those who practice] religion are kind of repulsive!" His talk is provocative and fervent at the same time.

It is certain that Arthur Hollands's masculinity does not represent all Protestant groups in the Tokyo area. There are a large number of women's schools founded and run by Protestant denominations in the Tokyo area that maintain a similar feminine image to the Catholic women's schools discussed previously. Similar to the elite schools run by Roman Catholic female orders, these Protestant women's schools are also attended by daughters of privileged families. These schools include Aoyama Gakuin, Ferris Jogakuin, and Toyo Eiwa Jogakuin.

Yet another angle of the historical perspective gives us a glimpse into the different dynamics between Catholic and Protestant churches during the re-evangelization period in Tokyo. During the Meiji, Taisho, and early Shōwa Periods, all Christian groups had to deal with the policy of State Shinto. Whereas the Roman Catholic Church maintained a low profile in criticizing governmental policies, Protestant groups tended to be more vocal, risking the imprisonment of their members and the disbanding of the groups. The incident already described in detail in chapter 1 may serve as an illustration of the position taken by the Roman Catholic Church. When one of the students from a Jesuit university refused to make obeisance to the national Yasukuni Shrine and was reprimanded by the authorities, this incident received national media attention. The Archbishop of Tokyo and an emissary from the Vatican responded by contacting the Ministry of Education, asking about the precise nature of the act of obeisance. The government explained that bowing down to the Yasukuni Shrine is not a religious act but an act of patriotism. The Church took this explanation at face value and allowed the members of the church to bow down at the Yasukuni Shrine. The leaders from the Protestant denominations also needed to make various compromises to survive. In their struggles for survival, however, some leaders from Protestant groups inevitably came into conflict with the government's official discourse. For example, when the leaders of the Protestant denominations discussed their unified catechism and agreed on its content, they realized that "it was impossible to alter the church's belief in the resurrection of Christ and the subordination (in effect) of the emperor to God and his Christ" (quoted in Drummond 1971, 266). In this political context, more than one hundred pastors from Holiness groups were arrested in 1942 because of their teaching on the Second Coming of Christ and the Thousand Year Kingdom. The authorities alleged that these teachings were contrary to the official monarchy of the reigning emperor. The detention of the pastors, which began in 1942, was prolonged, and some of them died in prison before their release (Drummond 1971, 268). When comparing Japanese Roman Catholic leaders and those from Protestant denominations at the time, it is apparent that there were several more direct confrontations with the government by the Protestant denominations.

The reader may find it odd to find the discussion of differing histories of Protestantism and Roman Catholicism in the section dealing with "Feminine Catholicism in Tokyo." My intention here is to emphasize the different gendered images that these two groups have maintained over time. While the Catholic Church has been obedient and less critical of mainstream public policies, Protestant groups have maintained the role of social critics. Speaking up against authority contradicts historically supported Japanese values. In addition, the Catholic Church in Tokyo is often associated with women's elite schools in the area and took on a feminine image. These factors have all contributed to the popular image of Roman Catholicism as quiet, docile, and obedient to authorities and more feminine than masculine in its gendered character.

Women as Priestesses and Men as Branches of the Grapevine

While we were walking down the stairs of the restaurant after lunch one day, Tanaka-san said to Kitami-san and me: "If there is one Catholic in the household, it would be okay. Because that person can pray for the entire family." Tanaka-san chuckled as if she had told us a secret. We had all attended the noon mass at Our Lady of the Assumption, and the three of us had decided to have lunch across the street from the church and spend some time together before Fr. Massey's class, which begins promptly at 2:00 p.m. As a devout Catholic who frequented charismatic meetings, Tanaka-san had strong faith in prayer. She was not exactly the only Catholic in her household—unlike the majority of the women in the same group—as her son had become Catholic before her conversion. Yet her words resonated with many other women in the group. As wives, mothers, and grandmothers, they constantly prayed for their loved ones. As we left the restaurant, we walked onto the crowded pavement, where many businessmen clad in dark-colored business suits hurried back to their offices. Tanaka-san was in her seventies and living with her retired husband, and Kitami-san, as we saw earlier, was in her fifties and living with her husband in downtown Tokyo. Although it has been more than two decades since the implementation of the Equal Employment Opportunty Law in 1986 promoted women's position in Japanese society, these generations were not affected by such relatively recent national policies. These are the women who were encouraged to marry, procreate, and then educate their sons and daughters while taking care of their husbands (Allison 1991, 1996; Borovoy 2005; Lebra 1984). In so doing, they enabled their husbands to work full-time outside the household domain during Japan's economic ascendancy in the international arena (Allison 1994, Brinton 1994, Ogasawara 1998).

As discussed so far in this chapter, Japan's state policies resulted in free time for women during the daytime, and the feminine image of Catholicism and the similarity between Catholic ideals of womanhood and traditional Japanese ideals of womanhood made it easier for women than for men to become Catholics in Tokyo. What are the implications of this situation for men? Recalling the initial conversation between the three housewives at the beginning of this chapter, it is evident that some men are certainly interested in becoming Catholic. Especially when the couple has a good marital relationship, a Catholic woman will encourage her husband to join her faith. (Not surprisingly, this is not the case when women find refuge in Roman Catholicism from difficult marriages.)

A typical husband's reaction to a wife who considers joining the Catholic Church is "Am I not good enough for you?" Some men would say, "I guess living with me is not sufficient salvation for you." It seems that the man in this context perceives himself to be in competition with another authority. Husbands are perhaps disappointed that they cannot be the sole authority figure for their wives. As the majority of the Japanese population does not have a clear picture of the church as an organization or Catholic doctrine, I am not sure what other figures these husbands perceive as their competitors. Possible choices are the Church, Jesus Christ, a priest of a particular parish, God the Father, or a particular friend of the wife who introduced her to the faith community. Husbands typically feel resentful when their wives attempt to go to mass on Sundays. In fact, many housewives I met through fieldwork said that they do not attend Sunday masses. For housewives, Sundays are one of few days during the week when they *have to* attend to the family, or at least to their husbands, full-time. Understanding these situations, some priests would tell housewives not to worry about attending masses on Sundays.[14]

Most of my research participants at Our Lady of the Assumption attended masses on weekdays. Most of the morning masses in Japan are held very early. Our Lady of the Assumption had morning masses at 6:00 a.m., 7:00 a.m., and 7:30 a.m., and Terada Church had mass at 6:30 a.m. This latter time is a common hour for weekday morning mass at many other parishes. This schedule makes sense, considering the long commutes in the Tokyo area. If mass were scheduled for 8:00 a.m., it would be more difficult for commuters to attend. Kitami-san was attending the noon mass before going to Fr. Massey's classes on Wednesdays, but when she cannot attend this class, she attended one of the morning masses before going to work. Mita-san attended two weekday noon masses at Our Lady of the Assumption, after which she would go downstairs to the crypt to join the rosary group and say a Hail Mary at her daughter's grave. She would then have lunch with this group after the rosary. I knew numerous other women who did not even think of attending Sunday masses. For them, it was not worth the trouble to try to attend Sunday masses, and the clergy do not criticize these women for not attending Sunday masses. It is tacitly accepted that it is difficult for Catholic wives who are the only Christians in their families to attend masses on Sundays (or Saturday evenings).

Not all men were uncomfortable pursuing a spiritual path through the classes offered by the Roman Catholic churches in Tokyo. Several young and middle-aged men attended night classes at Our Lady of the Assumption. One *sarariman* in his thirties or forties sat next to me in the very last row of the classroom. He was wearing a business suit and restlessly checked his cell phone. Halfway through the class, after checking his cell phone, he abruptly left the classroom and did not return.

During fieldwork, I heard many stories from women about men's deathbed conversions. This occurrence was humorously referred to as "heaven theft" (*tengoku dorobō*). The husband who converts on his deathbed is thought to go straight to heaven without exerting the effort involved in living a Catholic life. His entrance to heaven is ostensibly guaranteed through his deathbed baptism, because baptism washes away any sins committed during life. That is why this phenomenon is called "heaven theft," reflecting women's envious feeling toward these men who do not strive hard to gain faith. For these women, this action is akin to a "theft," not a legitimate way to gain a precious thing.

Izumi-san told me one of these stories of heaven theft. Izumi-san's chiropractor was a man who had no interest whatsoever in faith. His wife, however, was a devout Catholic and also the only Christian in the family. Approaching death, he said to his wife: "When I die, isn't it better if I go to the same place with you?" (*Yappari bokumo shindara kimito onajitokoroni ittahōga iiyonee.*) After this conversation, the wife called a Catholic priest from her church to baptize her husband. To the wife's great surprise, all of their children who were there at their father's deathbed expressed their desire to receive baptism together with their dying father. The priest accepted this wish of the family, and they were baptized at once. After telling me this story, Izumi-san said: "Isn't this mysterious? Nobody thought of this ending for my chiropractor! Look what happened, though. All the family, including the children, received baptism right there!" For Izumi-san, this episode was a miraculous act of divine origin.

Significantly, in this case, it was the woman of the house, the wife and mother, who became the catalyst for the baptism of the whole family. This kind of story is not unusual within the Archdiocese of Tokyo. The conversation among three housewives with which I opened this chapter also included the story of a man, Yoshimoto-san, who was visiting the church with his wife. He instantaneously accepted the priest's suggestion of baptism, and his son was envious of his father for receiving baptism without arduous catechism study. It is obvious that in both these examples, if the wife had not been a devout Catholic, nobody in the family would have become Catholic. In the case of deathbed conversions, it is difficult to ascertain whether the men involved share the Church's orthodox understanding of baptism and its significance or whether they accept baptism for personal reasons.

Many Catholic women in Tokyo state that their husbands promise to go to the church after retirement or promise to receive baptism on their deathbed. Mita-san's husband is a busy *sararīman* in Tokyo. According to Mita-san, he wakes up at 5:30 a.m., takes the 6:30 a.m. train to work, and after an hour and a half of commuting arrives in his office just after 8:00 a.m. He sorts out all incoming e-mails and returns some of the e-mails; then, by the time all other staff come in, it is 9:00 a.m., the official time to begin work. After a day's work, Mita-san's husband returns home at about 8:30 p.m. When she asked him about the possibility of conversion to Catholicism, he said, "perhaps later." She talked about his faith:

> I don't persuade him [to become Catholic] nor invite him [to the faith]. I don't like coercion. I think we have a freedom of faith and I don't like inviting somebody who is not interested. But my daughter became like this [i.e., she passed away and her remains are in the crypt of the church], and she had faith. When we have a memorial mass, he would come and attend.
>
> For now, it is difficult [for him] to have religion because of [the situations of] Japanese companies. If you acquire faith when you are young, it is manageable, but if you want to explore faith when you attain a certain age—especially when you are near retirement—it is difficult to keep the balance [between commitment to work and exploration of the faith].

As we saw earlier, Mita-san's daughter rests in the crypt of Our Lady of the Assumption. When her daughter passed away, the family purchased a large plot in the crypt that could house the ashes of up to five people. Mita-san thinks that her husband will come to catechism after his retirement and will eventually convert to the Catholic faith.[15] She explained that her husband is a graduate of the English literature department and thus is familiar with Christianity through reading English literature.

Fujimi-san's husband presents us with a different pattern. If you recall her story, he violently rejected his wife's visits to a Christian church. Later, when she asked if she could receive baptism, he said, "You may do so as long as you can pretend that I did not know." He then added that she could be baptized but was not allowed to attend church on Sundays. She continues to be the only Christian in the family. The husband repeatedly told his wife that he would have a Buddhist funeral for her if she died before him. Fujimi-san, however, believes that he has now changed his view. The change occurred in conjunction with the purchase of a cemetery plot. Her husband was the oldest son of his family, but the second son had taken over the family business. This succession by the second son took away the privilege and responsibility of Fujimi-san's husband to take over the family grave, because the second son took over the paternal succession line. Fujimi-san and her husband, therefore, needed to find a grave for themselves. The only plot they liked was in the crypt of Our Lady of the Assumption. After exhaustive research, Fujimi-san told her husband that he could be baptized just before he dies (therefore, he does not have to take any responsibility for being a Christian). To Fujimi-san's surprise, he agreed. The couple purchased the spot in the crypt, and she thinks that she did unexpectedly well to get her husband to consent to become Catholic when the time comes. She said mischievously, "I heard it later that you do not have to be a member of the church to be buried there. Well, I did quite well [to convince my husband to receive baptism], because I honestly thought you had to be a member." Fujimi-san now thinks that she would have a Catholic funeral even if she dies before her husband.

Analyzing the gender dichotomy within Japanese society, where husbands work long hours and women stay home to take care of children and other domestic affairs, Allison writes:

> Women who have endured affairs and long absences, with little companionship from their husbands, have often learned how to live and manage on their own. With children raised and money perhaps saved, they are less dependent on husbands than husbands are on them. A man at the age of retirement, by contrast, has been taken care of for long years by the company to which he's been attached, by women in the nightlife who have coddled and flattered him at night, and by a wife who has raised the children and managed the house largely by herself. For this he has obviously paid the price of his labor, but once he is no longer working and making the money to exchange for and justify these various dependencies, he is in a weakened and socially vulnerable position. (Allison 1994, 197)

Although my data are mostly drawn from interviews and interactions with women, I could discern vulnerable men behind these women whom I met in Tokyo. As Allison discovered studying men in a Tokyo nightclub (Allison 1994) and Ogasawara found in large Tokyo corporations (Ogasawara 1998), the extreme gendered division of labor, ironically enough, makes men dependent on women. Unlike the women I encountered in my study, who are able to pursue their spiritual interests, the majority of men cannot afford such freedom because of the time constraints of their long working hours. As Mita-san's husband's case shows, men consider the possibility of taking catechism classes after retirement and/or, like Fujimi-san's husband, promise to be baptized on their deathbed.

The home has been an important domain of cultic affairs in Japan. One of the major reasons behind this practice is historical. During the period of Christian persecution, each household (*ie*) had to register all the members of the household with a local temple to prove that there were no Christians. The practice of using the household (*ie*) as a unit of religious practice has continued to the present day, and contemporary Japanese Buddhists also maintain this practice. As I conduct my fieldwork, I learn that the practice of making the domain of home as a cultic sphere has many layers of meaning for the women I studied.

In the contemporary gendered division of labor, cultic affairs fall under the responsibilities of women. Women are the ones who follow annual calendrical rituals such as visiting Buddhist cemeteries, donating money to nearby Shinto shrines, and making sure the ancestors' rituals are conducted in prescribed years. Mita-san, for example, organized memorial masses for her deceased daughter by contacting a priest, ordering small gifts to give out to the visitors, and asking her church friends to come and participate in the mass. Hashimoto-san did the same for her husband's one-year anniversary, as her husband had also converted close to the end of his long life. Fujimi-san, who is the only Christian in her household, continues to carry out her duties by visiting Buddhist temples for both sides of her family. She says that she continues to visit temples for the week of *obon* (the midsummer week for the dead) and *higan* (the spring and autumn equinoxes). She adds that her husband's brothers have no idea that she is Christian; and for her part, she has no problem visiting both Buddhist temples and Christian churches.

Fujimi-san nicely summarized the position of these women when she told me about her morning prayers. She has set up her own Christian altar using a decorative shelf that she received when she was married. She wakes up every morning at 4:00 a.m. and offers freshly cooked rice when available and the first water to the Christian altar just like her mother did to a local Shinto deity. Fujimi-san then offers prayers to God. Describing her feelings toward this ritual, she said:

> I offer this [rice and water to the altar] on behalf of my family. Thank you. This rice is a source of life. Sacrifice from this world; something that sustains us in the path in which we are

transformed from the life that is given to death to the life of eternal living; [transformed from] the mind that inclined to sins to the mind of Jesus. I receive this [rice], and thank [God]. I offer thanks. This is a joy as a wife, mother, and housewife to be able to receive this rice as family food; I offer this [thanks and offering] with joy. We are also priests [*saishi*], given a spirit of the high priest [*daisaishi*] Jesus. I give thanks as a priest, for being given rice, for being blessed by Jesus, sustaining our lives. I give thanks.

Like Tanaka-san, who thought that one Christian in the household could keep the entire family safe with her prayers, Fujimi-san also believes in her role as a priestess in her household. She believes she received the spirit of Jesus through baptism, which makes her holy.[16] She calls herself "priest" and offers prayers on behalf of all of her family members, who are not necessarily Christian, let alone Catholic.

As I have illustrated in this chapter, the gender dichotomy seen in mainstream Japanese society is replicated within the Roman Catholic Church in Tokyo. The majority of church activities during the daytime are supported by women who can carve out free time during weekdays. Men, on the other hand, contribute much less time to the church before retirement, when they are free to participate in church activities. Two distinct gender ideals, formed through historical discursive processes in Japan, have different impacts on male and female conversion to Catholicism. Roman Catholicism in Tokyo has acquired the image of femininity over time. This image, along with Catholic teachings about meekness, which is a feminine attribute in the Japanese traditional Confucian-based worldview, makes it culturally appropriate for women to convert to Roman Catholicism. On the contrary, both the feminine image of Catholicism and its teaching of meekness are dissimilar to the popular ideal of manhood in Japan. This dissonance constitutes part of the reason why it is more difficult for men to convert to Catholicism in Tokyo. Often, women may remain only Christians in their households. As wives and mothers, however, their actions impact male members of the households, leading some men to eventually convert to Roman Catholicism.

In the next chapter, I continue to explore the ways in which Roman Catholics in Tokyo embrace a seemingly inherent contradiction of being Catholic and Japanese simultaneously. Striking a balance between a Confucian-based worldview and that of Catholicism, Tokyo Catholics negotiate their identity with a variety of means. In exploring this negotiation, I pay close attention to the historical consciousness of the laity, which significantly affects ways of being Catholic in Tokyo.

Chapter 5

Private Faith and the Legacy of Persecution

> "He who loves father or mother more than me is not worthy of me; and he who loves son or daughter more than me is not worthy of me; and he who does not take his cross and follow me is not worthy of me."
>
> —The Gospel according to Matthew 10, 37–39.

Kawamoto-san is a woman in her sixties. Like many other women I met in Tokyo, she is married with children, and her life is primarily rooted in her family. In the kitchen of the parish church that I was visiting, Kawamoto-san confided to me while we were doing dishes together: "I was a 'hidden Christian' at home for fourteen years." Instead of directly answering my questions, Kawamoto-san continued.

> I guess I did not want my family to prevent me from going to church. On Sundays, I told my family I was going shopping. Because, otherwise, they might have said something [against it] and I did not want to risk my opportunity to attend church."

Kawamoto-san originally had no intention of revealing her religious identity to her husband, but this situation came to an abrupt end. One of her husband's colleagues attended the same church as Kawamoto-san. Although she has a common family name, one of the *kanji* characters used in her name is uncommon. Noticing an unusual *kanji* character in her family name, her husband's colleague thought that she might be related to Mr. Kawamoto and posed the question to him. Kawamoto-san told me, "So, one day, my husband asked me: 'Are you Elizabeth?'" She laughed about this incident.

Kawamoto-san is not an isolated case. It is not uncommon among female members of the Catholic Church in Tokyo to conceal their religious identity from their family, relatives, and colleagues. As the only Catholics in their households or their workplace, these women frequently decide not to tell even their family members about their conversion. Building on previous scholarship on the Japanese sense of self as primarily "relational" (Kondo 1990), this chapter argues that by concealing their Catholic identity, these women maintain their socially assigned role as *yome*, or the wife and daughter-in-law of a household, in the primarily Buddhist cultic context of Japan.

One of the challenges that these women have to face is the issue of funerals and graves. Some Catholic women receive both a Buddhist funeral and a Christian memorial mass. Interestingly enough, this practice parallels that of the "hidden Christians" over the centuries who received Buddhist funerals to disguise their Catholic identity during the persecution period. This chapter demonstrates that the legacy of persecution of Japanese Christians in previous centuries still haunts present-day Catholics through their historical consciousness as a minority group and also through the strong ties that the government instituted between Buddhist temples, graves, and households. This chapter also relates contemporary religious expressions of Japanese Catholics in Tokyo to the changes instituted by the Second Vatican Council.

Private Faith in Tokyo

Kawamoto-san's story highlights the extent to which Japanese Catholics may strive to conceal their religious identity. As discussed in earlier chapters, many people hide their identity as Catholics in a variety of social settings. In chapter 4, we saw the case of Mr. Kikuchi, who was told by his baptismal sponsor that he did not have to reveal his new Catholic religious identity to anyone. Mr. Kikuchi was relieved to hear this instruction, as in his mind, a Catholic identity did not suit his role as president of a construction company (the meekness associated with Christian imagery contradicted the masculinity necessary for the president of a construction company).

A funeral is one of the occasions where one's religious identity becomes public. When Japanese Catholics attend Buddhist funerals in Tokyo, whether or not to take a *juzu* (Buddhist prayer beads) can pose a dilemma. During a discussion with five women, some said they would rather take a rosary to a Buddhist funeral and pray, but many said that they would prefer to take a *juzu*. Mika-san, for example, said that she could never imagine taking her rosary to a Buddhist funeral. In her words, "Well, for me, because it is a Buddhist funeral, and it [*juzu*] is a part of Buddhist funeral attire. There are a set of things to bring to a [Buddhist] funeral. I would never imagine taking a rosary [to a Buddhist funeral]." A few others said they take their rosaries and pray, but make sure that the crosses on their rosary are hidden from others' view.

Mrs. Kikuchi provided us with an interesting episode involving Mr. Kikuchi and a *juzu*. This episode suggests that even when most of one's immediate family is Christian, one may choose to pretend that he or she is part of the Buddhist-Shinto majority. Mr. Kikuchi took his *juzu* to his brother-in-law's Buddhist funeral. According to Mrs. Kikuchi, in the middle of a long Buddhist service, Mr. Kikuchi approached a Catholic priest who was attending the service and whispered to him. Here is what Mrs. Kikuchi said about this episode:

> So my husband was attending the funeral with a *juzu* in his hand because it was a Buddhist funeral. But, he goes to a [Catholic] father [who was attending the Buddhist funeral] and asked him something, right? "Father? Doesn't a *juzu* resemble a rosary?" And, the father goes, "Oh yes. Would you like me to change this *juzu* into a rosary?" Then, the father touched the rosary, said prayers, and then, "There you go, here is your rosary." Meanwhile, my mother-in-law was observing all this, and asking her son what he was doing. Then, she goes, "Could you change mine as well?" Then, the father [did the same to her mother-in-law's Buddhist prayer beads, and] goes, "Here you are" [giving her back a *juzu*-turned-into-a-rosary]. [laughter]

Mrs. Kikuchi, who told me this story, did not seem to have asked the priest to also perform this "transformation of *juzu* into a rosary" for herself. She was telling me about this episode in a spirit of poking fun and sharing some interesting stories for my research.[1] I should note that this practice of turning Buddhist prayer beads into rosaries is *not* a norm in the Archdiocese of Tokyo. The priest involved was well into his nineties and is known for his eccentric character, and Mrs. Kikuchi was also sharing this story as an illustration of this priest's humorous idiosyncrasies. For my part, I record this story to illustrate the ambivalence that Roman Catholics in Tokyo feel about their Catholic identity in what they perceive to be a hostile environment to Christians.

This issue of revealing one's identity as Catholic also arose during my interview with Okada-san, a mother of two whose husband suffers from a mental disability. She clearly stated that she would not tell her friends about attending church, for example, when they are making a date to play tennis. She said, "If I were asked why [I cannot play on a certain day], I would just say that I cannot make it on that day, and I wouldn't mention why I cannot make it." Okada-san was wearing many pieces of jewelry that either include a cross or resemble a rosary. I asked her reason for not telling others about her religious identity. She said: "I think what I know of the Catholic faith and what others would imagine as Catholicism are two different things. I do not want others to think that 'Ah, Okada-san is a Catholic . . .'" I further asked, "What do you mean by the 'Catholicism in other people's imagination'?" Okada-san responded: "The fact that I have 'religion' (*shūkyō*) would be considered special (*tokubetsu*). People would look at me as 'Catholic,' you know." But then, Okada-san added: "If I was asked whether I am a Catholic, I would say yes." While she was carrying on this conversation, I could not help but notice the obvious Christian symbols in her jewelry. I asked if she wears this jewelry only once a week when she goes to church. She answered in the negative to my question, stating, "Nobody would say anything about them [crosses or rosary]. Some people say, 'You must like crosses' and I say, 'Yes, I do.'" She smiled. On her neck, there was a cross on a chain, and on her wrist and fingers, there were more than five pieces of jewelry that had a rosary design.

This theme of what I call a "private faith" emerged early in my fieldwork and persisted until its end. In this chapter, I identify a few sociohistorical contexts that contribute to the formation of this tendency to conceal one's religious identity as Catholics in Tokyo. I should caution that my observations on private faith may not be valid beyond the Archdiocese of Tokyo and its surrounding areas. I speculate that this aspect of the Catholic faith might not be observed, for example, in the Archdiocese of Nagasaki, although it might exist in other urban centers such as Osaka. This type of individually oriented private faith could be intrinsically related to the conditions of urban life in Tokyo. To unravel the construction of "private faith," it is necessary to situate contemporary Tokyo Catholics in their historical and political contexts. First, I discuss the issue of religion in the context of postwar Japan.

Historical Consciousness and the Issue of Religion in Japan

Many Japanese Catholic women told me that they find a large gap between what they have experienced of the Christian faith and what others think of as Christianity or even as "religion." In Kawamoto-san's words, "ordinary non-Christian Japanese have a prejudice against [Christians]." Moreover, according to Okada-san, another convert to Catholicism, Japanese people "point fingers" at those who practice religion. Here, Okada-san does not mean people who participate in popular religious expressions such as going to Shinto shrines for New Year's and Buddhist temples for *obon*. She asked me frankly: "For example, if you find out that somebody belongs to Sōka Gakkai,[2] would you tell your friends that she or he is a Sōka Gakkai member?" Here, Okada-san is arguably placing Roman Catholicism and Sōka Gakkai on the same level by considering them both as religious institutions with which one can choose to be affiliated.[3]

As Robert Kisala (2006) has pointed out and as Okada-san's earlier comment illustrates, the popular image of the concept or category of "religion" (*shūkyō*) in Japan is negative to say the least. I even heard about a young girl in elementary school who pleaded with her mother not to tell anybody that she was a Christian after hearing her teacher talk about the Aum Affair and religion.[4] Christianity occupies an ambiguous position in this discourse on "religion" in contemporary Japan. For example, evangelical Christian messages are broadcast through loudspeakers at busy intersections of downtown Tokyo, and many people detest such an overt proclamation of an unfamiliar religious faith. Others accept the legitimacy of Roman Catholicism with a certain reverence because of its relationship to Western art and civilization. Historically, however, Christianity—regarded as "religion" par excellence—has been the main target of a general hostility toward "religion." Throughout the modern period, this hostility was sanctioned, and persecution of Christians was spearheaded, by the state of Japan. Starting in the early seventeenth century, the government enforced the outright and full-scale persecution of Christianity for roughly two and a half centuries. During this period, many Christians lost their lives to torture, execution, and starvation. As a means of survival, some Christians went underground to conceal their religious identity and disguised themselves as Buddhists. These underground Christians are called "hidden Christians" or *kakure kirishitan* (Gonoi 1990). Kawamoto-san, quoted earlier, in a humorous analogy referred to herself as a *kakure* of the twenty-first century, hiding from potential persecution from her own family. Although in the mid-nineteenth century the newly formed Meiji government was forced to rescind its anti-Christian decrees in response to condemnation from Western nations, in reality, the persecution of Christians continued during the Meiji (1868–1912), Taisho (1912–1926) and early Shōwa (1926–end of war) Periods. During the rise of nationalism and ultra-nationalism in the 1930s and 1940s, Christians were accused of pledging their loyalty to a figure other than the Japanese emperor, whom the state portrayed as a living deity. In the postwar period, Christianity never recovered from the damage to its popular image in the past.

Although the *kakure* appears to be part of the distant past, the notion of persecution still lingers among those Catholics I met in Tokyo. Kaneta-san told me of her family's experience of persecution in the southern island of Amami Ōshima during the 1940s. Located roughly midway between the Okinawa Islands and Kagoshima prefecture, her native island was a home to several Roman Catholic communities.[5] During World War II, the Japanese navy stationed forces on the island, and it promoted severe persecutions of Christians there. According to Kaneta-san, churches were burned, the church-run women's school was closed, and all the priests were expelled from the island on the allegation of being spies for enemy nations. In addition, she told me stories of houses being doused by water using a fire truck to intimidate Christians. Under the guise of "practice drills," the army targeted Christian homes to practice for "extinguishing an enemy fire."[6] When asked if she herself had experienced these persecutions, she answered in the negative. "No, no. The stories were told and retold." Kaneta-san had not even been born at the time. I asked her where she had heard these stories, and she said: "From my grandfather, and my mother. My uncle and my mother."

Then Kaneta-san added something intriguing: "Ah, and my mother and uncle did not step on *fumie*." *Fumie*, or the requirement of stepping on a Christian icon, was one of the methods used to identify Christians—who would refuse to commit this sacrilege—during the time of the shoguns. But according to Kaneta-san, the practice was in use even during the early years of the Shōwa. Later on, however, I learned that she was talking about a document called *Notice of Religious Conversion* (*shūkyō henkō todoke*). A Japanese writer, Kosakai Sumi, depicts how the "*fumie* of the Shōwa Period" was conducted in Amami in the 1940s in her book *The Island of "Mary of Sorrow"*:

> Eight days after the speech, on December 10, Commander Kasa and Kakuwa Staff Officer, accompanied by Provost Sergeant Yamamoto Tadayoshi who is the Director of Nase Division of Military Police came to Ōkuma again, and they gathered all villagers on the sea shore. They set up a rope in the middle, and they divided Christians on one side and non-Christians on the other. After another speech by these army personnel, the section head [of the village] raised his voice and said:

> "Because we have Catholics [in our community], our peace and order are at risk. At this time of [national] emergency, you [Catholics] must pledge to sign the *Notice of Religious Conversion* in front of Commander and Kakuwa Lieutenant Commander! Otherwise, we will kill you!" (Kosakai 1984, 174)

Kosakai reports that all the parishioners in this community reluctantly signed this document. She further notes that many interviewees confided to her that they felt they would have been killed otherwise (1984, 174). Kaneta-san did not refer to this document, but what her mother and uncle encountered must have been this "*fumie* of the Shōwa Period" and not the actual stepping on icons of Mary and Jesus practiced in the Edo Period. Kaneta-san's family, however, must have referred to this forceful signing of the document as *fumie* when she was growing up listening to these stories. Although Kaneta-san herself did not experience such severe persecution from the Imperial Japanese Army, she has kept this fearful memory alive by telling and retelling these stories to her family and her close friends.[7] Kaneta-san explained her fear about expressing her religious identity to non-Christian Japanese with illustrations from her family's legacy of persecution on Amami Ōshima.

References to hidden Christians or historical persecution were often made by other Catholics I met in Tokyo. Even people who, unlike Kaneta-san, have no family experience of political persecution make connections between themselves and hidden Christians and religious persecutions when talking about their Catholic identity. For example, Professor Ōnishi, who became Catholic when he heard the call from Christ at the Eiheiji Buddhist Temple during meditation,[8] told me about his determination to be a devout Catholic in the following terms:

> But being Catholic comes with numerous and different baggage. In the long history of the Church, so much has happened. As a continuation of that long journey, if there happens to be another impeachment or persecution, I am determined to accept that. Although, if it really were to happen, I am not sure if I would be able to truly stick with my determination [laughter]. But, as for now, I am determined.

As seen in the examples of Kaneta-san and Professor Ōnishi, references to hidden Christians or the possibility of persecution are often mentioned in discussions of one's identity as a Roman Catholic. The analogy that Kawamoto-san made between herself and hidden Christians should be understood within this context. Although the historical hidden Christians belong to the distant past, many Catholics I encountered in 2006 and 2007 still used this concept in conversations about their identity. Along with the negative profile of "religion" in Japan, the trajectory that the Roman Catholic Church has taken in Japanese history strongly influences contemporary Catholics' construction of religious identity in Tokyo.

Good *Yome* and Christian Simultaneously?

In chapter 4, I introduced the construction of Japanese womanhood. In particular, I discussed the ways in which ideals of Japanese womanhood resonate with Catholic ideals embodied in the figure of Mary, who can be understood, first and foremost, as a caring mother. In the current chapter, I explore yet another aspect of being a Japanese woman in contemporary Tokyo and being Catholic at the same time. This facet of womanhood relates to the construction of identity as a *yome*. The most common English translation of this word *yome* is "daughter-in-law." As the *kanji* character suggests,[9] however, what this word signifies in the Japanese context is a woman of the household who takes care of household affairs. In the context of urban Tokyo, where most households are nuclear families, the role of *yome* is more centered on the duties of a wife and mother and less on those of a daughter-in-law, because the in-laws do not reside in the same household. Nevertheless, a *yome* does play the role of daughter-in-law whenever needed. A woman's role as *yome* potentially conflicts with her identity as a Roman Catholic when she is the only Christian at home, because women often play a vital role in maintaining the cultic affairs of the household. Two areas of scholarship constitute the contexts of my discussion, namely, scholarship on the Japanese sense of self and scholarship on Japanese religious expressions. As I have noted in chapter 4, the majority of the women I studied in Roman Catholic parishes are the only Christians among their families. Building on ongoing scholarly discussions on the Japanese sense of self, it is in their "relational" roles as mothers and wives that I situate my interlocutors in describing their identity as Roman Catholics (cf. Allison 1991, 1996, Borovoy 2005, Hamabata 1990, Kondo 1990, Lebra 1984, Rosenberger 2001).

What would it take for a woman to be a good *yome* in the context of popular religious expressions in Tokyo? As discussed in chapter 4, in contemporary Tokyo, cultic affairs often fall under the responsibility of women in the gendered division of labor. Women are the ones who are responsible for various rituals such as visiting Buddhist cemeteries, donating money to nearby Shinto shrines, and making sure the ancestors' rituals are conducted in prescribed years (cf. Traphagan 2004). We saw Hashimoto-san organizing her husband's one-year anniversary mass and Mita-san organizing the anniversary of her daughter's death, distributing her memorial gifts at the end of the mass in chapter 2. In his work on the aging population in the Tōhoku area, Traphagan persuasively argues that "Japanese religious activity [. . .] should be viewed as a mean of enacting concern (emotional, obligational, or otherwise) through ritual performance." Observing various traditional religious activities in the Tōhoku area, Traphagan notes:

> The emphasis is fundamentally not directed towards the deities. Instead, one does *omairi* [to pray], purchases an *omamori* [talisman], or write an *ema* [votive note] as a means of expressing the interconnectedness of people with the world around them, particularly with the other people, both dead and alive, with whom one has a close relationship. (Traphagan 2004, 125)

In analyzing the dreams of ancestors that older women have, Traphagan further writes that middle-aged and older women often take on the role of caretaker of the collective well-being of the family and become the ones who enact these concerns for the living and the dead (2004, 130).

What Traphagan describes is also witnessed through the daily lives of my research participants. In making sure that the memory of her husband would live on, at his memorial mass, Hashimoto-san distributed booklets that narrated her husband's life achievements. Likewise, as we saw at the end of chapter 4, Fujimi-san offers freshly cooked rice and the first water to her house altar every morning and prays for the sake of the entire family. As Fujimi-san herself articulated, she does this as a wife, mother, and housewife who is responsible for the well-being of the family. In the case of Fujimi-san, her family came to appreciate her morning prayers. When she was hospitalized for a subarachnoid hemorrhage, her husband commanded his children to offer rice and water to Fujimi-san's Christian house altar. These rituals at home or at religious institutions can be construed as a "means of enacting concern through ritual performance" (cf. Traphagan 2004, 125). What may be different in these Catholic examples from Traphagan's cases is that Fujimi-san clearly directs her prayers to a deity: Jesus. It is noteworthy that her non-Christian husband ordered his children to offer rice and water to the altar, but did not direct them to pray to the deity.

Traditionally, various concerns are enacted by attending Buddhist house altars, washing Buddhist tombstones, and buying talismans at Shinto shrines (Reader 1991; 1995). By engaging in these activities, one is able to demonstrate to onlookers that he or she cares about the living and/or the dead. For example, a *yome* who offers tea and rice at her Buddhist house altar will be admired for her filial piety to her ancestors who are enshrined there. When women shift their religious allegiance from the traditionally prescribed Buddhist-centered one to Christianity, even if they are able to enact the same concern through ritual means at Christian churches, such behaviors may not register with their loved ones as being equivalent to traditional rituals. A woman praying on her own at church would not be viewed as "enacting concern"; on the contrary, she might look "selfish" because of the absence of traditional idioms associated with "enacting concerns." In other words, women can risk endangering their perceived role as the spiritual caretaker of the family. In particular, the family dead are not located in the churchyard but often at Buddhist cemeteries. A woman's religious affiliation, therefore, is not an issue for herself only, but also for the entire family. In other words, by becoming Catholic, these women have to risk the potential accusation of being an "irresponsible" *yome* who does not take proper care of the family's well-being.

Interestingly, none of my research participants explained how she dealt with the issue of family in these terms. Instead, many declared that there is no conflict between being Catholic and Japanese at the same time. In reality, however, Catholic women do resort to various strategies to overcome this conflict. I suggest that concealing their religious identity is one of the strategies they use to cope with the potential accusation of being an "irresponsible" *yome*. For example, Fujimi-san continued to visit Buddhist temples associated with both sides of the family during the prescribed seasons of *obon* and *higan*. She said that she felt no contradiction in doing so. And in addition, she said: "My husband's siblings know nothing [about her conversion to Catholicism]."

By attending to Buddhist cemeteries and [Buddhist] house altars, women fulfill their duties as daughters-in-laws and *yome*. For those women, therefore, it is easier not to reveal their identities and to fulfill expected roles. To learn more about their strategies and the dilemma of being a good *yome* and Catholic simultaneously, I turn to the issue of the grave.

"Grave" Problems

The strategy of concealing one's religious identity as Catholic may be adopted while one is alive, but what will happen at these Catholic women's funerals when they die? What about their burial plots? As devout Catholics, these women wish to receive Catholic funerals. Moreover, as many have told me, they think it would be ideal to be placed in one of the spots in the crypt of their parish church, above which masses are conducted daily. But in reality, the issues regarding funerals and graves are complicated matters when a woman is the only connection in the family to the Catholic Church. Many households still maintain the state-instituted links between households and Buddhist temples for funerals and burials that date from the Tokugawa Era[10] (cf. Covell 2005; Hur 2007; Sasaki 2004).

In his 1968 publication, Japanese ethnologist and historian Takeda Chōshū forthrightly argues that the *ie* has been a focal point of religious life in Japan throughout its modern history (1968). As Takeda has successfully illustrated, the *ie* has been a vehicle of religious practice in Japanese society, especially for ancestor worship. This importance continued after World War II, when the *ie* system was largely abolished (cf. Smith 1974, Traphagan 2004). Takeda identifies one of the historical moments that tied the knot between the unit of the *ie* and religion in the decrees of the Tokugawa Shogunate, which demanded that each *ie* maintain one *butsudan* or Buddhist house altar, conduct ancestor worship, and register its members with a local Buddhist temple. The decrees not only ensured that parishioners had formal ties to their temple, but also mandated the practice of domestic ancestor worship supplemented by the performance of important rituals by ritual specialists on certain memorial occasions (Takeda 1976; Hur 2007). In other words, this temple certification system (*danka seido*) instituted an intimate relationship between the household and the temple for subsequent generations. Takeda notes that through the implementation of these decrees, any household, even those with insignificant economic activities, became *ie*. In other words, the idea of *ie* took root among the populace through these policies. The implementation of these decrees ensured that no Christians survived the persecution by the Tokugawa government (Takeda 1976). Rowe states that this temple certification system "formed the basis of the social and political role of temples and has been the defining characteristic of temple-family relationship in Japan for the past 300 years" (Rowe 2009, 21). Even in 2006 and 2007 when I conducted fieldwork, the legacy of these anti-Christian decrees can be discerned through the ties that still conventionally exist between the *ie*, Japanese Buddhist temples, and graves.

I observed a variety of responses from Catholic women to the dilemma of where to be buried. Hashimoto-san (encountered in chapter 3) explained to me how she had managed to secure a spot in the crypt right next to a close female friend from the parish. I knew, however, that her husband's remains had been buried in Aoyama Municipal Cemetery a year earlier. When I asked about her husband's grave, she replied defensively that she needs to be buried with her husband in Aoyama Cemetery as a member of the House of Hashimoto. She continued by saying, however, that she will split her ashes in half and plans to place some in the Aoyama Cemetery, where her husband lies, and the rest in the crypt of her parish church, where she has secured a spot very close to those of several priests. Fujimi-san, like many other women, says that it does not matter whether she receives a Buddhist or Catholic funeral; God will know that she is a devout Catholic no matter what kind of ceremony she receives. As noted in the last chapter, however, Fujimi-san managed to convince her husband to promise to convert to Catholicism when the time comes for him to die. This promise, she assumes, increases her chance of receiving a Catholic funeral.

In his article "Grave Changes," Rowe (2003) comments on sociologist Inoue Haruyo's studies of the religious choices of women who are married into their husband's households. Inoue points out that these women do not possess freedom of belief in a true sense of the word. Referring to the remnant of the temple certification system, Inoue says that "it was not people, but rather graves that were held hostage" by the patron temple (quoted in Rowe 2003, 95–96). Inoue points to the importance of the household system in creating and sustaining funerary Buddhism in Japan and relates this to the discrimination that people without descendants face in buying a temple burial spot. The Catholic women I encountered in Tokyo did strive for freedom of belief by converting to Roman Catholicism. What they have to face in terms of their choice of grave site is yet another story.

One solution is to receive both Buddhist and Catholic rituals. According to several respondents, it is not uncommon to have a Buddhist funeral for the sake of the surviving family and then hold a Catholic memorial mass for the deceased's sake. Describing Buddhist funerary and memorial rites in Japan, Sasaki points out that "for general [Japanese] Buddhist lay people, funerary rites are the work to transform the family dead into a buddha (*hotoke*) or ancestor by entrusting them in the hands of Buddhism" (2004: 18). By undergoing Buddhist funerary rites, the dead themselves become solidly anchored in the Other World, the world of the dead. In due time and with repeated memorial rites, these dead family members will become guardian figures to protect their clans (Sasaki 2004, 18). I agree with Sasaki that this is a popular understanding of the role of Buddhist funerary and memorial rites in Japan.

I would add another element to Sasaki's descriptions of the Japanese popular understanding of death. Death in the context of Buddhist funerary and memorial rites is something to be tamed, and the dead person's spirit is something to be placated. In other words, there is an underlying fear of the dead. Buddhist rituals are conceived of as a mechanism to protect the living from the potential harm that the dead person's spirit may cause for the living (cf. Antoni 1993; Blacker 1986; Hardacre 1997; Mullins 2004). Viewed in the light of these popular (Buddhist) understandings of death, the funerary rites are conducted for the sake of the living. The family members need to transform the dead into an ancestor, anchored in the world of the dead, using familiar idioms of Buddhism, and at the hands of a Buddhist priest whose temple yard may be the resting place of the deceased.

For those Roman Catholic women I met, it seems that potential ritual efficacies that may be conceivably effected in a funeral mass—such as by having incense over one's casket or being sprinkled with holy water by a Catholic priest—seem not to be an issue. Those women seem resigned to the fact that they may not receive a Catholic funeral when they are the only Christians in their families. I should also note that these women are also under the influence of the Catholic Church, which teaches that death is a celebratory occasion through which one is transferred to a different realm. According to the catechism of the Catholic Church, when one dies a Christian, one is "away from the body and at home with the Lord" (CCC [Catechism of the Catholic Church] 1681). As in many other parts of the world, the priests in the Tokyo area tend to wear white vestments for funeral masses, signifying that funerals are celebratory occasions. This positive approach to death perhaps helps these women to care less about the actual rituals that they receive at the time of death, as seen in the case of Fujimi-san's utterance that it does not matter whether she receives a Buddhist or Catholic funeral.

In accommodating this reality, the Catholic Bishops' Conference of Japan authorizes Buddhist funerals for Catholic parishioners for the sake of the deceased's family in its *Catholic Church's Guide to Interreligious Dialogue: Practical Q & A* (Catholic Bishops' Conference of Japan 2009).

> Q:29 When the only Catholic in the family dies, what can we do in communicating with the church and asking for a Catholic funeral?
>
> A: We recommend that a Catholic member himself or herself talk about this beforehand with his or her family, Catholic friends, godparents, the parish priest and people who are relevant. It is advisable to ask your family to contact the church in advance.
>
> The parish church should conduct a funeral mass at the parish upon consultation with the deceased's family. When the family strongly wishes to conduct a Buddhist funeral, the parish may accept this. However, the parish members [*kyoukai kankeisha*] should conduct a memorial mass for the deceased person (2009, 66).

From this Q&A, it is apparent that having a Buddhist funeral and Catholic memorial mass afterward is a common occurrence (see also Catholic Bishops' Conference of Japan 1985, 22).[11]

It is somewhat ironic that contemporary Catholics need to have both a Buddhist funeral and Catholic memorial mass, as these dual rituals were practiced by hidden Christians. Until 1884, Christians were not allowed to conduct their own funerals. Even the Meiji government interpreted funerals as part of national rites, and its subjects had to conduct either Shinto or Buddhist funerals (Gonoi 1990, 266).

As seen in Hashimoto-san's narrative, where she expresses the necessity of being buried in a particular place as a member of the House of Hashimoto, Catholic women are willing to receive a Buddhist funeral and to be buried in a Buddhist cemetery as part of being a loyal member of the family. In the context of the *ie* and their role as *yome* within the *ie*, concealing their religious identity is a strategy and sometimes a necessity. Many married women would rather conceal their religious identity and perform their roles and fulfill responsibilities as *yome*. In response to these parishioners' realities, situated in the Buddhist majority of Japan, the Roman Catholic Church is also willing to compromise by accepting that its members receive Buddhist funerals. Now in this final section, I turn to the larger institutional context of the Roman Catholic Church in order to further situate private faith in Tokyo.

Religious Expressions in the Post-Vatican II Period

The historic meetings of the Second Vatican Council, or Vatican II, held by the leaders of the Church from 1962 to 1965 have brought a number of significant changes to the parish lives of ordinary Roman Catholics (Bokenkotter 2004, cf. Greeley 2004). These reforms, which aimed to modernize the Church, have had major implications on the religious expressions of contemporary Roman Catholics in Tokyo. To further contextualize "private faith" in Tokyo, two changes in the post–Vatican II period are discussed: the Church's position on non-Christian religious traditions and the emphasis on God's love instead of strict observance of rules.

Of the various major changes that were introduced as a result of the Second Vatican Council, one of the most influential for Japanese Catholics may have been the one set out in the Declaration on the Relationship of the Church to Non-Christian Religions (*Nostra Aetate*). Through this Declaration, the Church clearly departed from previously held positions in which it saw non-Christians as in need of conversion to Christianity. Robert A. Graham states: "[I]n this historic document, the Church affirms that all peoples of the earth with their various religions form one community; the Church respects the spiritual, moral, and cultural values of Hinduism, Buddhism and Islam" (Abbott 1966, 658). In other words, the Church now views the world as one community of humanity with diverse meaningful ideas about religion. This is a dramatic shift from previously held notions, which saw non-Christian traditions as fundamentally of a negative nature.

Describing Buddhism as the tradition that "acknowledges the radical insufficiency of this shifting world" (Abbott 1966, 662), the Declaration approves other religions as striving "variously to answer the restless searching of the human heart by proposing 'ways,' which consist of teachings, rules of life, and sacred ceremonies" (662). It is noteworthy that the Church not only gives explicit approval to Hinduism, Buddhism, Judaism, and Islam, but also tacitly approves of "other religions" as legitimate. The Church goes on to declare, "The Catholic Church rejects nothing which is true and holy in these religions" (662).

In response to this call for religious tolerance from the Vatican, the Catholic Bishops Conference of Japan has published a booklet titled *Catholic Guide regarding Ancestors and the Deceased* (1985) detailing for lay Catholics how to maintain the commemoration of deceased family members in the primarily Buddhist cultic context of Japan. Interestingly, in 2009, this booklet has been significantly expanded and published as *Catholic Church's Guide to Interreligious Dialogue: Practical Q & A* (2009). Unlike the booklet published in 1985, the newest book significantly enlarged its scope beyond the practice of "ancestor worship." The book includes such topics as Shinto, divination, the blessing of cars, prevention of suicide, and discrimination. The book covers detailed instructions on specific questions such as whether a child should carry a Shinto portable shrine (*mikoshi*) for a neighborhood festival when asked by neighbors (2009, 46) or whether it is acceptable to visit a Shinto shrine on January 1 (2009, 40). In addition, the latest book discusses other issues such as social justice, human rights, and, most interestingly, Islam.

Throughout the book, one witnesses the spirit of tolerance. The Bishops Conference of Japan approves of most of the traditional practices relating to "ancestor worship" in Japan, such as offering of rice, incense, and food to the house altar; requesting Buddhist monks to read Buddhist sutras at the family grave; and maintaining the existing Buddhist memorial tablets (called *ihai*). The Bishops' Conference allows Catholics in Japan to accompany non-Christian friends to offer respect at a Shinto shrine[12] on January 1, to set up a pair of *kadomatsu*,[13] or New Year decorations to welcome the spirit of the New Year, at one's gate, and even to donate money toward a local Shinto festival as a gesture of being a good neighbor. At Our Lady of the Assumption, the parish set up a pair of *kadomatsu* at the gate of the church for the New Year as if to set an example for its parishioners. For the Catholics who hide their religious identities in Tokyo, the official Church policies to approve accommodation of Buddhism and other religious traditions help, if not facilitate, in concealing their identities. Through these policies, one can say that Roman Catholics in Tokyo are allowed to behave like non-Christians, an option that may not be available to some Japanese Christians who belong to Protestant denominations.

Another aspect of the changes brought by the Church in the post–Vatican II period is the emphasis on the love of God and not on various rules and the hierarchical order of the Church. Writing about the Church before the Council, Greeley states: "in the minds of most of the laity and the clergy and those who were not Catholic, Catholicism before Vatican II was in fact a centralized, immutable, and sin- and rule-driven heritage" (2004, 50). According to Avery Dulles (Abbott 1966), this conception persisted in the work of the priests who were participating in the Council well into its early sessions. Commenting on the initial draft of the Dogmatic Constitution of the Church (*Lumen Gentium*), Dulles states that the initial draft reflected the centuries-old traditional emphasis on "the hierarchical and juridical aspects of the Church" (Abbott 1966, 10). During the meetings, however, this tendency was replaced by a "more biblical, more historical, more vital and dynamic" view of the Church. Eventually, the Constitution was written based on the idea of the Church as the "loving Mother of all" (Abbott 1966, 11).

Shimada-san, a woman who received an infant baptism in 1940 before the Second Vatican Council, described the difference between faiths in Tokyo and Nagasaki. She moved to Tokyo in 1964 when she was twenty-four years old while Vatican II was in progress. Although her narrative does not include the changes brought by the Second Vatican Council, the stark contrast between faith in Nagasaki pre-1964 and faith in Tokyo post-1964 that she discussed is suggestive of the changes that Vatican II brought to Roman Catholics in Tokyo:

> In Nagasaki, there are a lot of restrictions; you can't do this, or can't do that. But in Tokyo, it is stressed that you do not do things that others would dislike. In Tokyo, I think it is important to do things that would make others happy. The faith in Nagasaki is something that one goes inside [compared to that of Tokyo] (*uchini komoru shinkō*). For example, in Tokyo, people would say that it is better to attend your friend's wedding [on Sunday], but in Nagasaki, the church has to be an utmost priority on Sundays. So, I would say [to a friend], "I am sorry, but I cannot attend [your wedding]" or "I'll come a bit late." In Tokyo, [people would say that] it would be better to attend your friend's wedding to make your friend happy. In that case, it is more important to attend the wedding than to attend the church. That kind of difference? So, I have been relieved tremendously after I moved to Tokyo [as there are significantly less restrictions put on my social life by the Church].

Although Shimada-san's narrative does not specifically involve Shinto or Buddhist contexts, she describes the ethos of faith in Tokyo as tolerant and having an emphasis on caring for one's neighbor. She conveyed that it is therefore much easier to be Catholic in Tokyo compared to what she knows about Nagasaki. Similar sentiments were expressed by another devout Catholic, Seto-san, who lives in the city of Nagasaki. When he visited Tokyo in the summer of 2007, commenting on the joyous attitude of Tokyo Catholics, Seto-san said "Wow, faith in Tokyo is very different from that of Nagasaki!" Both Shimada-san and Seto-san are descendants of *kirishitan* who were incarcerated for their faith during the persecution periods. Shimada-san's great-grandfather was captured in the persecution during the Meiji Period, and Seto-san is a descendant of a samurai *kirishitan*. According to both of them, faith in Nagasaki still carries traditions that go back many generations.[14]

While the Church officially appreciates Buddhism as a different "way" to a similar spiritual truth, and lay Catholics in Tokyo appear to be rather lax in observing their religious precepts, Tokyo Catholics are still reluctant to reveal their Catholic identity. The *Catholic Church's Guide to Interreligious Dialogue* also points to general difficulties to reveal one's identity as a Catholic. Q4 reads: "How can I live in a society in which my faith is not accepted?" The book answers: "First, you must live your life as a Christian, and this will be your testimony. When an opportunity arises, you assess a situation, and reveal your faith with courage, and talk about Christ" (2009, 39). These Q&As presuppose that the laity do not normally reveal their religious identities and gently encourage them to do so in appropriate circumstances. Through these Q&As, we can see that the Bishops' Conference of Japan acknowledges that it is difficult for Japanese Catholics to "come out" as Catholics.

Devout Catholics in Tokyo continue to suffer from the legacy of the hidden Christians, particularly through the issue of funerals and graves. The *ie* system that crystallized with the state's anti-Christian decrees still haunts present-day Christians through the problem of funerary rituals and the family grave site. This is particularly true with those whose ancestors are buried in the cemeteries of Buddhist temples. Changes brought by the Second Vatican Council—especially changes in the Church's position with respect to non-Christian traditions and the Church's emphasis on God's love over obedience to rules—do not necessarily make it easier for Tokyo Catholics to reveal their Catholic identities in various social settings in Japan.

Conclusion and Implications

On October 20, 1967, at 11:50 a.m., the former prime minister of Japan, Yoshida Shigeru, passed away at his home in the town of Ōiso, Kanagawa Prefecture, at age eighty-nine. Upon his death, his daughter, Asō Kazuko, called Fr. Hamao Fumio and invited him to conduct a rite of baptism for her father. A future cardinal, Fr. Hamao, arrived at the house and baptized Yoshida Shigeru, and he became Joseph Thomas More Yoshida Shigeru after his death on October 20. The Christian name "Joseph" was chosen by Shigeru himself many years prior to his baptism, and "Thomas More" was added by his family. Joseph Thomas More Yoshida Shigeru's private funeral was conducted at St. Mary's Cathedral in Tokyo on October 23, 1967, and the mass was attended by about 1,000 people, including his family and relatives, Prime Minister Satō Eisaku, foreign ambassadors, and important figures from the Japanese financial sector (Asahi Shimbunsha 1967).

Eight days later, on October 31, 1967, Shigeru's state funeral was conducted at Nippon Budokan in Tokyo. Satō Eisaku served as the chief mourner. This was the first state funeral conducted in Japan in the postwar period (Okazaki 2003). Between 1946 and 1954, Yoshida Shigeru served as the prime minister of Japan for seven years and two months. During his tenure as prime minister, the nation was directly under the influence of the occupation forces for four and a half years (Hara 2005, 230). It was during Shigeru's tenure as the minister of foreign affairs or prime minister that Japan had to receive General Douglas MacArthur, Supreme Commander of the Allied Powers (SCAP), negotiate the status of the emperor of Japan with the occupation forces, and create a new constitution in which Japan had to refashion itself as a democratic country. Yoshida Shigeru is remembered fondly by many as a prime minister who managed this difficult phase of the country's history smoothly and led the postwar economic recovery of the nation.

Commenting on Shigeru's conversion to Catholicism, Fr. Hamao reminisced about a conversation with Yoshida Shigeru in which he said: "not while I am alive, but when I am about to die, I'd like to snatch heaven" (Asahi Shimbunsha 1967). This expression, "stealing heaven," refers to the act of baptism on one's deathbed among Roman Catholics in the Tokyo area, as we saw earlier in this book. According to the priest, it is permitted to baptize a person at death, if the will to be baptized was clearly communicated while alive. Fr. Hamao further revealed Shigeru's strong ties to the Roman Catholic Church. When St. Mary's Cathedral of the Tokyo Archdiocese was being rebuilt,[1] Shigeru served as the head of its supporters' association. All members of the House of Yoshida, with the exception of the first son, Ken'ichi, are Roman Catholic, and according to Fr. Hamao, Shigeru held a favorable view of Roman Catholicism (Asahi Shimbunsha 1967). It then seems appropriate that his funeral was conducted in the Cathedral for which he served as the head of the supporters' association.

It was highly likely that Shigeru was surrounded by women who were committed to the Roman Catholic faith. Shigeru's first wife, Yoshida Yukiko, who passed away twenty-six years prior to his death, was known to have been a Catholic (Asō 1993). His daughter, Asō Kazuko, who served her father both privately and publicly after her mother's demise, is also known to have been devout. Fr. Hamao in his interview revealed that he knew Kazuko well, but was not so close to Shigeru, although they met for the first time in Italy while Fr. Hamao was still a seminarian in Rome (Asahi Shimbunsha 1967), an episode that may suggest that there were ongoing relationships between the priest and the Yoshida family members.

The conversion story of former Prime Minister Yoshida Shigeru bears a strong resemblance to the stories of Roman Catholic laypeople in Tokyo that I heard during the course of this study. Although I do not have an access to the narratives of Yoshida Yukiko or Asō Kazuko on their relationship with Catholicism, it is not far-fetched to think that these two women covertly but unfailingly influenced the views of Shigeru. Through family relationships with his wife and daughter, Shigeru was moved enough to undergo baptism (but was unable to do so while alive). It is probable that it was Shigeru's wish to receive baptism because it seems from the story of Fr. Hamao that Shigeru chose his own Christian name long before his death. For the current study, the Yoshidas' story also serves as yet another illustration of the substantial influence that Roman Catholic women can exert on their family members. The episode also attests to the contradictions that many people experience when taking on a Roman Catholic identity in Japanese society, another theme that runs through this work.

In the introduction to his edited volume *Conversion to Christianity: Historical and Anthropological Perspectives on a Great Transformation* (1993), Robert W. Hefner develops a useful formula for understanding the processes through which people identify with Christianity. Instead of looking at conversion as a deeply psychological process of realigning one's system of meaning, Hefner suggests that it is important to look at the larger social context of those who convert. Hefner demonstrates that conversion assumes a variety of forms, as it is influenced by a larger interplay of identity, politics, and morality. In interesting ways, my research findings both confirm and contradict Hefner's assertion.

In my study of Roman Catholicism in the Tokyo area, I have focused on the transformative processes that Japanese lay Catholics undergo. I have argued that as members of the laity deepen their understanding of the Catholic worldview, the importance placed on a Neo-Confucian–based human hierarchy is diminished. As the laity submit themselves to divine authority, they are able to establish a fixed place from which they can act. While this may appear similar to a bound, individualistic sense of self, this newly established sense of self can be understood as a "realigned self" in which human relationships are still valid but with less intensity. I found that following conversion, Catholic laypeople in Tokyo go through an intense realignment of their value systems. These transformative processes are often accompanied by a sense of liberation and freedom. I have suggested that this sense of liberation and elation results from laypeople's perception that they are leaving behind the virtue of striving hard to fulfill their social roles. Here, however, Hefner's suggestion to look into the larger social context becomes useful. As I have shown, this sense of liberation can only be understood when studying the historical and social constraints imposed on people in the form of social ideals.

I have further argued that the sense of self as traditionally conceived of in Japan has been shaped and reshaped by discursive processes whereby the state and its elites have emphasized one's social and familial roles using Neo-Confucian idioms. Starting in the Tokugawa Era (1603–1868), Neo-Confucianism, along with other ideologies, served as a tool of governance until Japan's defeat at the end of World War II. Through the mobilization of Neo-Confucian–based ethics, the government and its elites managed to produce a sense of self that emphasized one's "proper position" and fulfilling one's roles in family and society. My study complements that of Kondo (1990) and is a response to her call for investigation of the larger discursive contexts that have shaped personhood in Japan. Kondo states:

> [The] discourse of self-transformation must be placed within a larger historical and political context. Ideologies of selfhood are not innocent with respect to power relationships, a factor little acknowledged in most studies of "the person" or "the self." Selves are produced through specific disciplines and transgressions elicit particular punishments, just as the ethics doctrines offer particular, compelling, and satisfying pathways to self-fulfillment. (Kondo 1990, 114)

It is my hope that I have traced at least some of the larger political and historical power relationships that Kondo pointed to in her work. My own project is also my attempt to enrich ongoing conversations about the ways in which power shapes the construction of the self, a topic that has increasingly been studied by anthropologists (Mageo 2002).

To portray the transformation that the laity experiences, I have depicted two dissimilar worldviews: 1) a conventional one marked by "one's proper position" in society; and 2) one that is anchored in the notion of the Christian God as the center of gravity. Although these two worldviews are distinct, as I have shown throughout the book, Japanese Catholics in Tokyo whom I encountered managed to embrace both. Some Catholic women do so by visiting their ancestors' and in-laws' graves during the prescribed seasons of *obon* and *higan*, taking care of household Buddhist altars, and attending masses at the Catholic Church. Although these women showed me that embracing these two worldviews is possible, I also witnessed some tensions between the distinct ideas and values embedded in these two traditions. These tensions often manifest around one's obligation to the household, as many converts in the Tokyo area often are the only Catholics in their households. I have argued that laypeople often conceal their Catholic identity as part of a strategy to cope with the tension arising from an individual religious identity that is different from that of the household. In this final chapter, I explore some of the implications of enacting socially approved ways of being a Japanese person as a member of the household, a workplace, and one's community while also practicing the Roman Catholic faith in contemporary Tokyo.

Implications of Maintaining Two Different Worldviews

What are the implications of maintaining two distinctly different worldviews? The answer differs based on the perspective of the person to whom one poses this question. For the Catholic community at large, and from an evangelizing Christian perspective, publicly silent, private faith poses a problem. In discussing the current state of the Catholic Church in Tokyo, Ōnishi-sensei shared his perspective, which is based on his experience as a Catholic in Tokyo for more than forty years. He is a long-standing lay leader of the Catholic Charismatic Renewal movement in Tokyo. He said his encounter with Roman Catholicism came during his search for alternative values at the height of the Student Movements in the 1960s.[2] Based on his experience, he said:

> I think today's members of the Church [in Tokyo] are content with their own salvation. They are happy with who they are, and the church has become like a [social] club. For example, at Our Lady of the Assumption, there are many priests [offering numerous classes] and by attending these classes, one can deepen his or her faith to a reasonable degree. And [they think that] that is good. I think that is the Church today; you do not go out from there [that comfortable cocoon].

From a Christian perspective, this type of faith goes against the main tenet of Christianity, which should entail evangelism. Professor Ōnishi, who does not hide his Catholic identity and devotes his life to the Charismatic Renewal movement, differs from the majority of laity whom I describe in this study.

A similar point was raised by the Master of Épopée, Shindō-san. At one occasion, I was asking about attending two Eucharists a day. Some eager Catholics at Our Lady of the Assumption were debating whether it is acceptable to take the sacrament twice on the same day. I directed this question to Mr. Shindō, as I knew he was conversant with the ecclesiastic rules as well as Catholic theology. In response to the question, Shindō-san pointed out that the root word for a "mass" in Latin is related to the English word "dismissal." As every mass is concluded with the priest's word of dismissal, the faithful are to go and spread the teachings of Christ. Shindō-san criticized the practice of indulging oneself by receiving two sacraments in a day and stated that Catholics instead are expected to go out from the Church and spread the good news.

For the majority of women I encountered, however, to lead a Christian life was something personal. Although they did not explicitly tell me, I noticed that several of them attended a yoga class together. Likewise, a weekly Bible study group became a sort of social club. A daily rosary prayer group was often followed by a lunch gathering at a nearby restaurant. In addition, I know, for a few women, the church was a refuge from their rocky marriages. These women did not want to invite their husbands to the church because they wanted to flee from them even for a short period of time.

There are, however, examples that counter such allegations about private faith in Tokyo. Our Lady of the Assumption had a group called *Onigiri no kai* or the Group of Rice Balls, through which the members made and distributed rice balls to homeless people every Saturday night. I also heard after I left the field that a group of volunteers at the same parish began making "rice and curry" (*karē raisu*) and distributing it to homeless people or anybody who would like to partake of their meals. In response to media reports on the increasing poverty rate among children in Japan,[3] members of Terada Catholic Church began a "soup kitchen for children" (*kodomo shokudō*) in 2016 to provide nutritional meals as well as a supportive community for children and their struggling families. These examples illustrate some efforts by Roman Catholics in Tokyo to reach outside their own Christian community, and the activities imply evangelization.

These examples are not numerous, but these activities continue, indicating that an effort to reach out to social others is alive in some Roman Catholic communities in Tokyo. At the same time, numerous members continue to keep their faith as a private matter by hiding in their comfortable cocoon when one is the sole Catholic in one's immediate social circle. This phenomenon of "private faith" (Omori 2014) may be understood when we look into the dimension of power and identity politics, to which I now turn.

Conclusion and Implications

Questions of Power and Identity Politics

Another and related significant finding in my ethnographic research is that Christianity in Japan does not possess any real social power. Although I embarked on my study with the assumption that Westernization and *akogare*, or longing, to emulate the West have played a large role in the conversion and maintenance of Roman Catholic identity in Tokyo, my research results point to a very different conclusion. The introduction of Christianity to non-Western parts of the world such as Asia, Africa, and Oceania has often been associated with colonial and neocolonial projects of both overt and covert forms (Comaroff and Comaroff 1997). Scholars have discussed the larger interplay of identity, politics, and morality, which come together in conversion (Hefner 1993, Meyer 1999, Robbins 2004, 2010). As I observed in chapter 5, in the case of Japan, the legacy of Christian persecution still lingers in twenty-first-century Tokyo. Although there are many Japanese people who have idealized Christianity because of its positive associations with Europe, staunch historically rooted opposition to Christianity was still apparent during my fieldwork.

As Bishop Mizobe points out, historically, Christianity was identified as antithetical to Japan's national policy or *kokuze* from its beginning under the rulership of Hideyoshi, Ieyasu, and their successors. This was also the case during the Meiji Period (Mizobe 2007). At the time of Hideyoshi's rule, the three traditions of Shinto, Buddhism, and Confucianism were considered to be one, which was associated with the idea of Japan as a *shinkoku*, or the "nation of kami." In conceptualizing the political unity of Japan, Christianity was carefully removed from the polity, and the tradition was labeled as foreign and antithetical to Japan's political goals (Mizobe 2007). Mizobe further argues that the numerous martyrs were aware of this antithetical relationship between Christianity and Japan's political goals and willingly committed the "crime" of conversion against the political will of the rulers (Mizobe 2007, 57).

As described earlier, this historical memory of persecution is still alive among many members of today's Roman Catholic Church in Japan. This historical consciousness regarding Christianity is arguably one of the major differences between Japanese and Korean Christianity. Some scholars have suggested that positive memories of Protestant opposition to the imposition of Japanese State Shinto in the Korean Peninsula during Japan's occupation period still provide legitimacy for Christian missions in

Korea (Kim 1996). In many ways, however, in Japan, being associated with Christianity does not come with much benefit to one's social life. This was the case during the lifetime of former Prime Minster Yoshida Shigeru, as noted at the beginning of this chapter. Similar situations continue at the beginning of the twenty-first century. Because of its lack of cultural capital, as I discussed in chapter 5, hiding one's identity as a Christian is not a rare occurrence. This fact is known among the ecclesiastic authorities of the Roman Catholic Church in Japan, as we have seen in the handbook published by the Catholic Bishops' Conference of Japan (2009).

Making of, or Absence of, the "Modern Subject"?

My ethnography also contributes to discussions of the making of, or absence of, the "modern subject" in relation to the spread of Christianity in non–Euro-American contexts. Relating to the discussion of the modern subject is the concept of agency. Studying Christianity located in East Asian contexts, both Clammer (2001) for Japan and Madsen (1998) for China touch on the absence of a notion of the "autonomous individual" in these contexts who can ostensibly be a vehicle of the Christian faith. Clammer quotes Maruyama's argument[4] that Japan has failed to produce the category of the autonomous individual in making its transition to modernity. Summarizing Maruyama's argument, Clammer states:

> The basis of this [i.e., Maruyama's] claim is his idea (remarkably close to a Weberian understanding of the development of the Christian West) that modernity is based on the historical and cultural creation of the autonomous individual. What instead has been produced in Japan is the privatized and atomistic individual. Modernity is seen by Maruyama as a psychological and ethical state as much as a socioeconomic one, the key to which is the achievement of *shutaisei*—independence of spirit and the ability to define and manage the individual self autonomously. In his view Japan has, with very few exceptions, failed to produce such individuals. (Clammer 2001, 168–69)

Surmising from other scholars' work on the sense of self in Japanese society, Clammer speculates that the Japanese sense of self is conceived of as relational, dependent on others, and often related to nature. Both the relational sense of self and the ways Japanese people conceive of nature in relation to the self are foreign to Christian soteriology, argues Clammer. He suggests that this point may contribute to the relative lack of success of Christianity in gaining converts in Japan.

While Clammer has asserted that lack of autonomy contributes to the relative absence of Christianity in Japan, my ethnographic research suggests that the process may be the other way around; the conversion to Christianity may facilitate the formation of what appears to be a more autonomous self in Japanese contexts. It is noteworthy that my work shares similar foci with that of Maruyama and Clammer, and, while our conclusions may differ, my work makes comparable observations about the Japanese sense of self and the autonomous individual. By depicting the processes through which converts and devout lay members of the Catholic minority in Japan gain more autonomy through deepening their faith, my work complements Clammer's assertion that broader Japanese society lacks the concept of the autonomous individual.

The backdrop to the relational sense of self in Japan is the unit of the *ie*. I have pursued the question of the *ie* to the extent that it relates to contemporary Catholics. I suggest that the influence of the *ie* should be explored further in relation to the construction of the relational self in Japan. As I completed my study of religious expression among Roman Catholics in Tokyo, I realized that the *ie* as a unit has played significant roles in constructing the relational sense of self. Up until the abolishment of the system in 1947, the *ie* existed as a legal entity (Nakamura 1978). Under the conception of the *ie* system, only one individual (ideally the first-born male child from a legitimate marriage) can inherit the property of the household.[5] As Nakamura points out, there was no unit other than the *ie* within the scheme of the Meiji Civil Code (1978, 185). In other words, the *ie* was the integral unit, and further division of it to the level of the individual was inconceivable (Nakamura 1978, 185).

Although legally obsolete at the present time, the *ie* system lingers on in the form of the household registration system (*koseki seido*) in today's Japan. Family members must be registered under the name of the *ie*, which is usually led by the father as the head of the household. This is not surprising when one learns that the current Civil Code is actually a continuation of the Meiji Civil Code. The abolishment of the *ie* system was part of the postwar amendment to this Code (Takeda 1976, 180). It is highly likely that the unit of the *ie*, which existed under the law until 1947, has influenced the construction of the Japanese emphasis on a relational sense of self. Scholars have started investigating various ways in which the household registration system has affected people's lives in Japan (Chapman and Krogness 2014). Further studies on how this powerful tool of state governance is shaping a sense of self in Japan would be valuable.

AGENCY AND PERSONHOOD

Another question that I have implicitly raised in this study is the concept of agency. In introducing the concept of "methodological individualism," Marcus and Fischer locate its inception and dominance in the early part of the twentieth century (1986). As they have pointed out, the notion of personhood is strongly implicated in the conception of agency. The social construction of the person varies cross-culturally (Dumont 1980; Shore 1982), and calling for a much more sensitive treatment of agency in the social scientific literature still seems apt. In recent years, we have seen some fruitful approaches to this topic, especially in discussions of subjects located outside Western liberal democratic culture (Mahmood 2005; Ortner 2006). While Japan practices democracy, the nation should also be located outside the Western liberal democratic sphere for the purposes of discussions of personal agency.

As somebody who grew up in the postwar era of rapid economic growth during the 1970s and 1980s in Japan when the country was becoming "Number One" (Vogel 1979), I did not have many opportunities to witness social justice movements. All the adults, it seemed to me at the time, were busy catching up with lost economic opportunities of the past and eager to work hard, raise children, and rebuild the nation. Robust students movements of the 1960s had largely died down, and the adults of my parents' generation around me persevered through long hours of work without resorting to any political activism to improve their work or living conditions. (I also grew up in the periphery of Japan, in the Tohoku region, where it is often believed that one should not express one's feelings and should persevere under existing conditions without complaining.)

In East Asian contexts in which Confucianism is valued, standing up against authority takes on a different meaning relative to its Western sense. Demonstration as a form of protest is less popular in Japan compared to the United States, Canada, or Europe. Strongly influenced by Neo-Confucian ideals, Japan does not celebrate the concept of the human being as an autonomous unit as explicitly as in the United States; rather, the conception of human beings as interdependent has greater resonance

(Cave 2007). During many years of living in Canada, I witnessed radically different ways of being a person from the way I knew in Japan. I was impressed by many ordinary citizens in Canada who take the notion of social justice seriously. Devoting one's life to social justice movements is an ethical way to live for many people I know in Canada. Through my fieldwork in Tokyo, however, I have relearned that relationships are the building blocks of society, and in Japanese society, a self is defined by relational terms. One's behavior is formed in relationships, and it makes sense that it is harder to stand up against authorities. This insight is not new, and many scholars have confirmed this point. My research, however, has added an insight to this area of scholarship by demonstrating that a religious worldview can alter one's behaviors regarding the relational sense of self. Creating a strong tie to a Christian God can give rise to a different sense of self that is less rooted in human relationships.

In recent years, however, several works have documented a trend toward a more autonomous, individual sense of self in Japan (Kelsky 2001; Mathews and White 2004; Nakano and Wagatsuma 2004; Rosenberger 2013; Rowe 2011). I should note that these works do not focus on religious conversion. In light of this body of scholarship, it may be possible to situate my respondents' conversion to Roman Catholicism within this trend toward the construction of an autonomous, individual sense of self in Japan. However, even among these recent works that document a slightly different orientation of personhood, conclusions are rather ambiguous. As Mathews and White (2004) conclude in their edited volume, it is difficult to say whether there is a definite trend. I agree with this assessment. For example, older women who seek to procure an independent space where they can maintain peace of mind separated from their in-laws and husbands need to buy a separate place for their afterlife in the form of an individual grave (Rowe 2011). Likewise, young women who seek to assert their unique, individual life course need to leave Japan (Kelsky 2001) or keep contemplating such opportunities (Rosenberger 2013). Similarly, my Catholic female research participants must maintain their cultic duties in Buddhist terms at home as the spiritual caretakers for the family ancestors. From these observations, it seems that transformations in self and society occur only at a slow pace.

I should stress that one of the important findings in my current work is that a slightly different sense of agency is discernible among my respondents within Japanese Catholic communities compared with their sense of self prior to the deepening of their faith. There were occasional suggestions, embedded in the form of jokes, among my research participants that they "became stronger" (*tsuyokunatta*) than before converting to Christianity. This strength is sometimes apparent in my research participants' newfound courage to express opinions of their own, or at other times in their husbands' appraisal of the changes that their wives had undergone. Often, narratives describe how wives became able to say "no" to their husbands' unreasonable demands whereas they were unable to do so before having faith in Catholicism. I suggest that this transformation is also related to the development of a sense of self that privileges the relationship with the Christian God, a much more powerful authority than their male, human husbands.

Finally, relating to the concept of personhood, I suggest that this differently conceived sense of self among Roman Catholics in Tokyo resonates with observations made about Christian conversion in several other non–Euro-American contexts and its implications on personhood (Keane 2007; Robbins 2004). Although the Japanese case is not as dramatic as some other cases like that of Ghana (Meyer 1999), a similar pattern in the shift of authority is clear. As converts subscribe to a new configuration of power centering on the divine, the moral authority structure previously adhered to is weakened. With the shift of authority from humans to a non-human source, Japanese Roman Catholics, like many of their other non–Euro-American counterparts, effectively retained more independence from social obligations and therefore gained agency. These cases resonate with the observation made by Bialecki et al. that "in cultures that have recently adopted Christianity, conversion often triggers a partial abandonment of social and cultural forms oriented towards the collective in favor of individualist modes of social organization" (Bialecki et al. 2008, 1141).

As I conclude this book, especially when I reflect on the transformative processes that often accompany the conversion to Roman Catholic faith in Tokyo—weakening of the existing moral framework rooted in human relationships and a possible simultaneous rise of one's agentive power—I must wonder about the implications of my study on ethical issues in Japan. In a society in which the notion of integrity is celebrated, as in many Western societies, ideas about individual responsibility or accountability should be understood fairly easily, as these concepts are built on the same understanding of how a good human being ought to be. However, when we turn our eyes to Japan, the situation is slightly different. If the ethical code is built on an ideal of the self that is strongly articulated in relational terms, do the same ideals of individual responsibility and accountability work? Do concepts such as justice, individual responsibility, and accountability take on a foreign overtone in Japan?

In 2017, the word *sontaku* became one of the most discussed words of the year in Japan. The word itself means to "discern the feelings of the others," but the news media discussed this word in connection with a high-profile political scandal.[6] According to news reports, an educational organization of a strong nationalist bent purchased a previously state-owned land from the transport ministry to build a new primary school. The transaction involved a disproportionately large discount, and members of the Opposition as well as the media alleged that there was some preferential treatment in the transaction. The controversy flared up, as the head of this educational body claimed his social connection to the wife of the prime minister.[7]

An underlying principle at work in the particular usage of the word *sontaku* in the scandal of 2017 was to give priority in social interaction to the human relationships that one is involved in, and not to the integrity of oneself as a human person. When the word *sontaku* caught media attention, the initial reaction by Japanese populace was that of perplexity, as the word itself was unfamiliar in daily conversations. Once the precise meaning of the word was explained by experts, and the usage of this word in relation to the scandal was elucidated by several TV commentators, there seemed to be a prevalent sense of empathy among general populace toward those who were involved in the scandal. It seems that for many Japanese people the idea of *sontaku* was something very familiar. As a result, one of the recurring media discourses emphasized how "Japanese" this concept was—"to surmise what others are thinking" and then act in accordance with that understanding. I hope that my own findings on personhood and autonomy may shed some light on situations involving the word *sontaku*. My research may suggest that the idea of *sontaku* is to be found at the opposite end of individual autonomy and agency. As such, the promotion of *sontaku* as a Japanese concept suggests the persistence of a relational concept of the self.

Although Roman Catholic communities in Tokyo may be a small segment of Japanese society, several themes encountered through this research—the Japanese sense of self, agency, and ethical frameworks—are fundamental to our understanding of being a human being in Japan. I hope that my present work makes a modest contribution to the study of personhood and agency (Marcus and Fischer 1986; Ortner 2006) and the production of distinctive subjectivities (cf. Foucault 1984, 7) in non-Western parts of the world. As religious traditions are often an important source of authority, and the shaping of personhood cannot be divorced from discourses of power (Kondo 1990; Mageo 2002), the study of personhood and religious traditions may yield further insights into our complex ways of being human.

Notes

Introduction

1. Throughout this book, I use pseudonyms for individuals and various parish churches where I conducted research in Japan to protect the privacy of individuals as well as that of groups within these organizations. I use actual names only when the publication of the individual is relevant to my discussions.

2. The authors characterize personhood as "the grounds of human capabilities and actions, ideas about the self, and the expression of emotions" (Marcus and Fischer 1986, 45).

3. I use the word "converts" in a broad sense of the term. Here, I am referring to those who become members of the Roman Catholic Church through baptism (as an adult or as an infant) and also through the rite of confirmation. I am aware that it is odd to use the word "converts" to denote some Roman Catholics who received infant baptism. I noticed, however, that many of these Catholics went through a period in which they made a conscious decision to come back to the Church. In this sense, my usage of the term "converts" to refer to this group of people may be justified. In the three venues in which I conducted fieldwork, there were many converts from Protestant denominations. In Tokyo, these people go through a mass called *tenkaishiki* or the "changing of the group." This mass can be the rite of confirmation or the rite of baptism. Protestant Christians are not required to be baptized again to become Roman Catholics, but many prefer to be re-baptized.

4. Please see my note on the usage of the term "Japanese" in this study found in the section titled "Theoretical Orientations" in this chapter.

5. French historians associated with the *Annales* School coined the term *longue durée* to refer to a long-term distinctive period in the history of a culture. By contrast, "conjuncture" is used by these historians to refer to specific shorter episodes of social change.

6. Christianity was banned and Christian missionaries were expelled from the Japanese islands by the Tokugawa government in a gradual process. The persecution of Christianity started in 1587. A total ban on Christianity was implemented

by the Tokugawa shogunate in 1614, and the ban continued to be effective until the Meiji government lifted it in 1873 (Drummond 1971; Gonoi 1990).

7. When the government was propagating the idea of State Shinto (1868–1945), Christianity was again portrayed in a negative light. See Hardacre (1989) for details of projects carried out in the name of State Shinto. The idea of State Shinto revolved around the figure of the Japanese emperor, conceived as the divine head of the nation-state. All Christians in Japan at the time had to deal with the question of to whom one pledges one's utmost loyalty. Many Christians as well as members of new religious movements were interrogated or arrested by the government on charges of *lèse majesté* when their actions contradicted the state ideology (Hardacre 2006). I discuss ethnographic data on this topic in chapter 5.

8. The "work of God" is often expressed in Japanese Catholics as *kami no miwaza* or *kamisama no ohakarai*.

9. The question of the Japanese sense of self is also a popular topic within Japan, providing a fertile discussion ground for the field of *nihonjinron*. Benedict's famous work the *Chrysanthemum and the Sword* (in Japanese, *Kiku to katana* 1967) was translated into Japanese and still ranks fairly high as a bestseller. Doi's work *Amae no kōzō* (in English, *the Anatomy of Dependence*) is also one of the classics, along with Nakane Chie's (1967) *Tateshakai no ningen kankei*.

10. I often learned about the religious expressions and aspirations of men through conversations with their wives and sisters.

11. In a way, my approach may appear apolitical. I hope to describe things from within, similar to what Janice Boddy attempted to do in depicting the lives of women in Sudan in her work *Wombs and Alien Spirits* (1989).

12. In many ways, Christianity is not a commonly discussed topic in wider Japanese society. One middle-aged convert told me that she had never known that Catholic priests had to be celibate. When she found out this requirement for priests, she was extremely impressed by this practice. As Buddhist monks in Japan often do marry (Jaffe 2001), the idea of remaining celibate is novel in Japan.

13. The Catholic Charismatic Renewal (CCR) is a movement within Roman Catholicism. The participants in this movement emphasize the presence and working of the Holy Spirit in their lives. The CCR in Melbourne, Australia, lists three gifts of the spirit: the gift of prophecy, the gift of praying in tongues, and the gift of healing (Catholic Charismatic Renewal Australia n.d.; cf. Csordas 1994, 1997). Among the members of the charismatic Catholics in Tokyo, prophecy, speaking in tongues and prayer healing are also important, and these three characteristics also distinguish charismatic Catholics from other Catholics.

Chapter 1

1. I personally had to undergo this experience on a busy street in the Ginza district. A woman and a man approached me, initially commenting on the

features of my face, followed by a question of whether I had a son. This question led to a series of other questions that eventually became a sales pitch for "spiritual cleansing," which would supposedly improve my current life condition. The underlying cultural assumptions here are that women should marry and bear a son to fulfill a culturally constructed notion of adult womanhood.

2. The term *karōshi* made it into the *Oxford English Dictionary* in 2002. *The Japan Times Online*, January 18, 2002, https://www.japantimes.co.jp/news/2002/01/18/national/karoshi-keiretsu-on-oxford-list/#.W-ofw_ZuKUk.

3. I discuss human relationships further in chapter 2.

4. Tomoko Kitagawa (2007) discusses the conversion of Gō, a daughter of the ruling shogun, Toyotomi Hideyoshi. Relying on the historical account of missionary Luis Frois and other Jesuits, she discusses the extent to which Hideyoshi's female court attendants were influenced by things Christian. According to Frois, at one point, almost all female attendants in Hideyoshi's court had a Christian name—although one was not even affiliated with the Church. They called each other by these Christian names, such as Magdalena, Joanna, and Catelina (Kitagawa 2007, 13). These elite women took Christianity as a rare novelty from foreign lands.

5. It should be noted that the initial two periods that I discuss here—the period of successful evangelization and the subsequent period of proscription—saw no competition from Protestant denominations or Eastern orthodox groups. Missionaries from these groups came to Japan only after Japan opened its doors to the West in the beginning of the Meiji Period.

6. The image used was often that of the crucified Christ or Mary and the Infant Jesus. Villagers were gathered at a village head's house or a Buddhist temple to step on these icons to prove that they did not harbor the Christian faith (Gonoi 1990). There were a few other policies also introduced at the time. These policies are listed and explained in Miyazaki (2003, 14).

7. Gonoi notes that the practice of *fumie* was abolished in Nagasaki in 1858 (1990, 236).

8. Some hidden Christians decided not to join the Roman Catholic Church when the faith was officially permitted. These groups of contemporary hidden Christians are documented in numerous articles. Japanese researchers on hidden Christians claim that they have confirmed the traces of Gregorian chants transmitted through early missions in contemporary Christian folk songs (*kirishitan minyō*) preserved in Ikutsuki Island (Ohta 2004, 87). Whelan (2005) filmed a documentary of the rite of Christmas Eve conducted by two remaining *kakure* priests on the Goto Islands in 1995. At the same time, we also hear that these *kakure* communities are on the verge of extinction. Ohta (2004) also reports that a *kakure* community in Ikutsuki Island conducted a "disbanding ceremony" in 2003 because of a lack of successors.

9. Making amendments to these "unequal treaties" became Japan's diplomatic obsession for the next several decades.

10. Scholars have continued to debate at which point the government decided to allow the practice of the Christian faith. Ohta points out that, according to recent scholarship, taking down the decrees was merely a change in communication media by a new government (Ohta 2004, 228). Gonoi, however, notes that the removal of the decree notice boards was communicated to the United States and Italy two days after the event. This indicates that the government did intend this policy change for the sake of diplomacy (Gonoi 1990, 266).

11. I am aware that this is a simplistic description of the inception of State Shinto. There are, however, numerous ideas that the Meiji government borrowed from Christianity in order to form State Shinto. For example, Emperor Meiji was considered to be the head of the national body (*kokutai*), of which Japanese citizens constitute the other parts, analogous to the Christian idea that Jesus is the head of the church and believers constitute the body of the church. Furthermore, the Shinto wedding, for example, can be dated the beginning of the Meiji Era. A Japanese scholar, Ema, has reported that the first Shinto wedding was held at Hibiya shrine in 1898 (Hendry 1981, 195). It is highly likely that the Shinto wedding was invented based on the model of the Christian wedding.

12. Please see chapter 5 for an ethnographic example of hostility to Christianity as part of anti-Western movements during the Pacific War.

13. The Paris Mission limited its membership to those whose native language was French. This organization consisted of parish priests from various parishes in France. The organization received its instruction for evangelization of the Far East directly from the Sacred Congregation for Propagation of the Faith in the Vatican. The Paris Mission's goal was to train local priests so that the respective dioceses could function with local populations independently of foreign missionaries (Ohta 2004, 177–78).

14. The apostolic vicariate is a territorial designation made by the Vatican for a region where a diocese cannot be put in place.

15. Ohta notes that the death rate from dysentery at the time was 30 percent to 40 percent. However, de Rotz cared for 210 patients afflicted with dysentery in Urakami Village, of whom only eight died, a death rate of 4 percent. This statistic is even more remarkable when we consider that those in Urakami had just returned from exile, and thus their health conditions were not optimal (Ohta 2004).

16. Yasukuni Shrine is a Shinto shrine located in central Tokyo. It was called Shōkonsha originally and located in Kyoto. The shrine was transferred to Tokyo in June 1879 and renamed Yasukuni Shrine (Antoni 1993: 121–22). The shrine is dedicated to the 2.5 million who died in the name of the country through participating in various wars such as the Russo-Japanese War, the Manchurian Incident, World War I, and World War II (Yasukuni Shrine 2008). The shrine has been a center of controversy because it also enshrines fourteen convicted

war criminals including former Prime Minister Tōjo Hideki. Visits to this shine by political leaders of Japan often anger Asian nations that were the subjects of Japan's political and military aggression in the past.

17. The number of converts made by each parish within the Archdiocese of Tokyo is not released publicly. I had access to this information through the Catholic Bishops' Conference of Japan.

18. Here, "converts" refers to two groups of people: 1) those who were not Christian but seek the Roman Catholic faith and receive the rite of baptism to officially join the Roman Catholic Church. This group includes both infants and adults; 2) those who are already affiliated with other Christian denominations but seek membership in the Roman Catholic Church. This latter group undergoes an almost identical period of inquiry and training by the Church. Adult converts—whether from a non-Christian background or already Christian through other denominations—all go through the process called the Rite of Christian Initiation for Adults (RCIA).

19. I use the expression Lord's Day instead of Sunday so that I can include a vigil mass on Saturday. It is the custom of the Roman Catholic Church to start the celebration of a feast day through a vigil mass on the day before the actual date of celebration. This pattern is also applicable to weekly Sunday masses, making Saturday evening masses part of the Lord's Day celebration.

20. Masses in Vietnamese and Polish were offered only on the first Sunday of the month.

21. All four stores are run by Catholic orders.

22. As the Terada Catholic Church is a pseudonym, so is the name of Terada village.

Chapter 2

1. "Fujiya fusei 'soshiki gurumi' kigen-gire arata ni 18-ken; shachō ga jii [Fujiya Accused of 'Organized Fraud: Eighteen More Concealed Cases of Expired Dates and the President Indicates Resignation]," *Yomiuri Shimbun*, January 16, 2007.

2. "Asashōryū shazai; shishō to nininsankyaku saishuppatsu [Asashōryū Apologized and Pledged to Have a Fresh Start Working Closely with His Master]," *Yomiuri Shimbun*, December 1, 2007.

3. "Donnani ayamattemo tsugunai kirenai [Any apologies is not sufficient for atonement]," Nihon Television, *Nittere News 24*, June 12, 2008.

4. A cultural ideal of young women to be *ojō-san* was still very popular in 2008. When you say somebody is an *ojō-san*, you mean she is from a good family and well brought up. Being "well brought up" may include being trained in many arts, such as music, tea ceremony, and flower arrangement. This particular

cultural construction of ideal young womanhood in Japan may have to do with the Victorian values that were emulated in earlier periods in Japan.

5. "Mimeini totsunyū, jūtōhō ihan yōgi de kumiin taiho; jisatsu hakari jūtai; Machida tatekomori 15-jikan [Stormed in the barricade and arrested a gang member for illegal possession of a gun; the man barricaded himself for 15 hours but in a critical condition because of his attempted suicide]," *Asahi Shimbun*, April 21, 2007.

6. See de Bary et al. for the decree issued by Hideyoshi in 1591 (2001, 462–63).

7. Please see my discussion of this topic in the introduction.

8. Hakuseki points to one of the Chinese texts, the Chapter on Mourning Cloth in the *Book of Etiquette*: "There are three followings for women, which are applicable to every woman. Therefore when the girl is yet to be married, she follows her father. After her marriage, she follows her husband. After the death of her husband, she follows her son. The father is heaven for the daughter, the husband is the heaven for the wife. A woman cannot wear her hemp cloth twice in deep mournings [for her father and husband]" (Lu 1997, 257).

9. The *Common Sense Teachings for Japanese Children* was written by Kaibara Ekken (1630–1714), who served the Kuroda family, a *daimyō* of the Fukuoka-han. He was a medical doctor first and later a Confucian scholar in residence (Lu 1997, 258).

10. In discussing the case in China, Yao further notes that the teaching of the rectification of the names was "extended and interpreted as a conservative bulwark for an authoritarian regime in which absolute subordination of subject-minister to ruler guaranteed an effective administration" (Yao 2000, 35).

11. Donald Keene observes that in the late Tokugawa Period, values such as *giri* and loyalty are parodied. He relates this to the general decline of morals and ideals at the time. Pointing to the theater scene, which suggests the unpopularity of Confucian values, nevertheless, Keene notes that "even when they [Confucian values] were most conspicuously ridiculed in the theater, they continued to affect the lives of most Japanese. The theater is a mirror of society, but it may magnify, diminish, or hopelessly distort. The one thing one can say with certainty is that as long as something appears in the mirror, no matter how crooked or warped, it still exists in society and has compelled the attention of the makers of mirrors" (Keene 1984, 137).

12. Such things as seating arrangements are an integral part of proper manners, and as a result there is the Examination for Secretary Skills or the Examination for Business Manners in today's Japan. The Association for the Examination of Practical Skills offers several examinations for business-related skills. The content of these examinations includes proper speech (both orally and literary) and seating arrangements, and could include proper body movements. At the time of writing,

the organization lists the following examinations for business: *Hisho ginō kentei* [Examination for Secretary Skills], *Bijinesu jitsumu manā kentei* [Examination for Business Manners], *Sābisu setsugū kentei* [Examination for Customer Services], bijinesu bunsho kentei [Examination for Business Letters], *Bijinesu denwa kentei* [Examination for Business Telephone Conversation], *Jitsumu gino kentei kyōkai* [Association for the Examination of Practical Skills], www.kentei.or.jp.

13. 200-tsubo is roughly 660 square meters.

14. The *kanji* character for a daughter-in-law, *yome*, consists of a part representing "woman" and a part representing the "house."

15. Amanuma's statement that the concept of *ganbaru* is uniquely Japanese and not seen in any other Asian countries is typical of *nihonjinron* discourse. Contrary to Amanuma, I do not claim any uniqueness for this concept. I do agree, however, that this concept has been a popular notion in postwar Japan.

16. In the aftermath of the Great East Japan Earthquake in 2011, there was a strong sentiment among many of the sufferers of the devastation that they would no longer be able to *ganbaru* in the face of the enormous destruction caused by both earthquakes and following tsunami of unprecedented scale.

17. Kamata Minoru's book *Ganbaranai* ("Not to Strive Hard," 2003) has become a bestseller in Japan. This book has ignited various conversations in Japanese society for not striving hard any longer.

Chapter 3

1. Akishino Temple is located in the city of Nara. In line with Hashimoto-san's narrative, I give the location as "Kyoto," which is not far from Nara City. The city of Nara was an ancient capital of Japan before the capital moved to Kyoto.

2. The word *zahyōjiku*, translated here as the "coordinate grid," itself refers to the coordinate graph in which one uses the horizontal x-axis and the vertical y-axis to indicate value. It is not uncommon to use the word *zahyōjiku* metaphorically to indicate one's value system in contemporary Japanese.

3. At Buddhist memorial rites, it is a convention that those who are invited bring an envelope containing a monetary gift and receive a return gift (i.e., goods) on their way home. In the case of the Catholic memorial rites for Mita-san's daughter, however, nobody from the parish brought any monetary gifts. I followed the other parishioners' lead. Mita-san seemed happy that there were people from the parish present, as none of her immediate family is Catholic. Needless to say, it is difficult to conduct a mass without a congregation, as a large part of the mass involves a verbal exchange between the clergy and the congregation. Mita-san also seemed happy to provide return gifts—gift giving falls under the domain of a housewife's job (see Rupp 2003) in Japan's gendered

society. In addition, even though her daughter is deceased, taking care of her memorial rites may have given Mita-san a sense of being a mother who cares for and nurtures her children (cf. Allison 1996; Borovoy 2005).

4. As Rosenberger (2001), Kondo (1990), and Borovoy (2005) have shown, many women of Honda-san's generation often conceive of themselves as the main caretaker of the family as the wife and the mother.

5. Kevin Hanlon, who conducted research on popular Catholicism in Japan, reports similar findings to those from my fieldwork in Tokyo. According to Hanlon, the story of the prodigal son is one of the most popular parables, and many respondents associated the image of God with love (2003). His research was conducted in several cities in Japan but did not include Tokyo.

6. The English translations for these two poems are taken from "Ogura Hyakunin Isshu—100 poems by 100 poets" (Japanese Text Initiative 2001) found at Japanese Texts Initiative, a Collaboration of the University of Virginia Library Etext Center and the University of Pittsburgh. These translations are edited by the Japanese Text Initiative. The original translations are taken from Clay MacCauley's book *Hyakunin Isshu* published in 1917 in Yokohama. The texts that I used are found at www.etext.lib.virginia.edu/japanese/hyakunin.

7. In Japanese, these three lines read "*Kamikoso makoto no oya, anatano subetewo aishiteru, umaretekite yokatta!*" As Japanese nouns often do not presuppose gender distinctions or singular/plural distinctions, my translation is an approximation. I purposefully rendered "parents" in the plural form instead of the singular. In addition, the second and third lines do not possess subjects, and my translations can be taken as approximations.

8. Murakami-san lost her own mother when she was twenty-three years old, many years before her marriage.

9. *Batsu-ichi* is a casual, playful term denoting those who are divorced. In Japanese family registries, which function as the record of births and deaths within the unit of the household, the name of the divorcing spouse will be removed from the registry. Because they officially cross out the name, "cross one" became a popular code denoting someone who divorced once. You can refer to someone who divorced twice as "strike two" (*batsu-ni*). The part denoting the shape of X, batsu, as in English, also means "no" and has a negative connotation.

10. Spiritual Exercises were developed by Ignatius of Loyola in the sixteenth century (Broderick 2005, 4367). Spiritual Exercises continue to be popular worldwide. There are books and online retreats readily available in different languages, including Japanese.

Chapter 4

1. In this chapter, admittedly, my usage of the word "gender" presupposes a binary model of "male" and "female." This binary model was applicable to the

majority of the research participants I encountered during the fieldwork. I am aware, however, that this binary model of gender excludes a minority few who did not fit into this conventional model.

2. This abandoning one's ego to surrender divine will was expected during the time of the Pacific War, as seen in the case of kamikaze pilots who were asked to be suicide bombers. Young soldiers took off from the airbase with fuel that covered only one way. This divine, however, was that of a human. During the time of the Pacific War, Emperor Shōwa was thought to be divine.

3. From the large number of classes offered at Our Lady of the Assumption, this site had the largest number of laypeople attending during weekdays within the Archdiocese.

4. It seems that there is not a prevalent sense of Sunday as the Sabbath or a day of rest. People tend to work very hard at church, too, reflecting the modern idea of *ganbaru* that I discussed in chapters 1 and 2.

5. Terada Catholic Church organizes its parish members into several neighborhood groups according to parishioners' address. These groupings are used when there are several tasks needed to be done.

6. Every parish has a position called the *kyōkai-iinchō*. This can be translated as the head of the church committees. This position is usually taken up by a male, and he would represent the lay members of the church. This position is often filled through an election process.

7. The government has introduced amendments to the maximum amount of money a spouse can earn in order to be eligible for a spousal tax benefit. A set of amendments took effect starting in 2018.

8. For example, when Fujimi-san warned her husband about her desire to be baptized, he reluctantly allowed her to do so on the condition that she would not attend church on Sundays. The husband apparently knew that becoming Christian might involve attending church on Sundays. In fulfilling this request, she would stay home to take care of her husband when he was off from work.

9. I do not want to confuse the reader with the words "muscular" and "masculine." Although Abe's argument is about muscular Christianity, I take this emphasis on muscular Christianity as "masculine" Christianity.

10. It is well-known that the book *Bushido* was first written in English by Nitobe Inazo for Western audiences to explain Japanese ethics. The content, however, was heavily influenced by Christian and European ethics, which Nitobe acquired through his training in the West. He was a Quaker who studied at Johns Hopkins University.

11. See his website for details, http://arthur-hollands.com. According to the website, he was born of an American father and was baptized in the United States.

12. I had asked Yabe-san about this group as an example of "masculine Christianity." My interlocutor did not come up with this term.

13. Often, having tattoos indicates one's affiliation with a *yakuza* group. I put the word "normal" in quotation marks because the question of whether the

economy of *yakuza* groups stands outside the the non-yakuza economy in Japan is very complicated.

14. A private conversation with a Jesuit priest.

15. Coincidentally, Mita-san's son met a young woman who is from a Catholic family. The two are now engaged, and Mita-san has gained one baptized member of the church in her family. She believes this happened as a result of her prayers.

16. This idea of receiving a spiritual essence from the main spiritual authority in Christianity resonates with an idea seen in contemporary Shinto. In spring or autumn local Shinto festivals, a spiritual entity transferred to a mobile carrier from the main shrine is often carried around local neighborhoods to clean the evil spirits and blessing the localities with abundance and prosperity.

Chapter 5

1. Another twist to this story is that her mother-in-law is a member of a Protestant church.

2. Sōka Gakkai is one of the most successful new religious movements in Japan. The original organization named Sōka Kyōiku Gakkai was founded in 1930 in Tokyo as an offshoot of a Buddhist sect called Nichiren shō-shū. After changing its name to Sōka Gakkai in 1946, the organization had enormous success in expanding its membership during Japan's postwar economic development. Its current membership numbers more than 8 million, making Sōka Gakkai one of the largest new religious movements within Japan (Shimada 2009).

3. There are a number of Catholics who received infant baptism in Tokyo. Those who were born Christians, however, tend to "revert" to nominal participation in "Japanese Buddhist-Shinto" practices unless they have an active interest in being Christian. In the Americas and Europe, where Christianity was traditionally the dominant religion, one can be a "nominal Christian," but this is not the case in Tokyo.

4. Aum Shinrikyo or Oumu Shinrikyō became the most notorious new religious movement in Japan when its members attacked and killed innocent commuters in the subway system with sarin gas in central Tokyo on March 20, 1995. The teachings of the group incorporated elements of Hinduism, Buddhism, and some Christianity and proclaimed the coming of "armageddon," the cosmic battle of the end time (Jurgensmeyer 2000; Shimada 2009). The core members of this group—including its founder and charismatic leader, Matumoto Chizuo—were arrested, jailed, and sentenced to death. All thirteen of them were executed in 2018.

5. Unlike Kagoshima and Nagasaki prefectures, where Christian missionaries arrived from Europe as early as the mid-sixteenth century, the Christianization of Amami Ōshima goes back only to the early Meiji. Therefore, Amami Ōshima has no history of *kirishitan*, or Christians from the initial successful evangelization

period between 1549 and 1639 and the succeeding proscription period between 1640 and 1738.

6. This practice, along with many other oral histories of persecution, was also recorded in *Kanashimi no maria no shima* (Kosakai 1984).

7. This is also a political act, and a form of resistance, on the part of Kaneta-san as a member of a minority group. By retelling these stories, she asserts the damage her group received at the hands of the state and the majority of the Japanese population on the island who were not Christian. See *Acts of Memory* for theoretical discussions on the political nature of narrative memory (Bal 1999).

8. While meditating, Professor Ōnishi heard the voice of Christ asking him: "Do you like to follow me?" (*Tsuitekurukai?*) He answered "yes" to this question.

9. The *kanji* character consists of two ideographs: "woman/women" and "household."

10. I do not mean here that households kept ties with the exact same Buddhist temples since the Edo Period. I mean that the nominal relationship between household and temple established in the Edo Period has a continued presence in contemporary Japan.

11. See Christina Rocha's discussions of Japanese Brazilians having both Buddhist and Catholic memorial rites for the same individual in Brazil (Rocha 2006).

12. The book makes a distinction as to what practices are permitted and what are not. For example, Catholics are allowed to put hands together, bow down, burn incense, and offer flowers at Shinto shrines and Buddhist temples, but it is recommended that they not offer *tamagushi* (tree branches used for Shinto rituals), take part in drinking *omiki* (an alcohol used in Shinto rituals), clap hands, or ring the gongs (Catholic Bishops' Conference of Japan 2009, 53).

13. *Kadomatsu* is a New Year's decoration placed on both sides of the gate of one's house. It is usually made of bamboo, pines, and rope.

14. I do not intend to draw any conclusion about faith in Nagasaki in this section. I am using these ethnographic data to depict faith in Tokyo, which is the focus of this study.

Conclusion

1. St. Mary Cathedral of the Archdiocese of Tokyo was rebuilt between 1960 and 1964. St. Mary Cathedral, http://cathedral-sekiguchi.jp/cathedral/cathedral-history.

2. Marxist movements were taking over the university campuses in the 1960s. In the midst of rapid social change, Professor Ōnishi was invited to a bible study group.

3. "Kodomo no hinkon-ritsu saiaku 2012-nen 16.3% Kōrōshō chōsa 'touji no setai shotoku-gen ga eikyō [The worst child poverty rate at 16.3% in 2012,

studies conducted by the ministry of health, labour and welfare. Influenced by 'the drop of household income at the time]," *Nihon Keizai Shimbun*, July 16, 2014.

4. The essay that Clammer refers to is Maruyama Masao's "Patterns of Individuation and the Case of Japan: A Conceptual Scheme," in *Changing Japanese Attitudes to Modernization* (1985).

5. It was unlikely that a woman would assume this role as the head of the household, or *koshu*, but it was possible. The head of the household was given the right to oversee the rest of the members of his household. For example, members of a household did not possess the freedom to choose where to reside (Igeta 1982, 59).

6. "Akie-fujin tsuki shokuin ga kanyo, zaimushō shōkai. Kagoike-shi kanmon de shōgen; Moritomo tochi mondai [Involvement of a government aide assigned to Mrs. Abe, making inquiries with the ministry of finance—Mr. Kagoike summoned to testify on Moritomo property scandal]," *Asahi Shimbun*, March 24, 2017. "A scandal over school, land and nationalism in Japan," *BBC News*, March 17, 2017, https://www.bbc.com/news/world-asia-39252192.

7. "Shushō & Kagoike-shi kuichigau setsumei; Akie-shi no kanyo & 100-man-en no kifu [The discrepancy between Prime Minister's and Mr. Kaoigke's explanations regarding the involvement of Mrs. Abe and the donation of 1 million yen], *Asahi Shimbun*, March 25, 2017.

Works Cited

Abe, Ikuo. 2008. "Muscular Christianity in Japan: The Growth of a Hybrid." In *Muscular Christianity in Colonial and Post-Colonial Worlds*, edited by John J. MacAloon, 14–38. London: Routledge.
Abbott, Walter M. 1966. *The Documents of Vatican II. With Notes and Comments by Catholic, Protestant, and Orthodox Authorities*, edited and translated by Very Rev. MSGR. Joseph Gallagher. New York: Guild Press.
Ahearn, Laura M. 2000. "Agency." *Journal of Linguistic Anthropology* 9(1–2):12–15.
Allison, Anne. 1991. "Japanese Mothers and Obentōs: The Lunch-Box as Ideological State Apparatus." *Anthropological Quarterly* 64(4):195–208.
———. 1994. *Nightwork: Sexuality, Pleasure, and Corporate Masculinity in a Tokyo Hostess Club*. Chicago: University of Chicago Press.
———. 1996. *Permitted and Prohibited Desires: Mothers, Comics, and Censorship in Japan*. Berkeley: University of California Press.
———. 2013. *Precarious Japan*. Durham: Duke University Press.
Amanuma Kaoru. 1987. *Ganbari no kōzō: Nihonjin no kōdō genri* [Structure of Striving Hard: Principles of Japanese Behaviour.] Tokyo: Yoshikawa Kōbunkan.
Amore, Roy C., and Julia Ching. 2007. "Chinese Religions: Confucianism and Daoism." In *A Concise Introduction to World Religions*, edited by Willard G. Oxtoby and Alan F. Segal, 440–99. Don Mills, ON: Oxford University Press.
Antoni, Klaus. 1993. "Yasukuni-Jinja and Folk Religion." In *Religion and Society in Modern Japan*, edited by Mark Mullins, Shimazono Susumu and Paul Swanson, 121–32. Berkeley, CA: Asian Humanities Press.
Asahi Shimbunsha. 1967. Kinkyū tokushū Yoshida Shigeru no shōgai [Special Edition on the life of Yoshida Shigeru], *Asahi Graph*, November 5.
Asō Kazuko. 1993. *Chichi Yoshida Shigeru* [My father, Yoshida Shigeru]. Tokyo: Shinchōsha.
Badone, Ellen. 1989. *The Appointed Hour: Death, Worldview, and Social Change in Brittany*. Berkeley: University of California Press.
———, ed. 1990. *Religious Orthodoxy and Popular Faith in European Society*. Princeton, NJ: Princeton University Press.

Bal, Mieke. 1999. "Introduction." In *Acts of Memory: Cultural Recall in the Present*, edited by Mieke Bal, Jonathan V. Crewe, and Leo Spitzer, vii–xvii. Hanover, NH: Dartmouth College: University Press of New England.

Ballhatchet, Helen J. 2003. "The Modern Missionary Movement in Japan: Roman Catholic, Protestant, Orthodox." In *Handbook of Christianity in Japan*, edited by Mark R. Mullins, 35–65. Leiden: Brill.

Barker, John, ed. 2007. *The Anthropology of Morality in Melanesia and Beyond*. London: Ashgate.

Benedict, Ruth. 1967. *Kiku to katana: nihon bunka no kata. The Chrysanthemum and the Sword*. Translated by Hasegawa Matsuharu. Tokyo: Shakai shisōsha.

———. (1947) 1974. *The Chrysanthemum and the Sword: Patterns of Japanese Culture*. Tokyo: Charles E. Tuttle Co., Publishers.

Bialecki, Jon, Naomi Haynes, and Joel Robbins. 2008. "The Anthropology of Christianity." *Religion Compass* 2(6):1139–58.

Bialecki, Jon, and Girish Daswani. 2015. "What Is an individual? The View from Christianity." *HAU: Journal of Ethnographic Theory* 5(1):271–94.

Blacker, Carmen. (1975) 1986. *The Catalpa Bow*. London: Allen and Unwin.

Boddy, Janice. 1989. *Wombs and Alien Spirits: Women, Men, and the Zar Cult in Northern Sudan*. Madison: University of Wisconsin Press.

Bokenkotter, Thomas. 2004. *A Concise History of the Catholic Church*. Revised and Expanded Edition. New York: Doubleday.

Borovoy, Amy. 2005. *The Too-Good Wife: Alcohol, Codependency, and the Politics of Nurturance in Postwar Japan*. Berkeley: University of California Press.

Boxer, Charles Ralph. 1951. *The Christian Century in Japan, 1549–1650*. Berkeley: University of California Press.

Braudel, Fernand. 1980. *On History*. Chicago: University of Chicago Press.

Brinton, Mary C. 1994. *Women and the Economic Miracle: Gender and Work in Postwar Japan*. Berkeley: University of California Press.

Broderick, John F. 2005. "Ignatius Loyola." In *Encyclopedia of Religion*, edited by Lindsay Jones, volume 7, 2nd ed., 4367–69. Detroit: Macmillan Reference USA.

Burke, Peter. 1990. *The French Historical Revolution: The Annales School, 1929–89*. Stanford, CA: Stanford University Press.

Canell, Fenella, ed. 2006. *Anthropology of Christianity*. Durham: Duke University Press.

Catholic Bishops' Conference of Japan, Division for Interreligious Dialogue, ed. 1985. *Catholic Guide regarding Ancestors and the Deceased*. Tokyo: Catholic Bishops' Conference of Japan.

———. 2009. *Catholic Church's Guide to Interreligious Dialogue: Practical Q & A*. Tokyo: Catholic Bishops' Conference of Japan.

Catholic Bishops' Conference of Japan. 2008. *Statistics of the Catholic Church in Japan 2007*. Tokyo: Catholic Bishops' Conference of Japan.

———. 2014. *Statistics of the Catholic Church in Japan 2013*. Tokyo: Catholic Bishops' Conference of Japan.
Cave, Peter. 2007. *Primary School in Japan: Self, Individuality and Learning in Elementary Education*. London: Routledge.
Chapman, David, and Karl Jacob Krogness, ed. 2014. *Japan's Household Registration System: Koseki, Identity and Documentation*. London: Routledge.
Chiba, Kaeko. 2011. *Japanese Women, Class and the Tea Ceremony: The Voices of Tea Practitioners in Northern Japan*. New York: Routledge.
Chua, Liana. 2012. *The Christianity of Culture: Conversion, Ethnic Citizenship and the Matter of Religion in Malaysian Borneo*. New York: Palgrave Macmillan.
Christian, William A. Jr. 1996. *Visionaries: The Spanish Republic and the Reign of Christ*. Berkeley, CA: University of California Press.
Clammer, John. 2001. "The Other Others: Japanese Christianity and the Negotiation of Modernity." In *Japan and Its Others: Globalization, Differences and the Critique of Modernity*, edited by John Clammer, 163–88. Melbourne: Trans Pacific Press.
Comaroff, John L., and Jean Comaroff. 1997. *Of Revelation and Revolution: The Dialectics of Modernity and South African Frontier*. Vol. 2. Chicago: University of Chicago Press.
Covell, Stephen G. 2005. *Japanese Temple Buddhism: Worldliness in a Religion of Renunciation*. Honolulu: University of Hawai'i Press.
Csordas, Thomas J. 1994. *The Sacred Self: A Cultural Phenomenology of Charismatic Healing*. Berkeley: University of California Press.
———. 1997. *Language, Charisma, and Creativity: Ritual Life in Catholic Charismatic Renewal*. Berkeley: University of California Press.
De Bary, Wm. Theodore, Donald Keene, George Tanabe, and Paul Verley. 2001. *Sources of Japanese Tradition, Second Edition, Volume One: From Earliest Times to 1600*. New York: Columbia University Press.
Davis, Winston Bradley. 1980. *Dōjō: Magic and Exorcism in Modern Japan*. Stanford, CA: Stanford University Press.
Doi, Takeo. 1971. *Amae no kozo. The Anatomy of Dependence*. Tokyo: Kobundo.
Drummond, Richard H. 1971. *A History of Christianity in Japan*. Grand Rapids, MI: William B. Eerdmans Publishing Company.
Dumont, Louis. (1970) 1980. *Homo Hierarchicus: The Caste System and Its Implications*. Complete Revised English Edition. Translated by Mark Sainsbury, Louis Dumont, and Basia Gulati. Chicago: University of Chicago Press.
———. 1985. "A Modified View of Our Origins: The Christian Beginning of Modern Individualism." *The Category of the Person: Anthropology, Philosophy, History*, 93–122. Cambridge: Cambridge University Press.
———. 1986. *Essays on Individualism: Modern Ideology in Anthropological Perspective*. Chicago: University of Chicago Press.

Durkheim, Emile. (1915) 1974. *The Elementary Forms of Religious Life*. Translated by Joseph Swain. Glencoe: Free Press.
Elisha, Omri. 2011. *Moral Ambition: Mobilizing Social Outreach in Evangelical Megachurches*. Berkeley: University of California Press.
Elisonas, Jurgis. 1991. "Christianity and the Daimyo." *The Cambridge History of Japan*. Vol. 4, Early Modern Japan, edited by John Whitney Hall, 301–72. Cambridge: Cambridge University Press.
Foucault, Michele. 1984. *The Foucault Reader*. Edited by Paul Rabinow. New York: Pantheon.
Geertz, Clifford. 1973. *The Interpretation of Cultures: Selected Essays*. New York: Basic Books.
Goldstein-Gidoni, Ofra. 2012. *Housewives of Japan: An Ethnography of Real Lives and Consumerized Domesticity*. New York: Palgrave Macmillan.
Gonoi Takashi. 1990. *Nihon Kirisutokyōshi* [History of Christianity in Japan]. Tokyo: Yoshikawa Kōbunkan.
Greeley, Andrew. 2004. *The Catholic Revolution: New Wine, Old Wineskins, and the Second Vatican Council*. Berkeley: University of California Press.
Hamabata, Matthews Masayuki. 1990. *Crested Kimono: Power and Love in the Japanese Business Family*. Ithaca: Cornell University Press.
Hanlon, Kevin J. 2003. Gaikokujin shisai ga mita nihon no shinto [Popular Catholicism in Japan]. Tokyo: Enderure shoten.
Hara, Yoshihisa. 2005. *Yoshida Shigeru: Sonnō no seiji-ka* [Yoshida Shigeru: A Politician Who Revered the Emperor]. Tokyo: Iwanami shoten.
Hardacre, Helen. 1989. *Shintō and the State, 1868–1988*. Princeton, NJ: Princeton University Press.
———. 1997. *Marketing the Menacing Fetus in Japan*. Berkeley: University of California Press.
———. 2006. "State and Religion in Japan." In *Nanzan Guide to Japanese Religions*, edited by Paul Swanson and Clark Chilson, 274–88. Honolulu: University of Hawai'i Press.
Haresaku Masahide. 2005. *Anata ni hanashitai*. [I want to talk to you]. Tokyo: Kyōyūsha.
———. 2006. *Kibō wa kokoni aru*. [Here is hope]. Tokyo: Kyōyūsha.
Hefner, Robert W. 1993. *Conversion to Christianity: Historical and Anthropological Perspectives on a Great Transformation*. Berkeley: University of California Press.
Hendry, Joy. 1981. *Marriage in Changing Japan: Community and Society*. New York: St. Martin's Press.
Hobsbawm, Eric, and Terence Ranger. 1983. *The Invention of Tradition*. Cambridge: Cambridge University Press.
Hur, Nam-lin. 2007. *Death and Social Order in Tokugawa Japan: Buddhism, Anti-Christianity, and the Danka System*. Cambridge, MA: Harvard University Press.

Igeta Ryōji. 1982. "Meiji minpō to josei no kenri [Meiji Civil Code and the Right of Women]." In *Nihon joseishi* [History of Women in Japan] 4, *Modern Period*, edited by Joseishi sōgō kenkyu-kai [Association for Multidisciplinary Research on Women's History], 41–76. Tokyo: Tokyo University Press.

Ikeuchi, Suma. 2017. "Accompanied Self: Debating Pentecostal Individual and Japanese Relational Selves in Transnational Japan." *Ethos* 45(1):3–23.

Inoue Tadashi. 1977. *'Sekentei' no kozo: Shakai shinrishi e no kokoromi* [The Structure of 'Sekentei': An attempt of social psychological history]. Tokyo: Nihon Hōsō Kyokai Shuppan.

Itō Susumu. 1996. *Nihonjin no ai* [Japanese Love]. Tokyo: Hokuju shuppan.

Itsuki, Hiroyuki. 2007. *Ningen no kankei* [Human Relations]. Tokyo: Popurasha.

Iwasaki, Kenji, Masaya Takahashi, and Akinori Nakata. 2006. "Health Problems due to Long Working Hours in Japan: Working Hours, Workers' Compensation (*Karoshi*), and Preventative Measures." *Industrial Health* 44:537–40.

Jaffe, Richard M. 2001. *Neither Monk nor Layman: Clerical Marriage in Modern Japanese Buddhism*. Princeton, NJ: Princeton University Press.

Josephson, Jason Ananda. 2012. *The Invention of Religion in Japan*. Chicago: University of Chicago Press.

Jugensmeyer, Mark. 2000. *Terror in the Mind of God: The Global Rise of Religious Violence*. Berkeley: University of California Press.

Kamata Minoru. 2003. *Ganbaranai* [Not to Strive Hard]. Tokyo: Shūeisha Bunko.

Kato, Etsuko. 2004. *The Tea Ceremony and Women's Empowerment in Modern Japan: Bodies Re-presenting the Past*. New York: Routledge.

Kawahashi Noriko. 2006. "Gender Issues in Japanese Religions." In *Nanzan Guide to Japanese Religions*, edited by Paul Swanson and Clark Chilson, 323–35. Honolulu: University of Hawai'i Press.

Keane, Webb. 2007. *Christian Moderns: Freedom and Fetish in the Mission Encounter*. Berkeley: University of California Press.

Keene, Donald. 1984. "Characteristic Responses to Confucianism in Tokugawa Literature." In *Confucianism and Tokugawa Culture*, edited by Peter Nosco, 120–37. Princeton, NJ: Princeton University Press.

Kelsky, Karen. 2001. *Women on the Verge: Japanese Women, Western Dreams*. Durham: Duke University Press.

Kertzer, David I. 1988. *Ritual, Politics, and Power*. New Haven and London: Yale University Press.

Kim Yang-sŏn. 1996. "Compulsory Shintō Shrine Worship and Persecution." In *Korea and Christianity*, edited by Chai-Shin Yu, 87–120. Seoul: Korean Scholar Press.

Kisala, Robert. 2006. "Japanese Religions." In *Nanzan Guide to Japanese Religions*, edited by Paul Swanson and Clark Chilson, 3–13. Honolulu: University of Hawai'i Press.

Kitagawa, Tomoko. 2007. "The Conversion of Hideyoshi's Daughter Gō." *Japanese Journal of Religious Studies* 34:9-25.

Kondo, Dorinne K. 1986. "Dissolution and Reconstitution of the Self: Implications for Anthropological Epistemology." *Cultural Anthropology* 1:74-88.

———. 1990. *Crafting Selves: Power, Gender, and Discourses of Identity in a Japanese Workplace*. Chicago: University of Chicago Press.

Kosakai Sumi. 1984. *Kanashimi no maria no shima—aru Shōwa no junan* [The Island of "Mary of Sorrow": A Persecution of Shōwa]. Tokyo: Shūeisha.

Kuwayama, 1992. "The Reference Other Orientation." In *Japanese Sense of Self*, edited by Nancy Rosenberger, 121-51. Cambridge: Cambridge University Press.

Lebra, Takie Sugiyama. 1984. *Japanese Women: Constraints and Fulfillment*. Honolulu: University of Hawai'i Press.

Lu, David John. 1997. *Japan: A Documentary History*. Armonk, NY: M. E. Sharpe.

MacLaine, Shirley. 1986. *Out on a Limb*. New York: Bantam Books.

Madsen, Richard. 1998. *China's Catholics: Tragedy and Hope in an Emerging Civil Society*. Berkeley: University of California Press.

Mageo, Jeannette, ed. 2002. *Power and the Self*. Cambridge: Cambridge University Press.

Mahmood, Saba. 2005. *Politics of Piety: The Islamic Revival and the Feminist Subject*. Princeton: Princeton University Press.

Marcus, George E., and Michael M. J. Fischer. 1986. *Anthropology as Cultural Critique: An Experimental Moment in the Human Sciences*. Chicago: University of Chicago Press.

Maruyama, Masao. 1985. "Patterns of Individuation and the Case of Japan: A Conceptual Scheme." In *Changing Japanese Attitudes to Modernization*, edited by M. B. Jansen, 489-531. Tokyo: Charles E. Tuttle.

Maruyama Masao, and Katō Shūichi. 1998. *Honyaku to nihon no kindai* [Translation and Japan's Modernity]. Tokyo: Iwanami shoten.

Mathews, Gordon, and Bruce White, eds. 2004. *Japan's Changing Generations: Are Young People Creating New Society?* London: Routledge Curzon.

Mauss, Maucel. 1985. "A Category of the Human Mind: The Notion of Person; the Notion of Self." In *The Category of the Person: Anthropology, Philosophy, History*, edited by Michael Carrithers, Steven Collins, and Steven Lukes; translated by W. D. Halls, 1-25. Cambridge: Cambridge University Press.

McFarland, H. Neil. 1967. *The Rush Hour of the Gods: A Study of New Religious Movements in Japan*. New York: Macmillan.

Meyer, Birgit. 1999. "Commodities and Powers of Prayer: Pentecostal Attitudes Toward Consumption in Contemporary Ghana." In *Globalization and Identity: Dialectics of Flow and Closure*, edited by Birgit Meyer and Peter Geschiere, 151-76. Oxford: Blackwell Publishers.

Miyazaki, Kentarō. 2003. "Roman Catholic Mission in Pre-modern Japan." Translated by Peter Knecht. In *Handbook of Christianity in Japan*, edited by Mark R. Mullins, 1–18. Leiden: Brill.
Mizobe, Osamu. 2007. "Kokuze to Hakugai—Rekishi-jō yorino Saikousatsu [National Policy and Persecution: Reconsideration from Historical Perspectives]." In *Shinkyō no jiyū to seikyō bunri* [Freedom of Religion and the Separation of Church and the State], edited by Catholic Bishops' Conference of Japan, 45–58. Tokyo: Catholic Bishops' Conference of Japan.
Moeran, Brian. (1986) 1998. "One Over the Seven: Sake Drinking in a Japanese Pottery Community." In *Interpreting Japanese Society: Anthropological Approaches*, 2nd ed., edited by Joy Hendry, 243–58. London: Routledge.
Mosko, Mark. 2010. "Partible Penitents: Dividual Personhood and Christian Practice in Melanesia and the West. *Journal of the Royal Anthropological Institute* 16:215–40.
Mullins, Mark R. 1998. *Christianity Made in Japan: A Study of Indigenous Movements*. Honolulu: University of Hawai'i Press.
———. 2004. "Japanese Christians and the World of the Dead." *Mortality* 9(1):62–75.
———. 2011. "Between Inculturation and Globalization: The Situation of Roman Catholicism in Contemporary Japanese Society." In *Xavier's Legacies: Catholicism in Modern Japanese Culture*, edited by Kevin M. Doak, 169–92. Vancouver: University of British Columbia Press.
Nakamura Kichiji. 1978. *Ie no rekishi* [The History of Ie]. Tokyo: Nōsan gyoson bunnka kyōkai.
Nakane Chie. 1967. *Tateshakai no ningenkankei: tanitsu shakai no riron* [*Japanese Society*]. Tokyo: Kodansha.
Nakano, Lynne and Moeko Wagatsuma. 2004. "Mothers and Their Unmarried Daughters: An Intimate Look at Generational Change." In *Japan's Changing Generations: Are Young People Creating a New Society?*, edited by Gordon Mathews and Bruce White, 137–154. London: Routledge Curzon.
Nelson, John K. 2000. *Enduring Identities: The Guise of Shinto in Contemporary Japan*. Honolulu: University of Hawai'i Press.
Nosco, Peter, ed. 1984. *Confucianism and Tokugawa Culture*. Princeton, NJ: Princeton University Press.
Ogasawara, Yuko. 1998. *Office Ladies and Salaried Men: Power, Gender and Work in Japanese Companies*. Berkeley: University of California Press.
Ohnuki-Tierney, Emiko. 1990. "The Ambivalent Self of the Contemporary Japanese." *Cultural Anthropology* 5(2):197–216.
———. 2001. *Rice as Self: Japanese Identities through Time*. Princeton, NJ: Princeton University Press.
Ohta Yoshiko, ed. 2004. *Nihon Kirisuto-kyō to no kaikō: futatsu no jidai ni miru juyō to kattou* [Japan's Encounter with Christianity: Acceptance and

Struggles Seen through Two Eras]. Tokyo: Oriens Institute for Religious Research.
Okazaki, Hisahiko. 2003. *Yoshida Shigeru to sono jidai* [Yoshida Shigeru and His Era]. Tokyo: PHP Kenkyūjo.
Omori, Hisako. 2014. "Private Faith: Social Memory, Gender, and the Roman Catholic Church in Contemporary Tokyo." *Culture and Religion* 15(1):39–57. https://doi.org/10.1080/14755610.2014.884011.
Omoto Kumi. 2006. "Gendai nihon ni okeru katorikku karisuma undo no tenkai: zenkoku taikai wo jireini [The Catholic Charismatic Renewal Movement in Contemporary Japan: The Case of A National Conference]." *Journal of Religious Studies* 25–41. Tokyo: Komazawa Religious Studies Institute.
Ono, Sayako. 2015. "Ballet as Liberation: Dream, Desire, and Resistance among Urban Japanese Women." PhD diss., SOAS, University of London.
Ooms, Herman. 1984. "Neo-Confucianism and the Formation of Early Tokugawa Ideology: Contours of a Problem." In *Confucianism and Tokugawa Culture*, edited by Peter Nosco, 27–61. Princeton, NJ: Princeton University Press.
Ortner, Sherry B. 2006. *Anthropology and Social Theory: Culture, Power, and the Acting Subject*. Durham, NC: Duke University Press.
Panourgiá, Neni. 1994. "A Native Narrative." *Anthropology and Humanism* 19(1):40–51.
Quero, Hugo Cordova, and Rafael Shoji, eds. 2014. *Transnational Faiths: Latin-American Immigrants and Their Religions in Japan*. Farnham, VT: Ashgate.
Reader, Ian. 1991. *Religion in Contemporary Japan*. Honolulu: University of Hawai'i Press.
———. 1995. "Cleaning Floors and Sweeping the Mind." In *Ceremony and Ritual in Japan: Religious Practices in an Industrialized Society*, edited by Jan van Bremen et al., 227–45. London: Routledge.
Reader, Ian, and George J. Tanabe, Jr. 1998. *Practically Religious: Worldly Benefits and the Common Religion of Japan*. Honolulu: University of Hawai'i Press.
Robbins, Joel. 2004. *Becoming Sinners: Christianity and moral torment in a Papua New Guinean society*. Berkeley: University of California Press.
———. 2010. "Melanesia, Christianity, and Cultural Change: A Comment on Mosko's 'Partible Penitents.'" *Journal of the Royal Anthropological Institute* 16: 241–43.
Rocha, Christina. 2006. *Zen in Brazil: The Quest of Cosmopolitan Modernity*. Honolulu: University of Hawai'i Press.
Rosenberger, Nancy R, ed. 1992. *Japanese Sense of Self*. Cambridge: Cambridge University Press.
———. 2001. *Gambling with Virtue: Japanese Women and the Search for Self in a Changing Nation*. Honolulu: University of Hawai'i Press.
———. 2013. *Dilemmas of Adulthood: Japanese Women and the Nuances of Long-term Resistance*. Honolulu: University of Hawai'i Press.

Rowe, Mark. 2003. "Grave Changes: Scattering Ashes in Contemporary Japan." *Japanese Journal of Religious Studies* 30(1-2):85-118.
———. 2009. "Death, Burial, and the Study of Contemporary Japanese Buddhism." *Religion Compass* 3(1):18-30.
———. 2011. *Bonds of the Dead: Temples, Burial, and the Transformation of Contemporary Japanese Buddhism*. Chicago: University of Chicago Press.
Rupp, Katherine. 2003. *Gift-giving in Japan: Cash, Connections, and Cosmologies*. Stanford, CA: Stanford University Press.
Ryang, Sonia. 2006. *Love in Modern Japan: Its Estrangement from Self, Sex, and Society*. London and New York: Routledge.
Sakamoto Takao. 1997. "Nihon no kindaika to shūkyō—Kirisuto-kyō wo chūshin ni [Japan's modernization and religion: The case of Christianity and other traditions]." In *Uchinaru mono to shiteno shūkyō* [Religion as Internal Affairs], edited by Kawai Hayao and Murakami Yoichiro, 45-76. *Gendai nihon bunka-ron* [Contemporary Japanese Culture Theories] 12. Tokyo: Iwanami Shoten.
Sasaki Kōkan. 2004. *Shinpojiumu—Sōsai: gendaiteki igi to kadai—Kiroku* [Record of Symposium, Funerary and Memorial Rites: Its Contemporary Meanings and Challenge]. Tokyo: Sōtō Zen Research Center.
Schnell, Scott. 1999. *The Rousing Drum: Ritual Practice in a Japanese Community*. Honolulu: University of Hawai'i Press.
Seat, Karen. 2003. Mission Schools and Education for Women. In *Handbook of Christianity in Japan*, edited by Mark Mullins, 321-42. Leiden: Brill.
Shimada Hiromi. 2009. *Yokuwakaru! Nihon no shinshūkyō* [Easy to Understand! New Religious Movements in Japan]. Tokyo: Kasakura shuppan.
Shimazono, Susumu. 1993. "Introduction to Part 4: New Religious Movement." In *Religion & Society in Modern Japan*. Edited by Mark R. Mullins, Shimazono Susumu, and Paul L. Swanson, 221-30. Berkeley: Asian Humanities Press.
———. 2004. *From Salvation to Spirituality: Popular Religious Movements in Modern Japan*. Melbourne: Trans Pacific Press.
———. 2006. "Contemporary Japanese Religions." In *Nanzan Guide to Japanese Religions*, edited by Paul Swanson and Clark Chilson, 220-31. Honolulu: University of Hawai'i Press.
Shore, Bradd. 1982. *Sala'ilua: A Samoan Mystery*. New York: Columbia University Press.
Smith, Robert. 1974. *Ancestor Worship in Contemporary Japan*. Stanford: Stanford University Press.
———. 1983. *Japanese society: Tradition, Self and the Social Order*. Cambridge: Cambridge University Press.
Smyers, Karen. 1999. *The Fox and the Jewel*. Honolulu: University of Hawai'i Press.
Sophia School Corporation Editorial Committee for New Catholic Encyclopedia. 2002. *New Catholic Encyclopedia*, Vol. 3. Tokyo: Kenkyūsha.

Statistics Bureau Japan. 2007. Kokusei chōsa jinkō zōgenritsu jinkō mitsudo (Shōwa 35-nen ~ Heisei 17-nen) [National census on population change and population density (1960–2005)], sōmushō tōkeikyoku [Statistics Bureau]. July 6, 2007. www.stat.go.jp/data/chiri/map/c_koku/index2.htm.

Sueki, Fumihiko. 2006. *Nihon shūkyōshi* [History of Japanese religions]. Tokyo: Iwanami shoten.

Taguchi Randy. 2007. "Supirichuaru toiu kaibutsu [A Monster called Spirituality]." In *Kaze no tabibito* [Traveler of Wind], 38–86. Tokyo: Round of Life Eurasia Travel Co. Ltd.

Takeda Chōshū. 1976. *Nihonjin no "ie" to shukyo* [Japanese "Ie" and Religion]. Tokyo: Hyōronsha.

Taylor, Lawrence J. 1995. *Occasions of Faith: An Anthropology of Irish Catholics*. Philadelphia: University of Pennsylvania Press.

Terada Takefumi. 2010. "Kaigai kara no ijūsha to shūkyō jissen: Tokyo daishikyō-ku no firipin-jin kyōdōtai wo chūshin ni shite [Migrants from overseas and their religious practices: Case of Filipino Community in the Archdiocese of Tokyo]." In *Grōbaru-ka no naka no shūkyō: Suitai, saisei, henbou* [Religion and Globalization: Decline, Regeneration and Transformation], edited by Masatoshi Kisaichi, Takefumi Terada, and Masayuki Akahori, 91–110. Tokyo: Sophia University Press.

Toda Yūko. 1978. *Shōto pantsu to kuromontsukito: aru tsūyaku no mita sengoshi* [Short Pants and Crested Kimono: Postwar Japan through the Eyes of An Interpreter]. Tokyo: Keisō shuppan sābisu sentā.

Tokyo Metropolitan Government. 2008. "Heisei 17-nen kokusei chōsa ni yoru 'Tokyo-to no hiruma jinkō' kekka gaiyō [A Result Summary of 2008 National Census on 'Daytime Population of Metropolitan Tokyo']." http://www.metro.tokyo.jp/INET/CHOUSA/2008/03/60i3r100.htm.

Traphagan, John W. 2004. *The Practice of Concern: Ritual, Well-being, and Aging in Rural Japan*. Durham, NC: Carolina Academic Press.

Tsunoda Ryusaku, Wm Theodore de Bary, and Donald Keene, eds. 1958. *Sources of Japanese Tradition, Volume II*. New York: Columbia University Press.

United Nations. 2009. *2007 Demographic Year Book*. New York: United Nations. https://unstats.un.org/unsd/demographic/products/dyb/dyb2007.htm.

United Nations Department of Economic and Social Affairs [UN DESA]. 2016. *The World's Cities in 2016: Data Booklet*. New York: United Nations. https://doi.org/10.18356/8519891f-en.

Varley, Paul. 2000. *Japanese Culture*, 4th ed. Updated and Expanded. Honolulu: University of Hawai'i Press.

Verdery, Katherine. 1999. *The Political Lives of Dead Bodies: Reburial and Postsocialist Change*. New York: Columbia University Press.

Vogel, Ezra F. 1979. *Japan as Number One: Lessons for America*. Cambridge: Harvard University Press.

Whelan, Christal. 2005. *Otai ya: Christmas Eve*. DVD. Directed by Christal Whelan. Watertown, MA: Documentary Educational Resource.

Yamaguchi Satoko. 2003. Christianity and Women in Japan. *Japanese Journal of Religious Studies* 30(3–4):315–38.

Yao, Xinzhong. 2000. *An Introduction to Confucianism*. Cambridge: Cambridge University Press.

Yasukuni Shrine. 2008. About Yasukuni Shrine. *Yasukuni Shrine*. October 3, 2010. www.yasukuni.or.jp/english/about/index.html.

Young, Richard Fox. 1993. Magic and Morality in Modern Japanese Exorcistic Technologies. In *Religion and Society in Modern Japan*, edited by Mullins, Mark, Shimazono Susumu, and Paul Swanson, 239–56. Berkeley, CA: Asian Humanities Press.

Index

Note: Page numbers in *italics* indicate illustrations.

Abe, Ikuo, 148, 201n9
adoptive children, 115
agency, 2, 186; definition of, 114; personhood and, 188–192
Ahearn, Laura, 114
Akishino Temple (Nara), 83, 109, 199n1
Allison, Anne, 136, 155
Amami Ōshima, 51, 164–165, 202n5
Amanuma, Kaoru, 76, 78–79, 199n15
ancestor worship, 167–170, 174–175
Angel's Club, 46
Angel's Forest store, 43–44, *44*
Annales School, 4, 60, 193n5
apology press conference (*shazai kaiken*), 54
Arai Hakuseki, 63, 198n8
Arima Harunobu, 23
Aum Shinrikyō, 30, 163, 202n4
authority, 15, 53, 60; divine, 2, 9–10, 113; of husbands, 151–152

Bachnik, Jane, 7, 62, 83, 84
baptism, 48, 193n3, 197n18; converts' descriptions of, 5–6, 104–106, 129–131; men's views about, 129, 130, 138–140; names taken at, 51, 160, 179–180; priest's description of, 139–140; sponsors of, 52, 91, 134, 138, 160, 172
batsu-ichi, 107, 200n9. *See also* divorce
Benedict, Ruth, 76, 194n9
benri (convenience), 20
Bialecki, Jon, 10, 190
Bible, 39, 55, 56, 141; Non-church Movement and, 49; passages in, 93, 95, 103, 120, 141, 159; Protestants and, 49, 126
Borovoy, Amy, 74
Boy Scouts, 46
Braudel, Fernand, 4, 60, 193n5
Buddhism, 5, 16; burial customs of, 160, 169–173, 177, 182; celibacy in, 194n12; Christianity and, 24, 36, 52, 161–162, 174–177; funeral rites of, 31–33, 91, 107–109, 111, 156, 199n3; new religious movements and, 30; Nichiren sect of, 50, 202n2; notion of love in, 98; prayer beads and, 161–162; sects of, 32–33; temple certification system of, 24, 156, 170–171, 177; after WWII, 31–32

217

Bushido, 148, 201n10
"business card reception" boxes, 88–90, *89*

catechism, 39, 46, 51, 97, 119–120, 156, 172; uneasy feelings toward, 130, 153
"Catholic bar," 36, 85–87
Catholic Bishops' Conference of Japan, 34, 46, 132; on Buddhist funerals, 172–173; on Catholics hiding identity, 186
Catholic Charismatic Renewal movement, 14, 41, 122–125, 194n13
"Catholic religious army" (*katorikku shūkyō butai*), 29
Catholicism, 34–37; acolytes' motivations for, 106–110; celibacy in, 194n12; characteristics of, 121–127; concealed identity of, 16; demographics of, 34–36, 85, 132, 146–147; educational institutions of, 23, 28, 144–148; female parishioners of, 16, 129–136, 150–157; feminine ideals of, 135, 143–150, 166–169; Japanese history of, 16, 22–29, 163–166; Jesuits and, 200n10; lapsed Buddhists and, 107–109; male parishioners of, 129–131, 134–135, 152–154; masculine ideals and, 139–143, 148–150, 157; during Meiji Period, 24–27, 30, 149, 163–164, 194n6; popular values of, 93–106; Protestant converts to, 109, 193n3; Protestant values and, 121–127, 148–150; World War II and, 27, 29–34, 149–150; worldview of, 6, 15–16, 94; Zen meditation and, 36, 52. *See also* Protestants
Cave, Peter, 65
celibacy, 194n12

cemeteries, 89, 170, 173; purchasing plots in, 32–33, 130, 154
children, 64; adoptive, 115; care of, 21–22, 136, 155. *See also* parents
"Christian century" (1549–1639), 22
Christianity, 9–10; Buddhism and, 24, 36, 52, 161, 174–177; historical prejudices against, 16, 22–29, 163–166; individualism and, 113–114; Korean, 185–186; meekness as virtue in, 139–143, 157; "muscular," 148–149, 201n9; Shinto and, 24, 30, 149–150, 156–157, 174, 194n7, 196n11; Tokugawa ban of, 5, 23–24, 193n6; worldview of, 15–16. *See also* Catholicism; "hidden" Christians
Clammer, John, 186–187
concealed faith. *See* "hidden" Christians
Confucius, 62, 67. *See also* Neo-Confucianism
Congrégation des Sœurs de l'Instruction Charitable du Saint Enfant Jésus, 28
"conjuncture," 4, 8, 193n5
convenience (*benri*), 20
conversion, 92, 131–132, 193n3; deathbed, 16, 129, 153–156, 179–181; motivations for, 106–110; notice of, 165; from Protestantism, 190, 193n3; of samurai, 28, 176; two-tier model of, 84–85
conversion experiences, 5–6, 81–82, 104–106, 117–121; Bialecki on, 10, 190; gender differences in, 129–132
"coordinate grid" (*zahyōjiku*), 83, 199n2

danka seido. *See* temple certification system

Declaration on the Relationship of the Church to Non-Christian Religions, 173–174
divorce, 74–75, 85, 104–107, 129, 133, 141. *See also* marriage
Dogmatic Constitution of the Church, 175
Doi, Takeo, 194n9
Dominican order, 27, 28, 107, 144
Dulles, Avery, 175
Dumont, Louis, 10, 113–114
Durkheim, Émile, 58

Edo Period (1603–1868), 4, 60–68, 198n11; ancestor worship during, 170; ban on Christianity during, 5, 23–24, 193n6; funeral rites during, 169; literature of, 67; masculine ideals during, 140
educational institutes, 64, 107–108, 110; Catholic, 23, 28, 144–148; Confucian, 66–67; Meiji, 65–66; Protestant, 149
elder care, 21, 22, 136
emperor, 150, 179; divinity of, 26–29, 64, 201n2
"emptying oneself" (*jibun wo karappo nishite*), 94
Endo Shūsaku, 86
"entrusting" (*yudaneru*), 84, 94–96, 106; perseverance and, 94–95, 116, 126
Equal Employment Opportunity Law (1986), 80, 151

faith, 12–13, 22, 42, 83; private, 162–163, 173; after Second Vatican Council, 175–177
"Fathers' Club," 45, 105
feminine ideals, 135, 143–150, 166–169. *See also* gender issues

filial piety (*kō*), 8, 64, 65, 97, 168
First Friday (*hatsukin*), 36, 45
Fischer, Michael M. J., 2
Foucault, Michel, 4, 5, 106, 191
Frois, Luis, 195n4
fumie, 24, 164–165, 195n7
funeral services, 31–33, 110–111, 154–156, 179–180; burial customs and, 160, 169–173, 177, 182; choir for, 51–52, 134; clothing for, 91, 198n8; gift exchange at, 111–113, 199n3; negative views of, 107–109; women's role in, 168–173

ganbaru (perseverance), 15, 94–97, 119–121; cult of, 76–80; as postwar concept, 199n15; Sabbath observance and, 201n4; *yudaneru* and, 94–95, 116, 126
gender issues, 129–158; binary of, 200n1; with childcare, 21–22, 136, 155; with elder care, 21, 22, 136; "Fathers' Clubs" and, 45, 105; female parishioners and, 16, 129–136, 150–157; feminine ideals and, 135, 143–150, 166–169; funeral rites and, 168–173; with *ganbaru*, 15, 80, 94–96; male parishioners and, 129–131, 134–135, 152–154; masculine ideals and, 139–143, 148–150, 157; *ojō-san* ideal as, 56–57, 67, 117, 197n4; parental love and, 101–103; social expectations and, 7–8, 85, 135–136, 155; women in workforce as, 133–134, 136–137, 151; women's education as, 145–147
gift exchange, 84, 87–90, 93; at funeral services, 111–113, 199n3
glossolalia (speaking in tongues), 41, 42, 122, 139, 194n13

God (Christian): authority of, 2, 9–10, 113; as love, 84, 97, 101–103, 106, 200n5; as new "third person," 15–16, 85–87; as society, 55–60; work of, 194n8
Gonoi Takashi, 23, 195n7
gossip, 58, 91–92
Gotō Islands, 14
Graham, Robert A., 174
Great East Japan Earthquake (2011), 199n16
Greeley, Andrew, 175
Green, T. H., 79

Hamabata, Matthews Masayuki, 68–71
Hamao Fumio, 179–180
handicaps, people with, 115–116
Hanlon, Kevin, 200n5
Hardacre, Helen, 66, 136, 194n7
Haresaku, Masahide, 101–103
Hayashi Razan, 61–62
Heart Sutra, 49
heaven, 62; parishioner views of, 96–97; "theft" of, 153, 180
Hefner, Robert W., 181
"hidden" Christians, 16, 24–25, 138–139, 164–166, 195n8; Buddhist burial customs and, 160, 169–173, 177, 182; Catholic conversions of, 109, 193n3; characteristics of, 121–127; Church support for, 174–177; within families, 159–160, 167–169, 172; gender roles and, 148–150; missionary efforts of, 26, 148–149; temple affiliation of, 24, 156, 170–171, 177; during World War II, 27, 29–34, 149–150
hierarchies. *See* social hierarchies
Hinduism, 174, 202n4
Holiness groups, 29, 150
Hollands, Arthur, 148–149
"holy family" (*seikazoku*), 131

household registration system (*koseki seido*), 187, 200n9, 204n5
housewives (*sengyō shufu*), 39, 47, 49, 90, 104, 115, 168; gift-giving responsibility of, 199n3; life course of, 137; prayer of, 157
human relationships. *See ningen kankei*
hymns, 42, 94, 103, 122, 134

identity politics, 181, 184–186
Ikutsuki Island, 195n8
Imperial Rescript on Education (*kyōiku chokugo*), 65–66, 72
"incense money" (*kōden*), 111
India, 113–114
individualism, 3, 10, 136; Christianity and, 113–114. *See also* sense of self
Inoue Haruyo, 171
"integrity," 12–13
Islam, 58, 174
Itō Susumu, 97–101
Iwakura Tomomi, 36
Iwakura Mission (1871–1873), 25

Japan: constitutions of, 26, 30, 53; dioceses of, 27, 34, 35; economy of, 21, 136–137, 149, 201n13; nationalism in, 5, 29, 51, 77, 101, 164
Japanese language: dialects of, 5, 53–54; social relationships reflected in, 7–8, 69, 87; words for *love* in, 97–101
Jesuits, 22–23, 28, 200n10
jibun sagashi (search for self), 11
jibun wo karappo nishite (emptying oneself), 94

kabuki theater, 61, 140
kadomatsu, 175, 203n13
Kagoshima Prefecture, 72

Kaibara Ekken, 198n9
kakure kirishitan. See "hidden" Christians
Kamakura City, 137–138
kamikaze pilots, 201n2
karōshi (death by overwork), 21, 195n2
Keene, Donald, 67, 198n11
Kisala, Robert, 33, 163
kōden ("incense money"), 111
Kōfuku no kagaku, 30
koi (love), 98, 100, 101
kokutai, 196n11
Kondo, Dorinne K., 6–9, 12, 68–71, 160, 182
Korea, 37, 185–186
Kosakai Sumi, 165
koseki seido (household registration system), 187–188, 200n9, 204n5
Kyoto, 23, 83

Light of Spiritual Wave (Reiha no hikari), 50
longue durée, 4, 8, 60, 193n5
Lourdes shrine, 43
love, 67, 97–103; forms of, 97; God as, 84, 97, 101–103, 106, 200n5; Japanese words for, 97–101; nationalism and, 101; parental, 101–103; Saint Paul on, 101
loyalty, personal, 88, 91–92
Loyola, Ignatius of, 120, 200n10
Lu, David John, 60–63

MacArthur, Douglas, 179
MacLaine, Shirley, 50
Manyōshū (poetry collection), 98
Marcus, George E., 2
marriage, 48, 133, 150–152, 155, 184; "couple culture" and, 133; divorce and, 74–75, 85, 104–107, 129, 133, 141; postponement of, 11; women's education and, 145

Maruyama, Masao, 186
Masako, Empress, 144, 148
masculine ideals, 140–143, 148–150. *See also* gender issues
Mathy, Francis, 94
meekness, as Christian virtue, 139–143, 157
Meiji Constitution, 26, 30
Meiji Period (1868–1912), 8, 56, 60, 64–68, 79; Catholicism during, 24–27, 30, 149, 163–164, 194n6; Civil Code of, 187; feminine ideals of, 135; gender roles during, 135; "sportsmanship" during, 148
mentalité, 60–61, 68, 76
Michiko, Empress Emerita, 143–144, 148
migrants, 15, 34, 36–37
mikoshi (Shinto portable shrine), 174
Miyoshi Masao, 72
Mizobe, Osamu, 185
Mukyōkai-ha (Non-church Movement), 48–49, 56
Mukyōkai-shungi (Non-Church Principle), 27
Mullins, Mark R., 10
mystical experiences, 1, 123–125

Nagasaki, 14, 23, 28, 94; Archdiocese of, 34, 35; churches of, 25, 27, 50–51, 175–176
Nakamura Kichiji, 187
Nakane Chie, 194n9
Nanbandera church, 23
nationalism, Japanese, 5, 29, 51, 77, 101, 164
Neo-Confucianism, 4, 60–68, 181–182; ethics of, 8, 55, 116, 198n11; masculine ideals of, 142; notion of love in, 98; social relationships and, 6, 15, 87, 103

New Age spirituality, 96; literature of, 50, 97; reincarnation and, 51
new religious movements, 10, 30–31, 34, 49, 202n2
new "third person," 15–16, 95–98
New Year festival, 32, 38, 163, 174–175, 203n13
Nichiren shō-shū (Buddhist sect), 50, 202n2
nihonjinron (theories of Japanese uniqueness), 5, 199n15
ningen kankei (human relationships), 19–20, 67–68, 84, 115; adoptive children and, 115; personal loyalty and, 88, 91–93; reciprocity in, 87
Nippon danji ("Japanese man"), 139–141
Nitobe Inazo, 201n10
Non-church Movement (Mukyōkai-ha), 48–49, 56
Non-Church Principle (Mukyōkai-shungi), 27
Nosco, Peter, 67
Notice of Religious Conversion, 165

obedience (*tei*), 63–64, 67, 142, 150, 177
ochanoma (Japanese-style living room), 44–46
Oda Nobunaga, 23
Ohta Yoshiko, 144, 195n8, 196n10
ojō-san (well brought up daughter), 56–57, 67, 117, 197n4. See also gender issues
Okinawa Islands, 5, 27, 164
Ōmura Sumitada, 23
Ooms, Herman, 61
"oracles," 93–94, 95
Ortner, Sherry B., 114
Osaka, 34, 35, 53, 144, 162

Ōtomo Sōrin, 23
Ōura Roman Catholic Church (Nagasaki), 50–51
overwork, 20–21, 155, 195n2

Pacific War. See World War II
Panourgiá, Neni, 13
parents, 63–65, 69, 101–103. See also children; filial piety
Paris Foreign Missions Society, 27–28, 43, 45, 144, 196n13
paternalism, 97
Paul (apostle), 94, 101, 103
Pentecostals, 122–123. See also Catholic Charismatic Renewal movement
persecution, 23–26, 51, 156, 159–160, 163, 165–166, 170, 175, 185, 193n6; Amami Ōshima and, 164–165, 203n6
perseverance (*ganbaru*), 15, 94–97, 119–124; cult of, 76–80; entrusting and, 94–95, 116, 126; as postwar concept, 199n15
personhood: agency and, 114, 188–192; definition of, 193n2; study of, 2, 9–10, 69. See also self
pilgrimage, 14, 50–51, 108
power, 2, 4; agentive, 132, 190; Confucianism and, 142; embedded in *seken*, 57–58, 93; in family/sexuality/gender, 70, 136; identity politics and, 184–186; Japanese Catholic Church and, 52; self and, 7, 69, 182, 192; subjectivity and, 114
Praise Meeting, 122, 123
prayer beads, 161–162
prodigal son parable, 102, 200n5
Protestants, 85, 117, 175; Catholic conversion of, 109, 193n3;

educational institutes of, 149;
Pentecostal, 122–123; values of,
121–127, 148–150

Rabinow, Paul, 4
reciprocity, 84, 87–90, 93. *See also* gift
exchange
Reiha no hikari (Light of Spiritual
Wave), 50
reincarnation beliefs, 51
Reiyū-kai movement, 30
"rejoice always," 84, 93–94, 103, 106
religion, 56, 58, 154, 163–166,
174–175; freedom of, 25, 26, 30; *ie*
and, 170; negative views of, 33, 149,
162; separation of state and, 30. *See
also* new religious movements
Risshō Kōseikai movement, 30
Rite of Christian Initiation of Adults
(RCIA), 92
Road Angels (motorcycle club),
148–149
Roman Catholicism. *See* Catholicism
rosaries, 51, 121, 152, 161–162
Rosenberger, Nancy, 21, 107, 136
Rowe, Mark, 31, 170, 171
Rupp, Katherine, 87–88, 111–112
Russian Orthodox Church, 26
Ryang, Sonia, 97, 101
ryōsai kenbo ("good wife and wise
mother"), 135

Sabbath observances, 201n4, 201n6
sacraments, 49, 102, 121, 138,
183–184; divorcees and, 75; lay
explanation of, 126
Sacred Heart school (Seishin Joshi
Gakuin), 71, 139, 143–146
Samoa, 69
samurais, 61; Christian converts
among, 28, 176

sararīman (businessmen), 86, 133–
134, 152, 154
Sasaki Kōkan, 171
Satō Eisaku, 179
Seat, Karen, 28, 144, 145
Seichō no ie, 30
seikazoku (holy family), 131
Seishin Joshi Gakuin (Sacred Heart
school), 71, 139, 143–146
seken (society), 54–60; authority of,
15, 53, 60, 113; definitions of, 57;
expressions with, 56–58; scope of,
110; social behavior in, 57
self, 94; identity politics and, 185–186;
integrity of, 12–13; search for, 11;
"sliding scale" of, 7, 62, 83, 84. *See
also* personhood
sense of self, 83–84, 194n9;
conversion experiences and, 132;
enhanced, 107–109; gendered, 136,
167–169; individualism and, 3, 10,
113–114, 136; *mentalité* and, 60–61;
"relational," 6–10, 68–76, 135, 160,
167; social roles and, 6–10
Setouchi Jakuchō, 31
shazai kaiken (apology press
conference), 54
Shimazono Susumu, 30–31, 33
Shinto, 49, 61; Christianity and, 24,
30, 149–150, 156–157, 174, 194n7,
196n11; emperor and, 26–29, 64;
festivals of, 156, 175, 202n16;
funeral rites of, 167, 172; in Korea,
185–186; new religious movements
and, 30; after WWII, 29–32, 65
Shirayuri Gakuen (women's school),
28, 47–48, 147
Shōkonsha Shrine, 196n16
Shokushi, Princess, 100
Shore, Bradd, 69, 70
Shōtoku Taishi, 53

Shōwa Period (1926–1989), 27, 51, 67, 149, 164–165
shutaisei (spirit of independence), 186
Sisters of St. Paul of Chartres, 28, 47, 48, 144
Smith, Robert J., 65, 66, 77, 79–80
social hierarchies, 68–69; Japanese grammar and, 7–8, 87; Neo-Confucianism and, 6, 15, 87; obedience and, 64; sense of self and, 7–10
Société de Marie, 28, 144
Société des Missions Étrangères. *See* Paris Foreign Missions Society
Sōka Gakkai, 30, 31, 49, 163, 202n2
sontaku (discern feelings of others), 191
speaking in tongues (glossolalia), 41, 42, 122, 139, 194n13
"spiritual cleansing," 195n1
Spiritual Exercises (Loyola), 120, 200n10
spirituality movements, 30–31, 34. *See also* new religious movements
"sportsmanship," 148
spousal tax benefit, 136, 201n7
State Shinto, 26, 65–66; Christianity and, 26–27, 149–150, 194n7, 196n11; dismantling of, 29–30, 65; in Korea, 185–186
Sueki Fumihiko, 26
suicide, 59, 63, 66, 174. *See also* death

Taguchi Yoshigorō, 29
Taisho Period (1912–1926), 79, 149, 164
Taizé community, 36
Takayama Ukon, 23
Takeda Chōshū, 169–170
tattoos, 149, 201n13
tea ceremony, 11
television talk shows, 31, 58–59

temple certification system, 24, 156, 170–171, 177
tengoku dorobō ("heaven theft"), 153, 180
tenkaishiki mass, 193n3
Tenshō Mission (1582), 23
terauke seido. *See* temple certification system
Toda Yūko, 98–100
Tokugawa Iemitsu, 24
Tokugawa Ieyasu, 23–24, 26, 185
Tokugawa Period. *See* Edo Period
Tokyo, 18–22; Archdiocese of, 34, 35, 36, 175–176, 197n17; population of, 19
Toyotomi Hideyoshi, 23–24, 26, 185, 195n4
Traphagan, John W., 167–168
Troeltsch, Ernst, 113–114

Uchimura Kanzō, 27, 48–49, 56

Vatican Council, Second, 3, 15, 173–177

Warring States Period (1460–1573), 22
work hours, 20–21, 155, 195n2
"work of God," 194n8
World War II, 4, 8, 98–99, 196n16; Holiness group arrests during, 150; Japanese Christianity during, 27, 29–34, 149–150, 164–165; kamikaze pilots of, 201n2; Neo-Confucianism and, 60; Tokyo after, 19

Xavier, Francis, 22

yakuza (organized crime group), 148, 201n13
Yasukuni Shrine, 28–29, 149–150, 196n16

Yokohama, 19, 27, 35, 138
yome, 72–73, 199n14; "hidden" Christians and, 160, 173; ideal of, 166–169
Yoshida Shigeru, 179–180, 186

yudaneru (entrusting), 84, 94–96, 106; *ganbaru* and, 94–95, 116, 126

zahyōjiku ("coordinate grid"), 83, 199n2
Zhu Xi, 60